GREAT
AMERICAN
WESTERN
STORIES

LYONS PRESS CLASSICS

GREAT AMERICAN WESTERN STORIES

EDITED AND WITH AN INTRODUCTION BY
STEVEN D. PRICE

GUILFORD
CONNECTICUT

An imprint of Globe Pequot

Distributed by NATIONAL BOOK NETWORK

Copyright © 2017 by Lyons Press

British Library Cataloguing in Publication Information Available

Library of Congress Cataloging-in-Publication Data Available

ISBN 978-1-4930-2946-4 (paperback)
ISBN 978-1-4930-2947-1 (e-book)

∞™ The paper used in this publication meets the minimum requirements
of American National Standard for Information Sciences—Permanence of
Paper for Printed Library Materials, ANSI/NISO Z39.48-1992.

Printed in the United States of America

CONTENTS

INTRODUCTION

STEVEN D. PRICE

Few images have permeated American culture more that the American West. We drive automobiles that bear the names Mustang, Wrangler, Bronco, and Dakota. We root for sports teams named the Rangers, Cowboys, Mavericks, and Braves. In the era when cigarettes were advertised on television and in print, the rugged Marlboro Man cowboy identified that brand with the West. We sing "Home on the Range" and thrill to bronc riders and calf ropers at rodeos.

Once upon a time, Westerns were staples of movies, radio, and television. Starting at the turn of the twentieth century, stars like Bronco Billy Anderson and William S. Hart galloped across the silver screen, to be followed by Tom Mix, Johnny Mack Brown, Randolph Scott, John Wayne, Joel McCrea, and Clint Eastwood. And there were Roy Rogers, Gene Autry, and other singing cowboys who were likely to burst into a sentimental ballad as fast as they could draw their Colt .45s. (My grandfather, an émigré from Czarist Russia, spent his free afternoons enthralled by Western movies where, according to family lore, he studied the English language from the likes of Hoot Gibson and Buck Jones. I never knew the man, so whether "head 'em off at the pass" entered his lexicon remains a mystery.)

One of the first TV shows I remember watching, and this goes back to the late 1940s, was *Six Gun Playhouse*, a pre-dinner hour of cowboy movies that provided plot lines for the kids in the neighborhood to reenact (without horses, alas) the next day. There was even a live TV Western called *Action in The Afternoon*. Though set in the Old West, it was filmed somewhere in suburban Philadelphia, where every now and then an airplane could be seen zooming above a cattle drive or gun duel. Thereafter came a herd of perennial network classics such as *Gunsmoke, Bonanza, Death Valley Days, The Lone Ranger, Hopalong Cassidy,* and *The Cisco Kid.*

What was the basis for America's media fascination and identification (sometimes real, often only spiritual) with the Old West? You hold a large part of the answer in your hands. Books and magazine articles and stories fed popular taste from post–Civil War days. You will recognize many of the authors in this volume: Better known for his Tarzan tales, Edgar Rice Burroughs wrote Westerns. So did the classic short-story writer O. Henry, creator of the Cisco Kid, who before being sanitized for television series and movie consumption was as cold-blooded a killer as the Old West ever produced.

Also represented are the great Western authors, such as Zane Grey, Bret Harte, and Joaquin Miller, as well as others—Theodore Roosevelt and Mark Twain—who are more associated with other subject areas.

How true to life are these tales? We can trust Roosevelt and Buffalo Bill Cody's daughter Helen Cody Wetmore for accurate portrayals, and Twain perhaps less so. Certainly Ned Buntline's treatment of Wild Bill Hickok and Alfred Henry Lewis's depiction of Bat Masterson are made up of whole cloth. But does it really matter? I much prefer the line from the classic John Wayne movie *The Man Who Shot Liberty Valence*, "when legend becomes fact, print the legend."

—Steven D. Price

1

THE VIRGINIAN

BY OWEN WISTER

Even though its title suggests otherwise, The Virginian *(1902) is frequently cited as the earliest Western novel, aside from the pulp fiction variety. Its hero is never named, but is referred to as "the tall man" or "the stranger" (although his nickname Jeff, for Jefferson Davis, suggests his early life). This second chapter introduces the hero and contains the deathless line, most famously uttered by Gary Cooper in the 1929 film adaptation, "When you call me that, smile!"*

We cannot see ourselves as other see us, or I should know what appearance I cut at hearing this from the tall man. I said nothing, feeling uncertain.

"I reckon I am looking for you, seh," he repeated politely.

"I am looking for Judge Henry," I now replied.

He walked toward me, and I saw that in inches he was not a giant. He was not more than six feet. It was Uncle Hughey that had made him seem to tower. But in his eye, in his face, in his step, in the whole man, there dominated a something potent to be felt, I should think, by man or woman.

"The Judge sent me afteh you, seh," he now explained, in his civil Southern voice; and he handed me a letter from my host. Had I not witnessed his facetious performances with Uncle Hughey, I should have judged him wholly ungifted with such powers. There was nothing external about him but what seemed the signs of a nature as grave as you could meet. But I had witnessed; and therefore supposing that I knew him in spite of his appearance, that I was, so to speak, in his secret and could give him a sort of wink, I adopted at once a method of easiness. It was so pleasant to be easy with a large stranger, who instead of shooting at your heels had very civilly handed you a letter.

"You're from old Virginia, I take it?" I began.

He answered slowly, "Then you have taken it correct, seh."

A slight chill passed over my easiness, but I went cheerily on with a further inquiry. "Find many oddities out here like Uncle Hughey?"

"Yes, seh, there is a right smart of oddities around. They come in on every train."

At this point I dropped my method of easiness.

"I wish that trunks came on the train," said I. And I told him my predicament.

It was not to be expected that he would be greatly moved at my loss; but he took it with no comment whatever. "We'll wait in town for it," said he, always perfectly civil.

Now, what I had seen of "town" was, to my newly arrived eyes, altogether horrible. If I could possibly sleep at the Judge's ranch, I preferred to do so.

"Is it too far to drive there to-night?" I inquired.

He looked at me in a puzzled manner.

"For this valise," I explained, "contains all that I immediately need; in fact, I could do without my trunk for a day or two, if it is not convenient to send. So if we could arrive there not too late by starting at once—"I paused.

"It's two hundred and sixty-three miles," said the Virginian.

To my loud ejaculation he made no answer, but surveyed me a moment longer, and then said, "Supper will be about ready now." He took my valise, and I followed his steps toward the eating-house in silence. I was dazed.

As we went, I read my host's letter—a brief hospitable message. He was very sorry not to meet me himself. He had been getting ready to drive over, when the surveyor appeared and detained him. Therefore in his stead he was sending a trustworthy man to town, who would look after me and drive me over. They were looking forward to my visit with much pleasure. This was all.

Yes, I was dazed. How did they count distance in this country? You spoke in a neighborly fashion about driving over to town, and it meant—I did not know yet how many days. And what would be meant by the term "dropping in," I wondered. And how many miles would be considered really far? I abstained from further questioning the "trustworthy man." My questions had not fared excessively well. He did not propose making me dance, to be sure: that would scarcely be trustworthy. But neither did he propose to have me familiar with him. Why was this? What had I done to elicit that veiled and skillful sarcasm about oddities coming in on every train? Having been sent to look after me, he would do so, would even carry my valise; but I could not be jocular with him. This handsome, ungrammatical son of the soil had set between us the bar of his cold and perfect civility. No polished person could have done it better. What was the matter? I looked at him, and suddenly it came to me. If he had tried familiarity with me the first two minutes of our acquaintance, I should have resented it; by what right, then, had I tried it with him? It smacked of patronizing: on this occasion he had come off the better gentleman of the two. Here in flesh and blood was a truth which I had long believed in words, but never met before. The creature we call a GENTLEMAN lies deep in the hearts of thousands that are born without chance to master the outward graces of the type.

Between the station and the eating-house I did a deal of straight thinking. But my thoughts were destined presently to be drowned in amazement at the rare personage into whose society fate had thrown me.

Town, as they called it, pleased me the less, the longer I saw it. But until our language stretches itself and takes in a new word of closer fit, town will have to do for the name of such a place as was Medicine Bow. I have seen and slept in many like it since. Scattered wide, they littered the frontier from the Columbia to the Rio Grande, from the Missouri to the Sierras. They lay stark, dotted over a planet of treeless dust, like soiled packs of cards. Each was similar to the next, as one old five-spot of clubs resembles another. Houses, empty bottles, and garbage, they were forever of the same shapeless pattern. More forlorn they were than stale bones. They seemed to have been strewn there by the wind and to be waiting till the wind should come again and blow them away. Yet serene above their foulness swam a pure and quiet light, such as the East never sees; they might be bathing in the air of creation's first morning. Beneath sun and stars their days and nights were immaculate and wonderful.

Medicine Bow was my first, and I took its dimensions, twenty-nine buildings in all,—one coal shute, one water tank, the station, one store, two eating-houses, one billiard hall, two tool-houses, one feed stable, and twelve others that for one reason and another I shall not name. Yet this wretched husk of squalor spent thought upon appearances; many houses in it wore a false front to seem as if they were two stories high. There they stood, rearing their pitiful masquerade amid a fringe of old tin cans, while at their very doors began a world of crystal light, a land without end, a space across which Noah and Adam might come straight from Genesis. Into that space went wandering a road, over a hill and down out of sight, and up again smaller in the distance, and down once more, and up once more, straining the eyes, and so away.

Then I heard a fellow greet my Virginian. He came rollicking out of a door, and made a pass with his hand at the Virginian's hat. The Southerner dodged it, and I saw once more the tiger undulation of body, and knew my escort was he of the rope and the corral.

"How are yu', Steve?" he said to the rollicking man. And in his tone I heard instantly old friendship speaking. With Steve he would take and give familiarity.

Steve looked at me, and looked away—and that was all. But it was enough. In no company had I ever felt so much an outsider. Yet I liked the company, and wished that it would like me.

"Just come to town?" inquired Steve of the Virginian.

"Been here since noon. Been waiting for the train."

"Going out tonight?"

"I reckon I'll pull out tomorro'."

"Beds are all took," said Steve. This was for my benefit.

"Dear me," said I.

"But I guess one of them drummers will let yu' double up with him." Steve was enjoying himself, I think. He had his saddle and blankets, and beds were nothing to him.

"Drummers, are they?" asked the Virginian.

"Two Jews handling cigars, one American with consumption killer, and a Dutchman with jew'lry."

The Virginian set down my valise, and seemed to meditate. "I did want a bed tonight," he murmured gently.

"Well," Steve suggested, "the American looks like he washed the oftenest."

"That's of no consequence to me," observed the Southerner.

"Guess it'll be when yu' see 'em."

"Oh, I'm meaning something different. I wanted a bed to myself."

"Then you'll have to build one."

"Bet yu' I have the Dutchman's."

"Take a man that won't scare. Bet yu' drinks yu' can't have the American's."

"Go yu'" said the Virginian. "I'll have his bed without any fuss. Drinks for the crowd."

"I suppose you have me beat," said Steve, grinning at him affectionately. "You're such a son-of-a—when you get down to work. Well, so long! I got to fix my horse's hoofs."

I had expected that the man would be struck down. He had used to the Virginian a term of heaviest insult, I thought. I had marveled to hear it come so unheralded from Steve's friendly lips. And now I marveled still more. Evidently he had meant no harm by it, and evidently no offence had been taken. Used thus, this language was plainly complimentary. I had stepped into a world new to me indeed, and novelties were occurring with scarce any time to get breath between them. As to where I should sleep, I had forgotten that problem altogether in my curiosity. What was the Virginian going to do now? I began to know that the quiet of this man was volcanic.

"Will you wash first, sir?"

We were at the door of the eating-house, and he set my valise inside. In my tenderfoot innocence I was looking indoors for the washing arrangements.

"It's out hyeh, seh," he informed me gravely, but with strong Southern accent. Internal mirth seemed often to heighten the local flavor of his speech. There were other times when it had scarce any special accent or fault in grammar.

A trough was to my right, slippery with soapy water; and hanging from a roller above one end of it was a rag of discouraging appearance. The Virginian caught it, and it performed one whirling revolution on its roller. Not a dry or clean inch could be found on it. He took off his hat, and put his head in the door.

"Your towel, ma'am," said he, "has been too popular."

She came out, a pretty woman. Her eyes rested upon him for a moment, then upon me with disfavor; then they returned to his black hair.

"The allowance is one a day," said she, very quietly. "But when folks are particular—" She completed her sentence by removing the old towel and giving a clean one to us.

"Thank you, ma'am," said the cow-puncher.

She looked once more at his black hair, and without any word returned to her guests at supper.

A pail stood in the trough, almost empty; and this he filled for me from a well. There was some soap sliding at large in the trough, but I got my own. And then in a tin basin I removed as many of the stains of travel as I was able. It was not much of a toilet that I made in this first wash-trough of my experience, but it had to suffice, and I took my seat at supper.

Canned stuff it was—corned beef. And one of my table companions said the truth about it. "When I slung my teeth over that," he remarked, "I thought I was chewing a hammock." We had strange coffee, and condensed milk; and I have never seen more flies. I made no attempt to talk, for no one in this country seemed favorable to me. By reason of something,—my clothes, my hat, my pronunciation, whatever it might be, I possessed the secret of estranging people at sight. Yet I was doing better than I knew; my strict silence and attention to the corned beef made me in the eyes of the cowboys at table compare well with the over-talkative commercial travellers.

The Virginian's entrance produced a slight silence. He had done wonders with the wash-trough, and he had somehow brushed his clothes. With all the roughness of his dress, he was now the neatest of us. He nodded to some of the other cowboys, and began his meal in quiet.

But silence is not the native element of the drummer. An average fish can go a longer time out of water than this breed can live without talking. One of them now looked across the table at the grave, flannel-shirted Virginian; he inspected, and came to the imprudent conclusion that he understood his man.

"Good evening," he said briskly.

"Good evening," said the Virginian.

"Just come to town?" pursued the drummer.

"Just come to town," the Virginian suavely assented.

"Cattle business jumping along?" inquired the drummer.

"Oh, fair." And the Virginian took some more corned beef.

"Gets a move on your appetite, anyway," suggested the drummer.

The Virginian drank some coffee. Presently the pretty woman refilled his cup without his asking her.

"Guess I've met you before," the drummer stated next.

The Virginian glanced at him for a brief moment.

"Haven't I, now? Ain't I seen you somewhere? Look at me. You been in Chicago, ain't you? You look at me well. Remember Ikey's, don't you?"

"I don't reckon I do."

"See, now! I knowed you'd been in Chicago. Four or five years ago. Or maybe it's two years. Time's nothing to me. But I never forget a face. Yes, sir. Him and me's met at Ikey's, all right." This important point the drummer stated to all of us. We were called to witness how well he had proved old acquaintanceship. "Ain't the world small, though!" he exclaimed complacently. "Meet a man once and you're sure to run on to him again. That's straight. That's no bar-room josh." And the drummer's eye included us all in his confidence. I wondered if he had attained that high perfection when a man believes his own lies.

The Virginian did not seem interested. He placidly attended to his food, while our landlady moved between dining room and kitchen, and the drummer expanded.

"Yes, sir! Ikey's over by the stock-yards, patronized by all cattlemen that know what's what. That's where. Maybe it's three years. Time never was nothing to me. But faces! Why, I can't quit 'em. Adults or children, male and female; onced I seen 'em I couldn't lose one off my memory, not if you were to pay me bounty, five dollars a face. White men, that is. Can't do nothing with niggers or Chinese. But you're white, all right." The drummer suddenly returned to the Virginian with this high compliment. The cow-puncher had taken out a pipe, and was slowly rubbing it. The compliment seemed to escape his attention, and the drummer went on.

"I can tell a man when he's white, put him at Ikey's or out loose here in the sage-brush." And he rolled a cigar across to the Virginian's plate.

"Selling them?" inquired the Virginian.

"Solid goods, my friend. Havana wrappers, the biggest tobacco proposition for five cents got out yet. Take it, try it, light it, watch it burn. Here." And he held out a bunch of matches.

The Virginian tossed a five-cent piece over to him.

"Oh, no, my friend! Not from you! Not after Ikey's. I don't forget you. See? I knowed your face right away. See? That's straight. I seen you at Chicago all right."

"Maybe you did," said the Virginian. "Sometimes I'm mighty careless what I look at."

"Well, py damn!" now exclaimed the Dutch drummer, hilariously. "I am ploom disappointed. I vas hoping to sell him somedings myself."

"Not the same here," stated the American. "He's too healthy for me. I gave him up on sight."

Now it was the American drummer whose bed the Virginian had in his eye. This was a sensible man, and had talked less than his brothers in the trade. I had little doubt who would end by sleeping in his bed; but how the thing would be done interested me more deeply than ever.

The Virginian looked amiably at his intended victim, and made one or two remarks regarding patent medicines. There must be a good deal of money in them, he supposed, with a live man to manage them. The victim was flattered. No other person at the table had been favored with so much of the tall cow-puncher's notice. He responded, and they had a pleasant talk. I did not divine that the Virginian's genius was even then at work, and that all this was part of his satanic strategy. But Steve must have divined it. For while a few of us still sat finishing our supper, that facetious horseman returned from doctoring his horse's hoofs, put his head into the dining room, took in the way in which the Virginian was engaging his victim in conversation, remarked aloud, "I've lost!" and closed the door again.

"What's he lost?" inquired the American drummer.

"Oh, you mustn't mind him," drawled the Virginian. "He's one of those box-head jokers goes around openin' and shuttin' doors that-a-way. We call him harmless. Well," he broke off, "I reckon I'll go smoke. Not allowed in hyeh?" This last he addressed to the landlady, with especial gentleness. She shook her head, and her eyes followed him as he went out.

Left to myself I meditated for some time upon my lodging for the night, and smoked a cigar for consolation as I walked about. It was not a hotel that we had supped in. Hotel at Medicine Bow there appeared to be none. But connected with the eating-house was that place where, according to Steve, the beds were all taken, and there I went to see for myself. Steve had spoken the truth. It was a single apartment containing four or five beds, and nothing else whatever. And when I looked at these beds, my sorrow that I could sleep in none of them grew less. To be alone in one offered no temptation, and as for this courtesy of the country, this doubling up—!

"Well, they have got ahead of us." This was the Virginian standing at my elbow.

I assented.

"They have staked out their claims," he added.

In this public sleeping room they had done what one does to secure a seat in a railroad train. Upon each bed, as notice of occupancy, lay some article of travel or of dress. As we stood there, the two Jews came in and opened and arranged their valises, and folded and refolded their linen dusters. Then a railroad employee entered and began to go to bed at this hour, before dusk had wholly darkened into night. For him, going to bed meant removing his boots and placing his overalls and waistcoat beneath his pillow. He had no coat. His work began at three in the morning; and even as we still talked he began to snore.

"The man that keeps the store is a friend of mine," said the Virginian; "and you can be pretty near comfortable on his counter. Got any blankets?"

I had no blankets.

"Looking for a bed?" inquired the American drummer, now arriving.

"Yes, he's looking for a bed," answered the voice of Steve behind him.

"Seems a waste of time," observed the Virginian. He looked thoughtfully from one bed to another. "I didn't know I'd have to lay over here. Well, I have sat up before."

"This one's mine," said the drummer, sitting down on it. "Half's plenty enough room for me."

"You're cert'nly mighty kind," said the cowpuncher. "But I'd not think o' disconveniencing yu'."

"That's nothing. The other half is yours. Turn in right now if you feel like it."

"No. I don't reckon I'll turn in right now. Better keep your bed to yourself."

"See here," urged the drummer, "if I take you I'm safe from drawing some party I might not care so much about. This here sleeping proposition is a lottery."

"Well," said the Virginian (and his hesitation was truly masterly), "if you put it that way—"

"I do put it that way. Why, you're clean! You've had a shave right now. You turn in when you feel inclined, old man! I ain't retiring just yet."

The drummer had struck a slightly false note in these last remarks. He should not have said "old man." Until this I had thought him merely an amiable person who wished to do a favor. But "old man" came in wrong. It had a hateful taint of his profession; the being too soon with everybody, the celluloid good-fellowship that passes for ivory with nine in ten of the city crowd. But not so with the sons of the sagebrush. They live nearer nature, and they know better.

But the Virginian blandly accepted "old man" from his victim: he had a game to play. "Well, I cert'nly thank yu'," he said. "After a while I'll take advantage of your kind offer."

I was surprised. Possession being nine points of the law, it seemed his very chance to intrench himself in the bed. But the cow-puncher had planned a campaign needing no intrenchments. Moreover, going to bed before nine o'clock upon the first evening in many weeks that a town's resources were open to you, would be a dull proceeding. Our entire company, drummer and all, now walked over to the store, and here my sleeping arrangements were made easily. This store was the cleanest place and the best in Medicine Bow, and would have been a good store anywhere, offering a multitude of things for sale, and kept by a very civil proprietor. He bade me make myself at home, and placed both of his counters at my disposal. Upon the grocery side there stood a cheese too large and strong to sleep near comfortably, and I therefore chose the dry-goods side. Here thick quilts were unrolled for me, to make it soft; and no condition was placed upon me, further than that I should remove my boots, because the quilts were new, and clean, and for sale. So now my rest was assured. Not an anxiety remained in my thoughts. These therefore turned themselves wholly to the other man's bed, and how he was going to lose it.

I think that Steve was more curious even than myself. Time was on the wing. His bet must be decided, and the drinks enjoyed. He stood against the grocery counter, contemplating the Virginian. But it was to me that he spoke. The Virginian, however, listened to every word.

"Your first visit to this country?"

I told him yes.

"How do you like it?"

I expected to like it very much.

"How does the climate strike you?

I thought the climate was fine.

"Makes a man thirsty though."

This was the sub-current which the Virginian plainly looked for.
But he, like Steve, addressed himself to me.

"Yes," he put in, "thirsty while a man's soft yet. You'll harden."

"I guess you'll find it a drier country than you were given to expect,"
said Steve.

"If your habits have been frequent that way," said the Virginian.

"There's parts of Wyoming," pursued Steve, "where you'll go
hours and hours before you'll see a drop of wetness."

"And if yu' keep a-thinkin' about it," said the Virginian, "it'll seem
like days and days."

Steve, at this stroke, gave up, and clapped him on the shoulder with
a joyous chuckle. "You old son-of-a!" he cried affectionately.

"Drinks are due now," said the Virginian. "My treat, Steve. But I
reckon your suspense will have to linger a while yet."

Thus they dropped into direct talk from that speech of the fourth
dimension where they had been using me for their telephone.

"Any cyards going to-night?" inquired the Virginian.

"Stud and draw," Steve told him. "Strangers playing."

"I think I'd like to get into a game for a while," said the Southerner.
"Strangers, yu' say?"

And then, before quitting the store, he made his toilet for this little
hand at poker. It was a simple preparation. He took his pistol from its
holster, examined it, then shoved it between his overalls and his shirt
in front, and pulled his waistcoat over it. He might have been combing

his hair for all the attention any one paid to this, except myself. Then the two friends went out, and I bethought me of that epithet which Steve again had used to the Virginian as he clapped him on the shoulder. Clearly this wild country spoke a language other than mine—the word here was a term of endearment. Such was my conclusion.

The drummers had finished their dealings with the proprietor, and they were gossiping together in a knot by the door as the Virginian passed out.

"See you later, old man!" This was the American drummer accosting his prospective bed-fellow.

"Oh, yes," returned the bed-fellow, and was gone.

The American drummer winked triumphantly at his brethren. "He's all right," he observed, jerking a thumb after the Virginian. "He's easy. You got to know him to work him. That's all."

"Und vat is your point?" inquired the German drummer.

"Point is—he'll not take any goods off you or me; but he's going to talk up the killer to any consumptive he runs across. I ain't done with him yet. Say," (he now addressed the proprietor), "what's her name?"

"Whose name?"

"Woman runs the eating-house."

"Glen. Mrs. Glen."

"Ain't she new?"

"Been settled here about a month. Husband's a freight conductor."

"Thought I'd not seen her before. She's a good-looker."

"Hm! Yes. The kind of good looks I'd sooner see in another man's wife than mine."

"So that's the gait, is it?"

"Hm! well, it don't seem to be. She come here with that reputation. But there's been general disappointment."

"Then she ain't lacked suitors any?"

"Lacked! Are you acquainted with cowboys?"

"And she disappointed 'em? Maybe she likes her husband?"

"Hm! well, how are you to tell about them silent kind?"

"Talking of conductors," began the drummer. And we listened to his anecdote. It was successful with his audience; but when he launched fluently upon a second I strolled out. There was not enough wit in this narrator to relieve his indecency, and I felt shame at having been surprised into laughing with him.

I left that company growing confidential over their leering stories, and I sought the saloon. It was very quiet and orderly. Beer in quart bottles at a dollar I had never met before; but saving its price, I found no complaint to make of it. Through folding doors I passed from the bar proper with its bottles and elk head back to the hall with its various tables. I saw a man sliding cards from a case, and across the table from him another man laying counters down. Near by was a second dealer pulling cards from the bottom of a pack, and opposite him a solemn old rustic piling and changing coins upon the cards which lay already exposed.

But now I heard a voice that drew my eyes to the far corner of the room.

"Why didn't you stay in Arizona?"

Harmless looking words as I write them down here. Yet at the sound of them I noticed the eyes of the others directed to that corner. What answer was given to them I did not hear, nor did I see who spoke. Then came another remark.

"Well, Arizona's no place for amatures."

This time the two card dealers that I stood near began to give a part of their attention to the group that sat in the corner. There was in me a desire to leave this room. So far my hours at Medicine Bow had seemed to glide beneath a sunshine of merriment, of easy-going jocularity. This was suddenly gone, like the wind changing to north in the middle of a warm day. But I stayed, being ashamed to go.

Five or six players sat over in the corner at a round table where counters were piled. Their eyes were close upon their cards, and one seemed to be dealing a card at a time to each, with pauses and betting between. Steve was there and the Virginian; the others were new faces.

"No place for amatures," repeated the voice; and now I saw that it was the dealer's. There was in his countenance the same ugliness that his words conveyed.

"Who's that talkin'?" said one of the men near me, in a low voice.

"Trampas."

"What's he?"

"Cow-puncher, bronco-buster, tin-horn, most anything."

"Who's he talkin' at?"

"Think it's the black-headed guy he's talking at."

"That ain't supposed to be safe, is it?"

"Guess we're all goin' to find out in a few minutes."

"Been trouble between 'em?"

"They've not met before. Trampas don't enjoy losin' to a stranger."

"Fello's from Arizona, yu' say?"

"No. Virginia. He's recently back from havin' a look at Arizona. Went down there last year for a change. Works for the Sunk Creek outfit." And then the dealer lowered his voice still further and said something in the other man's ear, causing him to grin. After which both of them looked at me.

There had been silence over in the corner; but now the man Trampas spoke again.

"AND ten," said he, sliding out some chips from before him. Very strange it was to hear him, how he contrived to make those words a personal taunt. The Virginian was looking at his cards. He might have been deaf.

"AND twenty," said the next player, easily.

The next threw his cards down.

It was now the Virginian's turn to bet, or leave the game, and he did not speak at once.

Therefore Trampas spoke. "Your bet, you son-of-a—."

The Virginian's pistol came out, and his hand lay on the table, holding it unaimed. And with a voice as gentle as ever, the voice that sounded almost like a caress, but drawling a very little more than usual, so that there was almost a space between each word, he issued his orders to the man Trampas: "When you call me that, SMILE." And he looked at Trampas across the table.

Yes, the voice was gentle. But in my ears it seemed as if somewhere the bell of death was ringing; and silence, like a stroke, fell on the large room. All men present, as if by some magnetic current, had become aware of this crisis. In my ignorance, and the total stoppage of my thoughts, I stood stock-still, and noticed various people crouching, or shifting their positions.

"Sit quiet," said the dealer, scornfully to the man near me. "Can't you see he don't want to push trouble? He has handed Trampas the choice to back down or draw his steel."

Then, with equal suddenness and ease, the room came out of its strangeness. Voices and cards, the click of chips, the puff of tobacco, glasses lifted to drink,—this level of smooth relaxation hinted no more plainly of what lay beneath than does the surface tell the depth of the sea.

For Trampas had made his choice. And that choice was not to "draw his steel." If it was knowledge that he sought, he had found it, and no mistake! We heard no further reference to what he had been pleased to style "amatures." In no company would the black-headed man who had visited Arizona be rated a novice at the cool art of self-preservation. One doubt remained: what kind of a man was Trampas? A public back-down is an unfinished thing,—for some natures at least. I looked at his face, and thought it sullen, but tricky rather than courageous. Something had been added to my knowledge also. Once again I had heard applied to the Virginian that epithet which Steve so freely used. The same words, identical to the letter. But this time they had produced a pistol. "When you call me that, SMILE!" So I perceived a new example of the old truth, that the letter means nothing until the spirit gives it life.

2

RIDERS OF THE PURPLE SAGE, CHAPTER 5

BY ZANE GREY

It is impossible to underestimate the importance of Zane Grey as an author of this book's genre. From 1917 to 1926, Grey was in the top ten best-seller list nine times, primarily with his stories of the Old West. Moreover, almost 100 movies were made based on his books and short stories, beginning with Riders of the Purple Sage. *In this chapter of the 1902 novel, the hero tracks a band of rustlers and then rescues a maiden in distress, both archetypal elements of Old West storytelling.*

Venters looked quickly from the fallen rustlers to the canyon where the others had disappeared. He calculated on the time needed for running horses to return to the open, if their riders heard shots. He waited breathlessly. But the estimated time dragged by and no riders appeared. Venters began presently to believe that the rifle reports had not penetrated into the recesses of the canyon, and felt safe for the immediate present.

He hurried to the spot where the first rustler had been dragged by his horse. The man lay in deep grass, dead, jaw fallen, eyes protruding—a sight that sickened Venters. The first man at whom he had ever aimed a weapon he had shot through the heart. With the clammy sweat oozing from every pore Venters dragged the rustler in among some boulders and covered him with slabs of rock. Then he smoothed out the crushed trail in grass and sage.

The rustler's horse had stopped a quarter of a mile off and was grazing.

When Venters rapidly strode toward the Masked Rider not even the cold nausea that gripped him could wholly banish curiosity. For he had shot Oldring's infamous lieutenant, whose face had never been seen. Venters experienced a grim pride in the feat. What would Tull say to this achievement of the outcast who rode too often to Deception Pass?

Venters's curious eagerness and expectation had not prepared him for the shock he received when he stood over a slight, dark figure. The rustler wore the black mask that had given him his name, but he had no weapons. Venters glanced at the drooping horse, there were no gun-sheaths on the saddle.

"A rustler who didn't pack guns!" muttered Venters. "He wears no belt. He couldn't pack guns in that rig. . . . Strange!"

A low, gasping intake of breath and a sudden twitching of body told Venters the rider still lived.

"He's alive! . . . I've got to stand here and watch him die. And I shot an unarmed man."

Shrinkingly Venters removed the rider's wide sombrero and the black cloth mask. This action disclosed bright chestnut hair, inclined to curl, and a white, youthful face. Along the lower line of cheek and jaw was a clear demarcation, where the brown of tanned skin met the white that had been hidden from the sun.

"Oh, he's only a boy! . . . What! Can he be Oldring's Masked Rider?"

The boy showed signs of returning consciousness. He stirred; his lips moved; a small brown hand clenched in his blouse.

Venters knelt with a gathering horror of his deed. His bullet had entered the rider's right breast, high up to the shoulder. With hands that shook, Venters untied a black scarf and ripped open the blood-wet blouse.

First he saw a gaping hole, dark red against a whiteness of skin, from which welled a slender red stream. Then the graceful, beautiful swell of a woman's breast!

"A woman!" he cried. "A girl! . . . I've killed a girl!"

Then came a spasm of vitality. She writhed in a torture of reviving strength, and in her convulsions she almost tore from Ventner's grasp. Slowly she relaxed and sank partly back. The ungloved hand sought the wound, and pressed so hard that her wrist half buried itself in her bosom. Blood trickled between her spread fingers. And she looked at Venters with eyes that saw him.

He cursed himself and the unerring aim of which he had been so proud. He had seen that look in the eyes of a crippled antelope which he was about to finish with his knife. But in her it had infinitely more—a revelation of mortal spirit. The instinctive bringing to life was there, and the divining helplessness and the terrible accusation of the stricken.

"Forgive me! I didn't know!" burst out Venters.

"You shot me—you've killed me!" she whispered, in panting gasps.

Upon her lips appeared a fluttering, bloody froth. By that Venters knew the air in her lungs was mixing with blood. "Oh, I knew—it would—come—some day! . . . Oh, the burn! . . . Hold me—I'm sinking—it's all dark. . . . Ah, God! . . . Mercy—"

Her rigidity loosened in one long quiver and she lay back limp, still, white as snow, with closed eyes.

Venters thought then that she died. But the faint pulsation of her breast assured him that life yet lingered. Death seemed only a matter of moments, for the bullet had gone clear through her.

Nevertheless, he tore sage leaves from a bush, and, pressing them tightly over her wounds, he bound the black scarf round her shoulder, tying it securely under her arm. Then he closed the blouse, hiding from his sight that blood-stained, accusing breast.

"What—now?" he questioned, with flying mind. "I must get out of here. She's dying—but I can't leave her."

He rapidly surveyed the sage to the north and made out no animate object. Then he picked up the girl's sombrero and the mask. This time the mask gave him as great a shock as when he first removed it from her face. For in the woman he had forgotten the rustler, and this black strip of felt-cloth established the identity of Oldring's Masked Rider. Venters had solved the mystery. He slipped his rifle under her, and, lifting her carefully upon it, he began to retrace his steps. The dog trailed in his shadow. And the horse, that had stood drooping by, followed without a call.

Venters chose the deepest tufts of grass and clumps of sage on his return. From time to time he glanced over his shoulder. He did not rest. His concern was to avoid jarring the girl and to hide his trail. Gaining the narrow canyon, he turned and held close to the wall till he reached his hiding-place. When he entered the dense thicket of oaks he was hard put to it to force a way through. But he held his burden almost upright, and by slipping side wise and bending the saplings he got in. Through sage and grass he hurried to the grove of silver spruces.

He laid the girl down, almost fearing to look at her. Though marble pale and cold, she was living. Venters then appreciated the tax that long carry had been to his strength. He sat down to rest. Whitie sniffed at the pale girl and whined and crept to Venters's feet. Ring lapped the water in the runway of the spring.

Presently Venters went out to the opening, caught the horse and, leading him through the thicket, unsaddled him and tied him with a long halter. Wrangle left his browsing long enough to whinny and toss his head. Venters felt that he could not rest easily till he had secured the other rustler's horse; so, taking his rifle and calling for Ring, he set out. Swiftly yet watchfully he made his way through the canyon to the oval and out to the cattle trail. What few tracks might have betrayed him he obliterated, so only an expert tracker could have trailed him. Then, with many a wary backward glance across the sage, he started to round up the rustler's horse. This was unexpectedly easy. He led the horse to lower ground, out of sight from the opposite side of the oval along the shadowy western wall, and so on into his canyon and secluded camp.

The girl's eyes were open; a feverish spot burned in her cheeks and she moaned something unintelligible to Venters, but he took the movement of her lips to mean that she wanted water. Lifting her head, he tipped the canteen to her lips. After that she again lapsed into unconsciousness or a weakness which was its counterpart. Venters noted, however, that the burning flush had faded into the former pallor.

The sun set behind the high canyon rim, and a cool shade darkened the walls. Venters fed the dogs and put a halter on the dead rustler's horse. He allowed Wrangle to browse free. This done, he cut spruce boughs and made a lean-to for the girl. Then, gently lifting her upon a blanket, he folded the sides over her. The other blanket he wrapped about his shoulders and found a comfortable seat against a spruce-tree that upheld the little shack. Ring and Whitie lay near at hand, one asleep, the other watchful.

Venters dreaded the night's vigil. At night his mind was active, and this time he had to watch and think and feel beside a dying girl whom he had all but murdered. A thousand excuses he invented for himself, yet not one made any difference in his act or his self-reproach.

It seemed to him that when night fell black he could see her white face so much more plainly.

"She'll go, presently," he said, "and be out of agony—thank God!"

Every little while certainty of her death came to him with a shock; and then he would bend over and lay his ear on her breast.

Her heart still beat.

The early night blackness cleared to the cold starlight. The horses were not moving, and no sound disturbed the deathly silence of the canyon.

"I'll bury her here," thought Venters, "and let her grave be as much a mystery as her life was."

For the girl's few words, the look of her eyes, the prayer, had strangely touched Venters.

"She was only a girl," he soliloquized. "What was she to Oldring?"

Rustlers don't have wives nor sisters nor daughters. She was bad— that's all. But somehow . . . well, she may not have willingly become the companion of rustlers. That prayer of hers to God for mercy! . . . Life is strange and cruel. I wonder if other members of Oldring's gang are women? Likely enough. But what was his game?

Oldring's Masked Rider! A name to make villagers hide and lock their doors. A name credited with a dozen murders, a hundred forays, and a thousand stealings of cattle. What part did the girl have in this? It may have served Oldring to create mystery.

Hours passed. The white stars moved across the narrow strip of dark-blue sky above. The silence awoke to the low hum of insects.

Venters watched the immovable white face, and as he watched, hour by hour waiting for death, the infamy of her passed from his mind. He thought only of the sadness, the truth of the moment.

Whoever she was—whatever she had done—she was young and she was dying.

The after-part of the night wore on interminably. The starlight failed and the gloom blackened to the darkest hour. "She'll die at the gray of dawn," muttered Venters, remembering some old woman's fancy. The blackness paled to gray, and the gray lightened and day peeped over the eastern rim. Venters listened at the breast of the girl. She still lived. Did he only imagine that her heart beat stronger, ever so slightly, but stronger? He pressed his ear closer to her breast. And he rose with his own pulse quickening.

"If she doesn't die soon—she's got a chance—the barest chance to live," he said.

He wondered if the internal bleeding had ceased. There was no more film of blood upon her lips. But no corpse could have been whiter. Opening her blouse, he untied the scarf, and carefully picked away the sage leaves from the wound in her shoulder. It had closed. Lifting her lightly, he ascertained that the same was true of the hole where the bullet had come out. He reflected on the fact that clean wounds closed quickly in the healing upland air. He recalled instances of riders who had been cut and shot apparently to fatal issues; yet the blood had clotted, the wounds closed, and they had recovered. He had no way to tell if internal hemorrhage still went on, but he believed that it had stopped.

Otherwise she would surely not have lived so long. He marked the entrance of the bullet, and concluded that it had just touched the upper lobe of her lung. Perhaps the wound in the lung had also closed. As he began to wash the blood stains from her breast and carefully rebandage the wound, he was vaguely conscious of a strange, grave happiness in the thought that she might live.

Broad daylight and a hint of sunshine high on the cliff-rim to the west brought him to consideration of what he had better do.

And while busy with his few camp tasks he revolved the thing in his mind. It would not be wise for him to remain long in his present hiding-place. And if he intended to follow the cattle trail and try to find the rustlers he had better make a move at once. For he knew that rustlers, being riders, would not make much of a day's or night's absence from camp for one or two of their number; but when the missing ones failed to show up in reasonable time there would be a search. And Venters was afraid of that.

"A good tracker could trail me," he muttered. "And I'd be cornered here. Let's see. Rustlers are a lazy set when they're not on the ride. I'll risk it. Then I'll change my hiding-place."

He carefully cleaned and reloaded his guns. When he rose to go he bent a long glance down upon the unconscious girl. Then ordering Whitie and Ring to keep guard, he left the camp. The safest cover lay close under the wall of the canyon, and here through the dense thickets Venters made his slow, listening advance toward the oval. Upon gaining the wide opening he decided to cross it and follow the left wall till he came to the cattle trail. He scanned the oval as keenly as if hunting for antelope.

Then, stooping, he stole from one cover to another, taking advantage of rocks and bunches of sage, until he had reached the thickets under the opposite wall. Once there, he exercised extreme caution in his surveys of the ground ahead, but increased his speed when moving. Dodging from bush to bush, he passed the mouths of two canyons, and in the entrance of a third canyon he crossed a wash of swift clear water, to come abruptly upon the cattle trail.

It followed the low bank of the wash, and, keeping it in sight, Venters hugged the line of sage and thicket. Like the curves of a serpent the canyon wound for a mile or more and then opened into a valley. Patches of red showed clear against the purple of sage, and farther out on the level dotted strings of red led away to the wall of rock.

"Ha, the red herd!" exclaimed Venters.

Then dots of white and black told him there were cattle of other colors in this inclosed valley. Oldring, the rustler, was also a rancher. Venters's calculating eye took count of stock that outnumbered the red herd.

"What a range!" went on Venters. "Water and grass enough for fifty thousand head, and no riders needed!"

After his first burst of surprise and rapid calculation Venters lost no time there, but slunk again into the sage on his back trail. With the discovery of Oldring's hidden cattle-range had come enlightenment on several problems. Here the rustler kept his stock, here was Jane Withersteen's red herd; here were the few cattle that had disappeared from the Cottonwoods slopes during the last two years. Until Oldring had driven the red herd his thefts of cattle for that time had not been more than enough to supply meat for his men. Of late no drives had been reported from Sterling or the villages north. And Venters knew that the riders had wondered at Oldring's inactivity in that particular field. He and his band had been active enough in their visits to Glaze and Cottonwoods; they always had gold; but of late the amount gambled away and drunk and thrown away in the villages had given rise to much conjecture. Oldring's more frequent visits had resulted in new saloons, and where there had formerly been one raid or shooting fray in the little hamlets there were now many. Perhaps Oldring had another range farther on up the pass, and from there drove the cattle to distant Utah towns where he was little known. But Venters came finally to doubt this. And, from what he had learned in the last few days, a belief began to form in Venters's mind that Oldring's intimidations of the villages and the mystery of the Masked Rider, with his alleged evil deeds, and the fierce resistance offered any trailing riders, and the rustling of cattle—these things were only the craft of the rustler-chief to conceal his real life and purpose and work in Deception Pass.

And like a scouting Indian Venters crawled through the sage of the oval valley, crossed trail after trail on the north side, and at last entered the canyon out of which headed the cattle trail, and into which he had watched the rustlers disappear.

If he had used caution before, now he strained every nerve to force himself to creeping stealth and to sensitiveness of ear. He crawled along so hidden that he could not use his eyes except to aid himself in the toilsome progress through the brakes and ruins of cliff-wall. Yet from time to time, as he rested, he saw the massive red walls growing higher and wilder, more looming and broken. He made note of the fact that he was turning and climbing. The sage and thickets of oak and brakes of alder gave place to pinyon pine growing out of rocky soil. Suddenly a low, dull murmur assailed his ears. At first he thought it was thunder, then the slipping of a weathered slope of rock. But it was incessant, and as he progressed it filled out deeper and from a murmur changed into a soft roar.

"Falling water," he said. "There's volume to that. I wonder if it's the stream I lost."

The roar bothered him, for he could hear nothing else. Likewise, however, no rustlers could hear him. Emboldened by this and sure that nothing but a bird could see him, he arose from his hands and knees to hurry on. An opening in the pinyons warned him that he was nearing the height of slope.

He gained it, and dropped low with a burst of astonishment.

Before him stretched a short canyon with rounded stone floor bare of grass or sage or tree, and with curved, shelving walls. A broad rippling stream flowed toward him, and at the back of the canyon waterfall burst from a wide rent in the cliff, and, bounding down in two green steps, spread into a long white sheet.

If Venters had not been indubitably certain that he had entered the right canyon his astonishment would not have been so great.

There had been no breaks in the walls, no side canyons entering this one where the rustlers' tracks and the cattle trail had guided him, and, therefore, he could not be wrong. But here the canyon ended, and presumably the trails also.

"That cattle trail headed out of here," Venters kept saying to himself. "It headed out. Now what I want to know is how on earth did cattle ever get in here?"

If he could be sure of anything it was of the careful scrutiny he had given that cattle track, every hoofmark of which headed straight west. He was now looking east at an immense round boxed corner of canyon down which tumbled a thin, white veil of water, scarcely twenty yards wide. Somehow, somewhere, his calculations had gone wrong. For the first time in years he found himself doubting his rider's skill in finding tracks, and his memory of what he had actually seen. In his anxiety to keep under cover he must have lost himself in this offshoot of Deception Pass, and thereby in some unaccountable manner, missed the canyon with the trails. There was nothing else for him to think. Rustlers could not fly, nor cattle jump down thousand-foot precipices. He was only proving what the sage-riders had long said of this labyrinthine system of deceitful canyons and valleys—trails led down into Deception Pass, but no rider had ever followed them.

On a sudden he heard above the soft roar of the waterfall an unusual sound that he could not define. He dropped flat behind a stone and listened. From the direction he had come swelled something that resembled a strange muffled pounding and splashing and ringing. Despite his nerve the chill sweat began to dampen his forehead. What might not be possible in this stonewalled maze of mystery? The unnatural sound passed beyond him as he lay gripping his rifle and fighting for coolness. Then from the open came the sound, now distinct and different. Venters recognized a hobble-bell of a horse, and the cracking of iron on submerged stones, and the hollow splash of hoofs in water.

Relief surged over him. His mind caught again at realities, and curiosity prompted him to peep from behind the rock.

In the middle of the stream waded a long string of packed burros driven by three superbly mounted men. Had Venters met these dark-clothed, dark-visaged, heavily armed men anywhere in Utah, let alone in this robbers' retreat, he would have recognized them as rustlers. The discerning eye of a rider saw the signs of a long, arduous trip. These men were packing in supplies from one of the northern villages. They were tired, and their horses were almost played out, and the burros plodded on, after the manner of their kind when exhausted, faithful and patient, but as if every weary, splashing, slipping step would be their last.

All this Venters noted in one glance. After that he watched with a thrilling eagerness. Straight at the waterfall the rustlers drove the burros, and straight through the middle, where the water spread into a fleecy, thin film like dissolving smoke.

Following closely, the rustlers rode into this white mist, showing in bold black relief for an instant, and then they vanished.

Venters drew a full breath that rushed out in brief and sudden utterance.

"Good Heaven! Of all the holes for a rustler! . . . There's a cavern under that waterfall, and a passageway leading out to a canyon beyond. Oldring hides in there. He needs only to guard a trail leading down from the sage-flat above. Little danger of this outlet to the pass being discovered. I stumbled on it by luck, after I had given up. And now I know the truth of what puzzled me most—why that cattle trail was wet!"

He wheeled and ran down the slope, and out to the level of the sage-brush. Returning, he had no time to spare, only now and then, between dashes, a moment when he stopped to cast sharp eyes ahead. The abundant grass left no trace of his trail. Short work he made of the distance to the circle of canyons. He doubted that he would ever see it again; he knew he never wanted to; yet he looked at the red corners and towers with the eyes of a rider picturing landmarks never to be forgotten.

Here he spent a panting moment in a slow-circling gaze of the sage-oval and the gaps between the bluffs. Nothing stirred except the gentle wave of the tips of the brush. Then he pressed on past the mouths of several canyons and over ground new to him, now close under the eastern wall. This latter part proved to be easy traveling, well screened from possible observation from the north and west, and he soon covered it and felt safer in the deepening shade of his own canyon. Then the huge, notched bulge of red rim loomed over him, a mark by which he knew again the deep cove where his camp lay hidden. As he penetrated the thicket, safe again for the present, his thoughts reverted to the girl he had left there. The afternoon had far advanced. How would he find her? He ran into camp, frightening the dogs.

The girl lay with wide-open, dark eyes, and they dilated when he knelt beside her. The flush of fever shone in her cheeks. He lifted her and held water to her dry lips, and felt an inexplicable sense of lightness as he saw her swallow in a slow, choking gulp. Gently he laid her back.

"Who—are—you?" she whispered, haltingly.

"I'm the man who shot you," he replied.

"You'll—not—kill me—now?"

"No, no."

"What—will—you—do—with me?"

"When you get better—strong enough—I'll take you back to the canyon where the rustlers ride through the waterfall."

As with a faint shadow from a flitting wing overhead, the marble whiteness of her face seemed to change.

"Don't—take—me—back—there!"

3

THE COMING OF CASSIDY

BY CLARENCE E. MULFORD

Generations of readers and viewers grew up with Hopalong Cassidy, beginning with his appearance in pulp fiction and then in the movies and a television series that is still shown on cable channels. However, unlike the squeaky-clean-cut heroic figure portrayed by actor William Boyd riding a snow-white steed named Topper, the original Hopalong was a ranch-hand cowboy who saw no reason to rely on judicial process when he could right wrongs his own way. This chapter of the 1908 novel Hopalong's Hop *describes how he acquired his nickname.*

Having sent Jimmy to the Bar-20 with a message for Buck Peters and seen the tenderfeet start for Sharpsville on the right trail and under escort, Bill Cassidy set out for the Crazy M ranch, by the way of Clay Gulch. He was to report on the condition of some cattle that Buck had been offered cheap and he was anxious to get back to the ranch. It was in the early evening when he reached Clay Gulch and rode slowly down the dusty, shack-lined street in search of a hotel. The town and the street were hardly different from other towns and streets that he had seen all over the cow-country, but nevertheless he felt uneasy. The air seemed to be charged with danger, and it caused him to sit even more erect in the saddle and assume his habit of indifferent alertness. The first man he saw confirmed the feeling by staring at him insolently and sneering in a veiled way at the low-hung, tied-down holsters that graced Bill's thighs. The guns proclaimed the gun-man as surely as it would have been proclaimed by a sign; and it appeared that gun-men were not at that time held in high esteem by the citizens of Clay Gulch. Bill was growing fretful and peevish when the man, with a knowing shake of his head, turned away and entered the harness shop. "Trouble's brewin' somewheres around," muttered Bill, as he went on. He had singled out the first of two hotels when another citizen, turning the corner, stopped in his tracks and looked Bill over with a deliberate scrutiny that left but little to the imagination. He frowned and started away, but Bill spurred forward, determined to make him speak.

"Might I inquire if this is Clay Gulch?" he asked, in tones that made the other wince.

"You might," was the reply. "It is," added the citizen, "an' th' Crazy M lays fifteen mile west." Having complied with the requirements of common politeness the citizen of Clay Gulch turned and walked into the nearest saloon. Bill squinted after him and shook his head in indecision.

"He wasn't guessin', neither. He shore knowed where I wants to go. I reckon Oleson must 'a' said he was expectin' me." He would have been somewhat surprised had he known that Mr. Oleson, foreman of the Crazy M, had said nothing to anyone about the expected visitor, and that no one, not even on the ranch, knew of it. Mr. Oleson was blessed with taciturnity to a remarkable degree; and he had given up expecting to see anyone from Mr. Peters.

As Bill dismounted in front of the "Victoria" he noticed that two men further down the street had evidently changed their conversation and were examining him with frank interest and discussing him earnestly. As a matter of fact they had not changed the subject of their conversation, but had simply fitted him in the place of a certain unknown. Before he had arrived they discussed in the abstract; now they could talk in the concrete. One of them laughed and called softly over his shoulder, whereupon a third man appeared in the door, wiping his lips with the back of a hairy, grimy hand, and focused evil eyes upon the innocent stranger. He grunted contemptuously and, turning on his heel, went back to his liquid pleasures. Bill covertly felt of his clothes and stole a glance at his horse, but could see nothing wrong. He hesitated: should he saunter over for information or wait until the matter was brought to his attention? A sound inside the hotel made him choose the latter course, for his stomach threatened to become estranged and it simply howled for food. Pushing open the door he dropped his saddle in a corner and leaned against the bar.

"Have one with me to get acquainted?" he invited. "Then I'll eat, for I'm hungry. An' I'll use one of yore beds to-night, too."

The man behind the bar nodded cheerfully and poured out his drink. As he raised the liquor he noticed Bill's guns and carelessly let the glass return to the bar.

"Sorry, sir," he said coldly. "I'm hall out of grub, the fire's hout, hand the beds are taken. But mebby 'Awley, down the strite, can tyke care of you."

Bill was looking at him with an expression that said much and he slowly extended his arm and pointed to the untasted liquor.

"Allus finish what you start, English," he said slowly and clearly. "When a man goes to take a drink with me, and suddenly changes his mind, why I gets riled. I don't know what ails this town, an' I don't care; I don't give a cuss about yore grub an' your beds; but if you don't drink that liquor you poured out to drink, why I'll natchurally shove it down yore British throat so cussed hard it'll strain yore neck. Get to it!"

The proprietor glanced apprehensively from the glass to Bill, then on to the business-like guns and back to the glass, and the liquor disappeared at a gulp. "Wy," he explained, aggrieved. "There hain't no call for to get riled hup like that, strainger. I bloody well forgot it."

"Then don't you go an' 'bloody well' forget this: Th' next time I drops in here for grub an' a bed, you have 'em both, an' be plumb polite about it. Do you get me?" he demanded icily.

The proprietor stared at the angry puncher as he gathered up his saddle and rifle and started for the door. He turned to put away the bottle and the sound came near being unfortunate for him. Bill leaped sideways, turning while in the air and landed on his feet like a cat, his left hand gripping a heavy Colt that covered the short ribs of the frightened proprietor before that worthy could hardly realize the move.

"Oh, all right," growled Bill, appearing to be disappointed. "I reckoned mebby you was gamblin' on a shore thing. I feels impelled to offer you my sincere apology; you ain't th' kind as would even gamble on a shore thing. You'll see me again," he promised. The sound of his steps on the porch ended in a thud as he leaped to the ground and then he passed the window leading his horse and scowling darkly. The proprietor mopped his head and reached twice for the glass before he found it. "Gawd, what a bloody 'eathen," he grunted. "'E won't be as easy as the lawst was, blime 'im."

Mr. Hawley looked up and frowned, but there was something in the suspicious eyes that searched his face that made him cautious. Bill dropped his load on the floor and spoke sharply. "I want supper an' a bed. You ain't full up, an' you ain't out of grub. So I'm goin' to get 'em both right here. Yes?"

"You shore called th' turn, stranger," replied Mr. Hawley in his Sunday voice. "That's what I'm in business for. An' business is shore dull these days."

He wondered at the sudden smile that illuminated Bill's face and half guessed it; but he said nothing and went to work. When Bill pushed back from the table he was more at peace with the world and he treated, closely watching his companion. Mr. Hawley drank with a show of pleasure and forthwith brought out cigars. He seated himself beside his guest and sighed with relief.

"I'm plumb tired out," he offered. "An' I ain't done much. You look tired, too. Come a long way?"

"Logan," replied Bill. "Do you know where I'm goin'? An' why?" he asked.

Mr. Hawley looked surprised and almost answered the first part of the question correctly before he thought. "Well," he grinned, "if I could tell where strangers was goin', an' why, I wouldn't never ask 'em where they come from. An' I'd shore hunt up a li'l game of faro, you bet!"

Bill smiled. "Well, that might be a good idea. But, say, what ails this town, anyhow?"

"What ails it? Hum! Why, lack of money for one thing; scenery, for another; wimmin, for another. Oh, h—l, I ain't got time to tell you what ails it. Why?"

"Is there anything th' matter with me?"

"I don't know you well enough for to answer that kerrect."

"Well, would you turn around an' stare at me, an' seem pained an' hurt? Do I look funny? Has anybody put a sign on my back?"

"You looks all right to me. What's th' matter?"

"Nothin', yet," reflected Bill slowly. "But there will be, mebby. You was mentionin' faro. Here's a turn you can call: somebody in this wart of a two-by-nothin' town is goin' to run plumb into a big surprise. There'll mebby be a loud noise an' some smoke where it starts from; an' a li'l round hole where it stops. When th' curious delegation now holdin' forth on th' street slips in here after I'm in bed, an' makes inquiries about me, you can tell 'em that. An' if Mr. Victoria drops in casual, tell him I'm cleanin' my guns. Now then, show me where I'm goin' to sleep."

Mr. Hawley very carefully led the way into the hall and turned into a room opposite the bar. "Here she is, stranger," he said, stepping back. But Bill was out in the hall listening. He looked into the room and felt oppressed.

"No she ain't," he answered, backing his intuition. "She is upstairs, where there is a li'l breeze. By th' Lord," he muttered under his breath. "This is some puzzle." He mounted the stairs shaking his head thoughtfully. "It shore is, it shore is."

The next morning when Bill whirled up to the Crazy M bunkhouse and dismounted before the door a puncher was emerging. He started to say something, noticed Bill's guns and went on without a word. Bill turned around and looked after him in amazement. "Well, what th' devil!" he growled. Before he could do anything, had he wished to, Mr. Oleson stepped quickly from the house, nodded and hurried toward the ranch house, motioning for Bill to follow. Entering the house, the foreman of the Crazy M waited impatiently for Bill to get inside, and then hurriedly closed the door.

"They've got onto it some way," he said, his taciturnity gone; "but that don't make no difference if you've got th' sand. I'll pay you one hundred an' fifty a month, furnish yore cayuses an' feed you. I'm losin' more 'n two hundred cows every month an' can't get a trace of th' thieves. Harris, Marshal of Clay Gulch, is stumped, too. He can't move without proof; you can. Th' first man to get is George Thomas, then his brother Art. By that time you'll know how things lay. George Thomas is keepin' out of Harris' way. He killed a man last week over in Tuxedo an' Harris wants to take him over there. He'll not help you, so don't ask him to." Before Bill could reply or recover from his astonishment Oleson continued and described several men. "Look out for ambushes. It'll be th' hardest game you ever went up ag'in, an' if you ain't got th' sand to go through with it, say so."

Bill shook his head. "I got th' sand to go through with anythin' I starts, but I don't start here. I reckon you got th' wrong man. I come up here to look over a herd for Buck Peters; an' here you go shovin' wages like that at me. When I tells Buck what I've been offered he'll fall dead." He laughed. "Now I knows th' answer to a lot of things."

"Here, here!" he exclaimed as Oleson began to rave. "Don't you go an' get all het up like that. I reckon I can keep my face shut. An' lemme observe in yore hat-like ear that if th' rest of this gang is like th' samples I seen in town, a good gun-man would shore be robbin' you to take all that money for th' job. Fifty a month, for two months, would be a-plenty."

Oleson's dismay was fading, and he accepted the situation with a grim smile. "You don't know them fellers," he replied. "They're a bad lot, an' won't stop at nothin'."

"All right. Let's take a look at them cows. I want to get home soon as I can."

Oleson shook his head. "I gave you up, an' when I got a better offer I let 'em go. I'm sorry you had th' ride for nothin', but I couldn't get word to you."

Bill led the way in silence back to the bunk house and mounted his horse. "All right," he nodded. "I shore was late. Well, I'll be goin'."

"That gun-man is late, too," said Oleson. "Mebby he ain't comin'. You want th' job at my figgers?"

"Nope. I got a better job, though it don't pay so much money. It's steady, an' a hull lot cleaner. So-long," and Bill loped away, closely watched by Shorty Allen from the corral. And after an interval, Shorty mounted and swung out of the other gate of the corral and rode along the bottom of an arroyo until he felt it was safe to follow Bill's trail. When Shorty turned back he was almost to town, and he would not have been pleased had he known that Bill knew of the trailing for the last ten miles. Bill had doubled back and was within a hundred yards of Shorty when that person turned ranchward.

"Huh! I must be popular," grunted Bill. "I reckon I will stay in Clay Gulch till t'morrow mornin'; an' at the Victoria," he grinned. Then he laughed heartily. "Victoria! I got a better name for it than that, all right."

When he pulled up before the Victoria and looked in the proprietor scowled at him, which made Bill frown as he went on to Hawley's. Putting his horse in the corral he carried his saddle and rifle into the barroom and looked around.

There was no one in sight, and he smiled. Putting the saddle and rifle back in one corner under the bar and covering them with gunny sacks he strolled to the Victoria and entered through the rear door. The proprietor reached for his gun but reconsidered in time and picked up a glass, which he polished with exaggerated care. There was something about the stranger that obtruded upon his peace of mind and confidence. He would let some one else try the stranger out.

Bill walked slowly forward, by force of will ironing out the humor in his face and assuming his sternest expression. "I want supper an' a bed, an' don't forget to be plumb polite," he rumbled, sitting down by the side of a small table in such a manner that it did not in the least interfere with the movement of his right hand. The observing proprietor observed and gave strict attention to the preparation of the meal. The gun-man, glancing around, slowly arose and walked carelessly to a chair that had blank wall behind it, and from where he could watch windows and doors.

When the meal was placed before him he glanced up. "Go over there an' sit down," he ordered, motioning to a chair that stood close to the rifle that leaned against the wall. "Loaded?" he demanded. The proprietor could only nod. "Then sling it acrost yore knees an' keep still. Well, start movin'."

The proprietor walked as though he were in a trance but when he seated himself and reached for the weapon a sudden flash of understanding illumined him and caused cold sweat to bead upon his wrinkled brow. He put the weapon down again, but the noise made Bill look up.

"Acrost yore knees," growled the puncher, and the proprietor hastily obeyed, but when it touched his legs he let loose of it as though it were hot. He felt a great awe steal through his fear, for here was a gun-man such as he had read about. This man gave him all the best of it just to tempt him to make a break. The rifle had been in his hands, and while it was there the gun-man was calmly eating with both hands on the table and had not even looked up until the noise of the gun made him!

"My Gawd, 'e must be a wizard with 'em. I 'opes I don't forget!" With the thought came a great itching of his kneecap; then his foot itched so as to make him squirm and wear horrible expressions. Bill, chancing to glance up carelessly, caught sight of the expressions and growled, whereupon they became angelic. Fearing that he could no longer hold in the laughter that tortured him, Bill arose.

"Shoulder, arms!" he ordered, crisply. The gun went up with trained precision. "Been a sojer," thought Bill. "Carry, arms! About, face! To a bedroom, march!" He followed, holding his sides, and stopped before the room. "This th' best?" he demanded. "Well, it ain't good enough for me. About, face! Forward, march! Column, left! Ground, arms! Fall out." Tossing a coin on the floor as payment for the supper Bill turned sharply and went out without even a backward glance.

The proprietor wiped the perspiration from his face and walked unsteadily to the bar, where he poured out a generous drink and gulped it down. Peering out of the door to see if the coast was clear, he scurried across the street and told his troubles to the harness-maker.

Bill leaned weakly against Hawley's and laughed until the tears rolled down his cheeks. Pushing weakly from the building he returned to the Victoria to play another joke on its proprietor. Finding it vacant he slipped upstairs and hunted for a room to suit him. The bed was the softest he had seen for a long time and it lured him into removing his boots and chaps and guns, after he had propped a chair against the door as a warning signal, and stretching out flat on his back, he prepared to enjoy solid comfort. It was not yet dark, and as he was not sleepy he lay there thinking over the events of the past twenty-four hours, often laughing so hard as to shake the bed. What a reputation he would have in the morning! The softness of the bed got in its work and he fell asleep, for how long he did not know; but when he awakened it was dark and he heard voices coming up from below. They came from the room he had refused to take. One expression banished all thoughts of sleep from his mind and he listened intently.

"'Red-headed Irish gunman.' Why, they means me! 'Make him hop into h—l.' I don't reckon I'd do that for anybody, even my friends."

"I tried to give 'im this room, but 'e wouldn't tyke it" protested the proprietor, hurriedly. "'E says the bloody room wasn't good enough for 'im, hand 'e marches me out hand makes off. Likely 'e's in 'Awley's."

"No, he ain't," growled a strange voice. "You've gone an' bungled th' whole thing."

"But I s'y I didn't, you know. I tries to give 'im this werry room, George, but 'e wouldn't 'ave it. D'y think I wants 'im running haround this blooming town? 'E's worse nor the other, hand Gawd knows 'e was bad enough. 'E's a coldblooded beggar, 'e is!"

"You missed yore chance," grunted the other. "Wish Z had that gun you had."

"I was wishing to Gawd you did," retorted the proprietor. "It never looked so bloody big before, d—n 'is 'ide!"

"Well, his cayuse is in Hawley's corral," said the first speaker. "If I ever finds Hawley kept him under cover I'll blow his head off. Come on; we'll get Harris first. He ought to be gettin' close to town if he got th' word I sent over to Tuxedo. He won't let us call him. He's a man of his word."

"He'll be here, all right. Fred an' Tom is watchin' his shack, an' we better take th' other end of town there's no tellin' how he'll come in now," suggested Art Thomas. "But I wish I knowed where that cussed gun-man is."

As they went out Bill, his chaps on and his boots in his hand, crept down the stairs, and stopped as he neared the hall door. The proprietor was coming back. The others were outside, going to their stations and did not hear the choking gasp that the proprietor made as a pair of strong hands reached out and throttled him. When he came to he was lying face down on a bed, gagged and bound by a rope that cut into his flesh with every movement. Bill, waiting a moment, slipped into the darkness and was swallowed up. He was looking for Mr. Harris, and looking eagerly.

The moon arose and bathed the dusty street and its crude shacks in silver, cunningly and charitably hiding its ugliness; and passed on as the skirmishing rays of the sun burst into the sky in close and eternal pursuit. As the dawn spread swiftly and long, thin shadows sprang across the sandy street, there arose from the dissipated darkness close to the wall of a building an armed man, weary and slow from a tiresome vigil. Another emerged from behind a pile of boards that faced the marshal's abode, while down the street another crept over the edge of a dried-out water course and swore softly as he stood up slowly to flex away the stiffness of cramped limbs. Of vain speculation he was empty; he had exhausted all the whys and hows long before and now only muttered discontentedly as he reviewed the hours of fruitless waiting. And he was uneasy; it was not like Harris to take a dare and swallow his own threats without a struggle. He looked around apprehensively, shrugged his shoulders and stalked behind the shacks across from the two hotels.

Another figure crept from the protection of Hawley's corral like a slinking coyote, gun in hand and nervously alert. He was just in time to escape the challenge that would have been hurled at him by Hawley, himself, had that gentleman seen the skulker as he grouchily opened one shutter and scowled sleepily at the kindling eastern sky. Mr. Hawley was one of those who go to bed with regret and get up with remorse, and his temper was always easily disturbed before breakfast. The skulker, safe from the remorseful gentleman's eyes, and gun, kept close to the building as he walked and was again fortunate, for he had passed when Mr. Hawley strode heavily into his kitchen to curse the cold, rusty stove, a rite he faithfully performed each morning. Across the street George and Art Thomas walked to meet each other behind the row of shacks and stopped near the harness shop to hold a consultation. The subject was so interesting that for a few moments they were oblivious to all else.

A man softly stepped to the door of the Victoria and watched the two across the street with an expression on his face that showed his smiling contempt for them and their kind. He was a small man, so far as physical measurements go, but he was lithe, sinewy and compact. On his opened vest, hanging slovenly and blinking in the growing light as if to prepare itself for the blinding glare of midday, glinted a five-pointed star of nickel, a lowly badge that every rural community knows and holds in an awe far above the metal or design. Swinging low on his hip gleamed the ivory butt of a silver-plated Colt, the one weakness that his vanity seized upon. But under the silver and its engraving, above and before the cracked and stained ivory handles, lay the power of a great force; and under the casing of the marshal's small body lay a virile manhood, strong in courage and determination. Toby Harris watched, smilingly; he loved the dramatic and found keen enjoyment in the situation. Out of the corner of his eye he saw a carelessly dressed cowpuncher slouching indolently along close to the buildings on the other side of the street with the misleading sluggishness of a panther. The red hair, kissed by the slanting rays of the sun where it showed beneath the soiled sombrero, seemed to be a flaming warning; the half -closed eyes, squinting under the brim of the big hat, missed nothing as they darted from point to point.

The marshal stepped silently to the porch and then on to the ground, his back to the rear of the hotel, waiting to be discovered. He had been in sight perhaps a minute. The cowpuncher made a sudden, eye-baffling movement and smoke whirled about his hips. Fred, turning the corner behind the marshal, dropped his gun with a scream of rage and pain and crashed against the window in sudden sickness, his gunhand hanging by a tendon from his wrist. The marshal stepped quickly forward at the shot and for an instant gazed deeply into the eyes of the startled rustlers. Then his Colt leaped out and crashed a fraction of a second before the brothers fired. George Thomas reeled, caught sight of the puncher and fired by instinct. Bill, leaving Harris to watch the other side of the street, was watching the rear corner of the Victoria and was unprepared for the shot. He crumpled and dropped and then the marshal, enraged, ended the rustler's earthly career in a stream of flame and smoke. Tom, turning into the street further down, wheeled and dashed for his horse, and Art, having leaped behind the harness shop, turned and fled for his life. He had nearly reached his horse and was going at top speed with great leaps when the prostrate man in the street, raising on his elbow, emptied his gun after him, the five shots sounding almost as one. Art Thomas arose convulsively, steadied himself and managed to gain the saddle. Harris looked hastily down the street and saw a cloud of dust racing northward, and grunted. "Let them go they won't never come back no more." Running to the cowpuncher he raised him after a hurried examination of the wounded thigh.

"Hop along, Cassidy," he smiled in encouragement. "You'll be a better man with one good laig than th' whole gang was all put together."

The puncher smiled faintly as Hawley, running to them, helped him toward his hotel. "Th' bone is plumb smashed. I reckon I'll hop along through life. It'll be hop along, for me, all right. That's my name, all right. Huh! Hopalong Cassidy! But I didn't hop into it, did I, Harris?" he grinned bravely.

And thus was born a nickname that found honor and fame in the cow-country a name that stood for loyalty, courage and most amazing gun-play. I have Red's word for this, and the endorsement of those who knew him at the time. And from this on, up to the time he died, and after, we will forsake "Bill" and speak of him as Hopalong Cassidy, a cowpuncher who lived and worked in the days when the West was wild and rough and lawless; and who, like others, through the medium of the only court at hand, Judge Colt, enforced justice as he believed it should be enforced.

4

THE RUSTLER OF WIND RIVER

BY GEORGE W. OGDEN

George W. Ogden was a Midwestern newspaperman whose career spanned the end of the nineteenth and early twentieth centuries. He wrote more than 30 novels and many more pulp fiction stories, most of which were set in the Old West. Here, in The Rustler of Wind River, *published in 1917, he painted a vivid picture of a feisty young women and a realistic multicultural setting.*

Fort Shakie was on its downhill way in those days, and almost at the bottom of the decline. It was considered a post of penance by enlisted men and officers alike, nested up there in the high plateau against the mountains in its place of wild beauty and picturesque charm.

But natural beauty and Indian picturesqueness do not fill the place in the soldierly breast of fair civilian lady faces, nor torrential streams of cold mountain water supply the music of the locomotive's toot. Fort Shakie was being crept upon by civilization, true, but it was coming all too slow for the booted troopers and belted officers who must wear away the months in its lonely silences.

Within the memory of officers not yet gray the post had been a hundred and fifty miles from a railroad. Now it was but twenty; but even that short leap drowned the voice of the locomotive, and the dot at the rails' end held few of the endearments which make soldiering sweet.

Soon the post must go, indeed, for the need of it had passed. The Shoshones, Arapahoes, and Crows had forgotten their old animosities, and were traveling with Buffalo Bill, going to college, and raising alfalfa under the direction of a government farmer. The Indian police were in training to do the soldiers' work there. Soon the post must stand abandoned, a lonely monument to the days of hard riding, long watches, and bleak years. Not a soldier in the service but prayed for the hastening of the day.

No, there was not much over at Meander, at the railroad's end, to cheer a soldier's heart. It was an inspiring ride, in these autumn days, to come to Meander, past the little brimming lakes, which seemed to lie without banks in the green meadows where wild elk fed with the shy Indian cattle; over the white hills where the earth gave under the hoofs like new-fallen snow. But when one came to it through the expanding, dusty miles, the reward of his long ride was not in keeping with his effort.

Certainly, privates and subalterns could get drunk there, as speedily as in the centers of refinement, but there were no gentlemanly diversions at which an officer could dispel the gloom of his sour days in garrison.

The rough-cheeked girls of that high-wind country were well enough for cowboys to swing in their wild dances; just a rung above the squaws on the reservation in the matter of loquacity and gum.

Hardly the sort for a man who had the memory of white gloves and gleaming shoulders, and the traditions of the service to maintain.

Of course there was the exception of Nola Chadron, but she was not of Meander and the railroad's end, and she came only in flashes of summer brightness, like a swift, gay bird. But when Nola was at the ranchhouse on the river the gloom lifted over the post, and the sour leaven in the hearts of unmarried officers became as sweet as manna in the cheer of the unusual social outlet thus provided.

Nola kept the big house in a blaze of joy while she nested there through the summer days. The sixteen miles which stretched between it and the post ran out like a silver band before those who rode into the smile of her welcome, and when she flitted away to Cheyenne, champagne, and silk hats in the autumn, a grayness hovered again over the military post in the corner of the reservation.

Later than usual Nola had lingered on this fall, and the social outlet had remained open, like a navigable river over which the threat of ice hung but had not yet fallen. There were not lacking those who held that the lodestone which kept her there at the ranchhouse, when the gaieties of the season beckoned elsewhere, was in the breast of Major Cuvier King. Fatal infatuation, said the married ladies at the post, knowing, as everybody knew in the service, that Major King was betrothed to Frances Landcraft, the colonel's daughter.

No matter for any complications which might come of it, Nola had remained on, and the major had smiled on her, and ridden with her, and cut high capers in the dance, all pending the return of Frances and her mother from their summering at Bar Harbor in compliance with the family traditions. Now Frances was back again, and fortune had thrown a sunburst of beauty into the post by centering her and Nola here at once. Nola was the guest of the colonel's daughter, and there were flutterings in uniformed breasts.

Beef day was an event at the agency which never grew old to the people at the post. Without beef day they must have dwindled off to acidulous shadows, as the Indians who depended upon it for more solid sustenance would have done in the event of its discontinuation by a paternal government.

There were phases of Indian life and character which one never saw save on beef day, which fell on Wednesday of each week. Guests at the post watched the bright picture with the keen interest of a pageant on the stage; tourists came over by stage from Meander in the summer months by the score to be present; the resident officers, and their wives and families—such as had them—found in it an ever-recurring source of interest and relief from the tedium of days all alike.

This beef day, the morning following the meeting between Saul Chadron and his mysterious guest, a chattering group stood on the veranda of Colonel Landcraft's house in the bright friendly sun. They were waiting for horses to make the short journey to the agency—for one's honesty was questioned, his sanity doubted, if he went afoot in that country even a quarter of a mile—and gayest among them was Nola Chadron, the sun in her fair, springing hair.

Nola's crown reached little higher than a proper soldier's heart, but what she lacked in stature she supplied in plastic perfection of body and vivacity of face. There was a bounding joyousness of life in her; her eager eyes reflecting only the anticipated pleasures of today. There was no shadow of yesterday's regret in them, no cloud of tomorrow's doubt.

On the other balance there was Frances Landcraft, taller by half a head, soldierly, too, as became her lineage, in the manner of lifting her chin in what seemed a patrician scorn of small things such as a lady should walk the world unconscious of. The brown in her hair was richer than the clear agate of her eyes; it rippled across her ear like the scroll of water upon the sand.

There was a womanly dignity about her, although the threshold of girlhood must not have been far behind her that bright autumnal morning. Her nod was equal to a stave of Nola's chatter, her smile worth a league of the light laughter from that bounding little lady's lips. Not that she was always so silent as on that morning, there among the young wives of the post, at her own guest's side. She had her hours of overflowing spirits like any girl, but in some company she was always grave.

When Major King was in attendance, especially, the seeing ones made note. And there were others, too, who said that she was by nature a colonel among women, haughty, cold and aloof. These wondered how the major ever had made headway with her up to the point of gaining her hand. Knowing ones smiled at that, and said it had been arranged.

There were ambitions on both sides of that match, it was known— ambition on the colonel's part to secure his only child a station of dignity, and what he held to be of consequence above all achievements in the world. Major King was a rising man, with two friends in the cabinet. It was said that he would be a brigadier-general before he reached forty.

On the major's side, was the ambition to strengthen his political affiliations by alliance with a family of patrician strain, together with the money that his bride would bring, for Colonel Landcraft was a weighty man in this world's valued accumulations. So the match had been arranged.

The veranda of the colonel's house gave a view of the parade grounds and the long avenue that came down between the officers' houses, cottonwoods lacing their limbs above the road. There was green in the lawns, the flash of flowers between the leaves and shrubs, white-gleaming walls, trim walks, shorn hedges. It seemed a pleasant place of quiet beauty that bright September morning, and a pity to give it up by and by to dust and desolation; a place where men and women might be happy, but for the gnawing fire of ambition in their hearts.

Mrs. Colonel Landcraft was not going. Indians made her sick, she said, especially Indians sitting around in the tall grass waiting for the carcasses to be cut up and apportioned out to them in bloody chunks. But there seemed to be another source of her sickness that morning, measuring by the grave glances with which she searched her daughter's face. She wondered whether the major and Frances had quarreled; and if so, whether Nola Chadron had been the cause.

They were off, with the colonel and a lately-assigned captain in the lead. There was a keener pleasure in this beef day than usual for the colonel, for he had new ground to sow with its wonders, which were beginning to pale in his old eyes which had seen so much of the world.

"Very likely we'll see the minister's wife there," said he, as they rode forward, "and if so, it will be worth your while to take special note of her. St. John Mathews, the Episcopalian minister over there at the mission—those white buildings there among the trees—is a full-blooded Crow. One of the pioneer missionaries took him up and sent him back East to school, where in time he entered the ministry and married this white girl. She was a college girl, I've been told, glamoured by the romance of Mathews' life. Well, it was soon over."

The colonel sighed, and fell silent. The captain, feeling that it was intended that he should, made polite inquiry.

"The trouble is that Mathews is an Indian out of his place," the colonel resumed. "He returned here twenty years or so ago, and took up his work among his people. But as he advanced toward civilization, his wife began to slip back. Little by little she adopted the Indian ways and dress, until now you couldn't tell her from a squaw if you were to meet her for the first time. She presents a curious psychological study—or perhaps biological example of atavism, for I believe there's more body than soul in the poor creature now. It's nature maintaining the balance, you see. He goes up; she slips back.

"If she's there, she'll be squatting among the squaws, waiting to carry home her husband's allotment of warm, bloody beef. She doesn't have to do it, and it shames and humiliates Mathews, too, even though they say she cuts it up and divides it among the poorer Indians. She's a savage; her eyes sparkle at the sight of red meat."

They rounded the agency buildings and came upon an open meadow in which the slaughterhouses stood at a distance from the road. Here, in the grassy expanse, the Indians were gathered, waiting the distribution of the meat. The scene was barbarically animated. Groups of women in their bright dresses sat here and there on the grass, and apart from them in gravity waited old men in moccasins and blankets and with feathers in their hair. Spry young men smoked cigarettes and talked volubly, garbed in the worst of civilization and the most useless of savagery.

One and all they turned their backs upon the visitors, the nearest groups and individuals moving away from them with the impassive dignity of their race. There is more scorn in an Indian squaw's back, turned to an impertinent stranger, than in the faces of six matrons of society's finest-sifted under similar conditions.

Colonel Landcraft led his party across the meadow, entirely unconscious of the cold disdain of the people whom he looked down upon from his superior heights. He could not have understood if any there had felt the trespass from the Indians' side—and there was one, very near and dear to the colonel who felt it so—and attempted to explain.

The colonel very likely would have puffed up with military consequence almost to the bursting-point.

Feeling, delicacy, in those smeared, smelling creatures! Surliness in excess they might have, but dignity, not at all. Were they not there as beggars to receive bounty from the government's hand?

"Oh, there's Mrs. Mathews!" said Nola, with the eagerness of a child who has found a quail's nest in the grass. She was off at an angle, like a hunter on the scent. Colonel Landcraft and his guest followed with equal rude eagerness, and the others swept after them, Frances alone hanging back. Major King was at Nola's side. If he noted the lagging of his fiancée he did not heed.

The minister's wife, a shawl over her head, her braided hair in front of her shoulders like an Indian woman, rose from her place in startled confusion. She looked as if she would have fled if an avenue had been open, or a refuge presented. The embarrassed creature was obliged to stand in their curious eyes, and stammer in a tongue which seemed to be growing strange to her from its uncommon use.

She was a short woman, growing heavy and shapeless now, and there was gray in her black hair. Her skin was browned by sun, wind, and smoke to the hue of her poor neighbors and friends. When she spoke in reply to the questions which poured upon her, she bent her head like a timid girl.

Frances checked her horse and remained behind, out of range of hearing. She was cut to the heart with shame for her companions, and her cheek burned with the indignation that she suffered with the harried woman in their midst. A little Indian girl came flying past, ducking and dashing under the neck of Frances' horse, in pursuit of a piece of paper which the wind whirled ahead of her. At Frances' stirrup she caught it, and held it up with a smile.

"Did you lose this, lady?" she asked, in the very best of mission English.

"No," said Frances, bending over to see what it might be. The little girl placed it in her hand and scurried away again to a beckoning woman, who stood on her knees and scowled over her offspring's dash into the ways of civilized little girls.

It was a narrow strip of paper that she had rescued from the wind, with the names of several men written on it in pencil, and at the head of the list the name of Alan Macdonald. Opposite that name some crude hand had entered, with pen that had flowed heavily under his pressure, the figures "$500."

Frances turned it round her finger and sat waiting for the others to leave off their persecution of the minister's wife and come back to her, wondering in abstracted wandering of mind who Alan Macdonald might be, and for what purpose he had subscribed the sum of five hundred dollars.

"I think she's the most romantic little thing in the world!" Nola was declaring, in her extravagant surface way as they returned to where Frances sat her horse, her wandering eyes on the blue foothills, the strip of paper prominent about her finger. "Oh, honey! what's the matter? Did you cut your finger?"

"No," said Frances, her serious young face lighting with a smile, "it's a little subscription list, or something, that somebody lost. Alan Macdonald heads it for five hundred dollars. Do you know Alan Macdonald, and what his charitable purpose may be?"

Nola tossed her head with a contemptuous sniff.

"They call him the 'king of the rustlers' up the river," said she.

"Oh, he *is* a man of consequence, then?" said Frances, a quickening of humor in her brown eyes, seeing that Nola was up on her high horse about it.

"We'd better be going down to the slaughter-house if we want to see the fun," bustled the colonel, wheeling his horse. "I see a movement setting in that way."

"He's just a common thief!" declared Nola, with flushed cheek and resentful eye, as Frances fell in beside her for the march against the abattoir.

Frances still carried the paper twisted about her finger, reserving her judgment upon Alan Macdonald, for she knew something of the feuds of that hard-speaking land.

"Anyway, I suppose he'd like to have his paper back," she suggested. "Will you hand it to him the next time you meet him?"

Frances was entirely grave about it, although it was only a piece of banter which she felt that Nola would appreciate. But Nola was not in an appreciative mood, for she was a full-blooded daughter of the baronial rule. She jerked her head like a vicious bronco and reined hurriedly away from Frances as she extended the paper.

"I'll not touch the thing!" said Nola, fire in her eyes.

Major King was enjoying the passage between the girls, riding at Nola's side with his cavalry hands held precisely.

"If I'm not mistaken, the gentleman in question is there talking to Miller, the agent," said he, nodding toward two horsemen a little distance ahead. "But I wouldn't excite him, Miss Landcraft, if I were you. He's said to be the quickest and deadliest man with a weapon on this range."

Major King smiled over his own pleasantry. Frances looked at Nola with brows lifted inquiringly, as if waiting her verification. Then the grave young lady settled back in her saddle and laughed merrily, reaching across and touching her friend's arm in conciliating caress.

"Oh, you delightful little savage!" she said. "I believe you'd like to take a shot at poor Mr. Macdonald yourself."

"We never start anything on the reservation," Nola rejoined, quite seriously.

Miller, the Indian agent, rode away and left Macdonald sitting there on his horse as the military party approached. He spurred up to meet the colonel, and to present his respects to the ladies—a hard matter for a little round man with a tight paunch, sitting in a Mexican saddle. The party halted, and Frances looked across at Macdonald, who seemed to be waiting for Miller to rejoin him.

Macdonald was a supple, sinewy man, as he appeared across the few rods intervening. His coat was tied with his slicker at the cantle of his saddle, his blue flannel shirt was powdered with the white dust of the plain. Instead of the flaring neckerchief which the cowboys commonly favored, Macdonald wore a cravat, the ends of it tucked into the bosom of his shirt, and in place of the leather chaps of men who ride breakneck through brush and bramble, his legs were clad in tough brown corduroys, and fended by boots to his knees. There were revolvers in the holsters at his belt.

Not an unusual figure for that time and place, but something uncommon in the air of unbending severity that sat on him, which Frances felt even at that distance. He looked like a man who had a purpose in his life, and who was living it in his own brave way. If he was a cattle thief, as charged, thought she, then she would put her faith against the world that he was indeed a master of his trade.

They were talking around Miller, who was going to give them places of vantage for the coming show. Only Frances and Major King were left behind, where she had stopped her horse to look curiously across at Alan Macdonald, king of the rustlers, as he was called.

"It may not be anything at all to him, and it may be something important," said Frances, reaching out the slip to Major King. "Would you mind handing it to him, and explaining how it came into my hands?"

"I'll not have anything to do with the fellow!" said the major, flushing hotly. "How can you ask such a thing of *me*? Throw it away, it's no concern of yours—the memorandum of a cattle thief!"

Frances drew herself straight. Her imperious chin was as high as Major King ever had carried his own in the most self-conscious moment of his military career.

"Will you take it to him?" she demanded.

"Certainly not!" returned the major, haughtily emphatic. Then, softening a little, "Don't be silly, Frances; what a row you make over a scrap of blowing paper!"

"Then I'll take it myself!"

"Miss Landcraft!"

"*Major* King!"

It was the steel of conventionality against the flint of womanly defiance. Major King started in his saddle, as if to reach out and restrain her. It was one of those defiantly foolish little things which women and men—especially women—do in moments of pique, and Frances knew it at the time. But she rode away from the major with a hot flush of insubordination in her cheeks, and Alan Macdonald quickened from his pensive pose when he saw her coming.

His hand went to his hat when her intention became unmistakable to him. She held the little paper out toward him while still a rod away.

"A little Indian girl gave me this; she found it blowing along—they tell me you are Mr. Macdonald," she said, her face as serious as his own. "I thought it might be a subscription list for a church, or something, and that you might want it."

"Thank you, Miss Landcraft," said he, his voice low-modulated, his manner easy.

Her face colored at the unexpected way of this man without a coat, who spoke her name with the accent of refinement, just as if he had known her, and had met her casually upon the way.

"I have seen you a hundred times at the post and the agency," he explained, to smooth away her confusion. "I have seen you from afar."

"Oh," said she, as lame as the word was short.

He was scanning the written paper. Now he looked at her, a smile waking in his eyes. It moved in slow illumination over his face, but did not break his lips, pressed in their stern, strong line. She saw that his long hair was light, and that his eyes were gray, with sandy brows over them which stood on end at the points nearest his nose, from a habit of bending them in concentration, she supposed, as he had been doing but a moment before he smiled.

"No, it isn't a church subscription, Miss Landcraft, it's for a cemetery," said he.

"Oh," said she again, wondering why she did not go back to Major King, whose horse appeared restive, and in need of the spur, which the major gave him unfeelingly.

At the same time she noted that Alan Macdonald's forehead was broad and deep, for his leather-weighted hat was pushed back from it where his fair, straight hair lay thick, and that his bony chin had a little croft in it, and that his face was long, and hollowed like a student's, and that youth was in his eyes in spite of the experience which hardships of unknown kind had written across his face. Not a handsome man, but a strong one in his way, whatever that way might be.

"I am indebted to you for this," said he, drawing forth his watch with a quick movement as he spoke, opening the back cover, folding the little paper carefully away in it, "and grateful beyond words."

"Good-bye, Mr. Macdonald," said she, wheeling her horse suddenly, smiling back at him as she rode away to Major King.

Alan Macdonald sat with his hat off until she was again at the major's side, when he replaced it over his fair hair with slow hand, as if he had come from some holy presence. As for Frances, her turn of defiance had driven her clouds away. She met the major smiling and radiant, a twinkling of mischief in her lively eyes.

The major was a diplomat, as all good soldiers, and some very indifferent ones, are. Whatever his dignity and gentler feelings had suffered while she was away, he covered the hurt now with a smile.

"And how fares the bandit king this morning?" he inquired.

"He seems to be in spirits," she replied.

The others were out of sight around the buildings where the carcasses of beef had been prepared. Nobody but the major knew of Frances' little dash out of the conventional, and the knowledge that it was so was comfortable in his breast.

"And the pe-apers," said he, in melodramatic whisper, "were they the thieves' muster roll?"

"He isn't a thief," said she, with quiet dignity, "he's a gentleman. Yes, the paper *was* important."

"Ha! the plot deepens!" said Major King.

"It was a matter of life and death," said she, with solemn rebuke for his levity, speaking a truer word than she was aware.

5

THE CABALLERO'S WAY

BY O. HENRY

Admirers of the justice-seeking Cisco Kid of films and television would never recognize the cold-blooded killer character created by master storyteller O. Henry. But, as this 1907 short story demonstrates, he was just such a desperado. But then again, bad guys are usually more interesting to read about than their law-abiding counterparts.

The Cisco Kid had killed six men in more or less fair scrimmages, had murdered twice as many (mostly Mexicans), and had winged a larger number whom he modestly forbore to count. Therefore a woman loved him.

The Kid was twenty-five, looked twenty; and a careful insurance company would have estimated the probable time of his demise at, say, twenty-six. His habitat was anywhere between the Frio and the Rio Grande. He killed for the love of it—because he was quick-tempered—to avoid arrest—for his own amusement—any reason that came to his mind would suffice. He had escaped capture because he could shoot five-sixths of a second sooner than any sheriff or ranger in the service, and because he rode a speckled roan horse that knew every cow-path in the mesquite and pear thickets from San Antonio to Matamoras.

Tonia Perez, the girl who loved the Cisco Kid, was half Carmen, half Madonna, and the rest—oh, yes, a woman who is half Carmen and half Madonna can always be something more—the rest, let us say, was humming-bird. She lived in a grass-roofed jacal near a little Mexican settlement at the Lone Wolf Crossing of the Frio. With her lived a father or grandfather, a lineal Aztec, somewhat less than a thousand years old, who herded a hundred goats and lived in a continuous drunken dream from drinking mescal. Back of the jacal a tremendous forest of bristling pear, twenty feet high at its worst, crowded almost to its door. It was along the bewildering maze of this spinous thicket that the speckled roan would bring the Kid to see his girl. And once, clinging like a lizard to the ridge-pole, high up under the peaked grass roof, he had heard Tonia, with her Madonna face and Carmen beauty and humming-bird soul, parley with the sheriff's posse, denying knowledge of her man in her soft melange of Spanish and English.

One day the adjutant-general of the State, who is, ex offico, commander of the ranger forces, wrote some sarcastic lines to Captain Duval of Company X, stationed at Laredo, relative to the serene and undisturbed existence led by murderers and desperadoes in the said captain's territory.

The captain turned the colour of brick dust under his tan, and forwarded the letter, after adding a few comments, per ranger Private Bill Adamson, to ranger Lieutenant Sandridge, camped at a water hole on the Nueces with a squad of five men in preservation of law and order.

Lieutenant Sandridge turned a beautiful couleur de rose through his ordinary strawberry complexion, tucked the letter in his hip pocket, and chewed off the ends of his gamboge moustache.

The next morning he saddled his horse and rode alone to the Mexican settlement at the Lone Wolf Crossing of the Frio, twenty miles away.

Six feet two, blond as a Viking, quiet as a deacon, dangerous as a machine gun, Sandridge moved among the Jacales, patiently seeking news of the Cisco Kid.

Far more than the law, the Mexicans dreaded the cold and certain vengeance of the lone rider that the ranger sought. It had been one of the Kid's pastimes to shoot Mexicans "to see them kick": if he demanded from them moribund Terpsichorean feats, simply that he might be entertained, what terrible and extreme penalties would be certain to follow should they anger him! One and all they lounged with upturned palms and shrugging shoulders, filling the air with "quien sabes" and denials of the Kid's acquaintance.

But there was a man named Fink who kept a store at the Crossing—a man of many nationalities, tongues, interests, and ways of thinking.

"No use to ask them Mexicans," he said to Sandridge. "They're afraid to tell. This hombre they call the Kid—Goodall is his name, ain't it?—he's been in my store once or twice. I have an idea you might run across him at—but I guess I don't keer to say, myself. I'm two seconds later in pulling a gun than I used to be, and the difference is worth thinking about. But this Kid's got a half-Mexican girl at the Crossing that he comes to see. She lives in that jacal a hundred yards down the arroyo at the edge of the pear. Maybe she—no, I don't suppose she would, but that jacal would be a good place to watch, anyway."

Sandridge rode down to the jacal of Perez. The sun was low, and the broad shade of the great pear thicket already covered the grass-thatched hut. The goats were enclosed for the night in a brush corral near by. A few kids walked the top of it, nibbling the chaparral leaves. The old Mexican lay upon a blanket on the grass, already in a stupor from his mescal, and dreaming, perhaps, of the nights when he and Pizarro touched glasses to their New World fortunes—so old his wrinkled face seemed to proclaim him to be. And in the door of the jacal stood Tonia. And Lieutenant Sandridge sat in his saddle staring at her like a gannet agape at a sailorman.

The Cisco Kid was a vain person, as all eminent and successful assassins are, and his bosom would have been ruffled had he known that at a simple exchange of glances two persons, in whose minds he had been looming large, suddenly abandoned (at least for the time) all thought of him.

Never before had Tonia seen such a man as this. He seemed to be made of sunshine and blood-red tissue and clear weather. He seemed to illuminate the shadow of the pear when he smiled, as though the sun were rising again. The men she had known had been small and dark. Even the Kid, in spite of his achievements, was a stripling no larger than herself, with black, straight hair and a cold, marble face that chilled the noonday.

As for Tonia, though she sends description to the poorhouse, let her make a millionaire of your fancy. Her blue-black hair, smoothly divided in the middle and bound close to her head, and her large eyes full of the Latin melancholy, gave her the Madonna touch. Her motions and air spoke of the concealed fire and the desire to charm that she had inherited from the gitanas of the Basque province. As for the humming-bird part of her, that dwelt in her heart; you could not perceive it unless her bright red skirt and dark blue blouse gave you a symbolic hint of the vagarious bird.

The newly lighted sun-god asked for a drink of water. Tonia brought it from the red jar hanging under the brush shelter. Sandridge considered it necessary to dismount so as to lessen the trouble of her ministrations.

I play no spy; nor do I assume to master the thoughts of any human heart; but I assert, by the chronicler's right, that before a quarter of an hour had sped, Sandridge was teaching her how to plaint a six-strand rawhide stake-rope, and Tonia had explained to him that were it not for her little English book that the peripatetic padre had given her and the little crippled chivo, that she fed from a bottle, she would be very, very lonely indeed.

Which leads to a suspicion that the Kid's fences needed repairing, and that the adjutant-general's sarcasm had fallen upon unproductive soil.

In his camp by the water hole Lieutenant Sandridge announced and reiterated his intention of either causing the Cisco Kid to nibble the black loam of the Frio country prairies or of haling him before a judge and jury. That sounded business-like. Twice a week he rode over to the Lone Wolf Crossing of the Frio, and directed Tonia's slim, slightly lemon-tinted fingers among the intricacies of the slowly grow-ing lariata. A six-strand plait is hard to learn and easy to teach.

The ranger knew that he might find the Kid there at any visit. He kept his armament ready, and had a frequent eye for the pear thicket at the rear of the jacal. Thus he might bring down the kite and the humming-bird with one stone.

While the sunny-haired ornithologist was pursuing his studies, the Cisco Kid was also attending to his professional duties. He moodily shot up a saloon in a small cow village on Quintana Creek, killed the town marshal (plugging him neatly in the centre of his tin badge), and then rode away, morose and unsatisfied. No true artist is uplifted by shooting an aged man carrying an old-style .38 bulldog.

On his way the Kid suddenly experienced the yearning that all men feel when wrong-doing loses its keen edge of delight. He yearned for the woman he loved to reassure him that she was his in spite of it. He wanted her to call his bloodthirstiness bravery and his cruelty devotion. He wanted Tonia to bring him water from the red jar under the brush shelter, and tell him how the chivo was thriving on the bottle.

The Kid turned the speckled roan's head up the ten-mile pear flat that stretches along the Arroyo Hondo until it ends at the Lone Wolf Crossing of the Frio. The roan whickered; for he had a sense of locality and direction equal to that of a belt-line street-car horse; and he knew he would soon be nibbling the rich mesquite grass at the end of a forty-foot stake-rope while Ulysses rested his head in Circe's straw-roofed hut.

More weird and lonesome than the journey of an Amazonian explorer is the ride of one through a Texas pear flat. With dismal monotony and startling variety the uncanny and multiform shapes of the cacti lift their twisted trunks, and fat, bristly hands to encumber the way. The demon plant, appearing to live without soil or rain, seems to taunt the parched traveller with its lush grey greenness. It warps itself a thousand times about what look to be open and inviting paths, only to lure the rider into blind and impassable spine-defended "bottoms of the bag," leaving him to retreat, if he can, with the points of the compass whirling in his head.

To be lost in the pear is to die almost the death of the thief on the cross, pierced by nails and with grotesque shapes of all the fiends hovering about.

But it was not so with the Kid and his mount. Winding, twisting, circling, tracing the most fantastic and bewildering trail ever picked out, the good roan lessened the distance to the Lone Wolf Crossing with every coil and turn that he made.

While they fared the Kid sang. He knew but one tune and sang it, as he knew but one code and lived it, and but one girl and loved her. He was a single-minded man of conventional ideas. He had a voice like a coyote with bronchitis, but whenever he chose to sing his song he sang it. It was a conventional song of the camps and trail, running at its beginning as near as may be to these words: 'Don't you monkey with my Lulu girl, Or I'll tell you what I'll do. . . .' and so on. The roan was inured to it, and did not mind.

But even the poorest singer will, after a certain time, gain his own consent to refrain from contributing to the world's noises. So the Kid, by the time he was within a mile or two of Tonia's jacal, had reluctantly allowed his song to die away—not because his vocal performance had become less charming to his own ears, but because his laryngeal muscles were aweary.

As though he were in a circus ring the speckled roan wheeled and danced through the labyrinth of pear until at length his rider knew by certain landmarks that the Lone Wolf Crossing was close at hand. Then, where the pear was thinner, he caught sight of the grass roof of the jacal and the hackberry tree on the edge of the arroyo. A few yards farther the Kid stopped the roan and gazed intently through the prickly openings. Then he dismounted, dropped the roan's reins, and proceeded on foot, stooping and silent, like an Indian. The roan, knowing his part, stood still, making no sound.

The Kid crept noiselessly to the very edge of the pear thicket and reconnoitered between the leaves of a clump of cactus.

Ten yards from his hiding-place, in the shade of the jacal, sat his Tonia calmly plaiting a rawhide lariat. So far she might surely escape condemnation; women have been known, from time to time, to engage in more mischievous occupations. But if all must be told, there is to be added that her head reposed against the broad and comfortable chest of a tall red-and-yellow man, and that his arm was about her, guiding her nimble fingers that required so many lessons at the intricate six-strand plait.

Sandridge glanced quickly at the dark mass of pear when he heard a slight squeaking sound that was not altogether unfamiliar. A gun-scabbard will make that sound when one grasps the handle of a six-shooter suddenly. But the sound was not repeated; and Tonia's fingers needed close attention.

And then, in the shadow of death, they began to talk of their love; and in the still July afternoon every word they uttered reached the ears of the Kid.

"Remember, then," said Tonia, "you must not come again until I send for you. Soon he will be here. A vaquero at the tienda said to-day he saw him on the Guadalupe three days ago. When he is that near he always comes. If he comes and finds you here he will kill you. So, for my sake, you must come no more until I send you the word."

"All right," said the stranger. "And then what?"

"And then," said the girl, "you must bring your men here and kill him. If not, he will kill you."

"He ain't a man to surrender, that's sure," said Sandridge. "It's kill or be killed for the officer that goes up against Mr. Cisco Kid."

"He must die," said the girl. "Otherwise there will not be any peace in the world for thee and me. He has killed many. Let him so die. Bring your men, and give him no chance to escape."

"You used to think right much of him," said Sandridge.

Tonia dropped the lariat, twisted herself around, and curved a lemon-tinted arm over the ranger's shoulder.

"But then," she murmured in liquid Spanish, "I had not beheld thee, thou great, red mountain of a man! And thou art kind and good, as well as strong. Could one choose him, knowing thee? Let him die; for then I will not be filled with fear by day and night lest he hurt thee or me."

"How can I know when he comes?" asked Sandridge.

"When he comes," said Tonia, "he remains two days, sometimes three. Gregorio, the small son of old Luisa, the lavendera, has a swift pony. I will write a letter to thee and send it by him, saying how it will be best to come upon him. By Gregorio will the letter come. And bring many men with thee, and have much care, oh, dear red one, for the rattlesnake is not quicker to strike than is 'El Chivato,' as they call him, to send a ball from his pistola."

"The Kid's handy with his gun, sure enough," admitted Sandridge, "but when I come for him I shall come alone. I'll get him by myself or not at all. The Cap wrote one or two things to me that make me want to do the trick without any help. You let me know when Mr. Kid arrives, and I'll do the rest."

"I will send you the message by the boy Gregorio," said the girl. "I knew you were braver than that small slayer of men who never smiles. How could I ever have thought I cared for him?"

It was time for the ranger to ride back to his camp on the water hole. Before he mounted his horse he raised the slight form of Tonia with one arm high from the earth for a parting salute. The drowsy stillness of the torpid summer air still lay thick upon the dreaming afternoon. The smoke from the fire in the jacal, where the frijoles blubbered in the iron pot, rose straight as a plumb-line above the clay-daubed chimney. No sound or movement disturbed the serenity of the dense pear thicket ten yards away.

When the form of Sandridge had disappeared, loping his big dun down the steep banks of the Frio crossing, the Kid crept back to his own horse, mounted him, and rode back along the tortuous trail he had come.

But not far. He stopped and waited in the silent depths of the pear until half an hour had passed. And then Tonia heard the high, untrue notes of his unmusical singing coming nearer and nearer; and she ran to the edge of the pear to meet him.

The Kid seldom smiled; but he smiled and waved his hat when he saw her. He dismounted, and his girl sprang into his arms. The Kid looked at her fondly. His thick, black hair clung to his head like a wrinkled mat. The meeting brought a slight ripple of some undercurrent of feeling to his smooth, dark face that was usually as motionless as a clay mask.

"How's my girl?" he asked, holding her close.

"Sick of waiting so long for you, dear one," she answered. "My eyes are dim with always gazing into that devil's pincushion through which you come. And I can see into it such a little way, too. But you are here, beloved one, and I will not scold. Que mal muchacho! not to come to see your alma more often. Go in and rest, and let me water your horse and stake him with the long rope. There is cool water in the jar for you."

The Kid kissed her affectionately. "Not if the court knows itself do I let a lady stake my horse for me," said he. "But if you'll run in, chica, and throw a pot of coffee together while I attend to the caballo, I'll be a good deal obliged."

Besides his marksmanship the Kid had another attribute for which he admired himself greatly. He was muy caballero, as the Mexicans express it, where the ladies were concerned. For them he had always gentle words and consideration. He could not have spoken a harsh word to a woman. He might ruthlessly slay their husbands and brothers, but he could not have laid the weight of a finger in anger upon a woman. Wherefore many of that interesting division of humanity who had come under the spell of his politeness declared their disbelief in the stories circulated about Mr. Kid. One shouldn't believe everything one heard, they said. When confronted by their indignant men folk with proof of the caballero's deeds of infamy, they said maybe he had been driven to it, and that he knew how to treat a lady, anyhow.

Considering this extremely courteous idiosyncrasy of the Kid and the pride he took in it, one can perceive that the solution of the problem that was presented to him by what he saw and heard from his hiding-place in the pear that afternoon (at least as to one of the actors) must have been obscured by difficulties. And yet one could not think of the Kid overlooking little matters of that kind.

At the end of the short twilight they gathered around a supper of frijoles, goat steaks, canned peaches, and coffee, by the light of a lantern in the jacal. Afterward, the ancestor, his flock corralled, smoked a cigarette and became a mummy in a grey blanket. Tonia washed the few dishes while the Kid dried them with the flour-sacking towel. Her eyes shone; she chatted volubly of the inconsequent happenings of her small world since the Kid's last visit; it was as all his other home-comings had been.

Then outside Tonia swung in a grass hammock with her guitar and sang sad canciones de amor.

"Do you love me just the same, old girl?" asked the Kid, hunting for his cigarette papers.

"Always the same, little one," said Tonia, her dark eyes lingering upon him.

"I must go over to Fink's," said the Kid, rising, "for some tobacco. I thought I had another sack in my coat. I'll be back in a quarter of an hour."

"Hasten," said Tonia, "and tell me—how long shall I call you my own this time? Will you be gone again to-morrow, leaving me to grieve, or will you be longer with your Tonia?"

"Oh, I might stay two or three days this trip," said the Kid, yawning. "I've been on the dodge for a month, and I'd like to rest up."

He was gone half an hour for his tobacco. When he returned Tonia was still lying in the hammock.

"It's funny," said the Kid, "how I feel. I feel like there was somebody lying behind every bush and tree waiting to shoot me. I never had mullygrubs like them before. Maybe it's one of them presumptions. I've got half a notion to light out in the morning before day. The Guadalupe country is burning up about that old Dutchman I plugged down there."

"You are not afraid—no one could make my brave little one fear."

"Well, I haven't been usually regarded as a jack-rabbit when it comes to scrapping; but I don't want a posse smoking me out when I'm in your jacal. Somebody might get hurt that oughtn't to."

"Remain with your Tonia; no one will find you here."

The Kid looked keenly into the shadows up and down the arroyo and toward the dim lights of the Mexican village.

"I'll see how it looks later on," was his decision. . . .

At midnight a horseman rode into the rangers' camp, blazing his way by noisy "halloes" to indicate a pacific mission. Sandridge and one or two others turned out to investigate the row. The rider announced himself to be Domingo Sales, from the Lone Wolf Crossing. He bore a letter for Senor Sandridge. Old Luisa, the lavendera, had persuaded him to bring it, he said, her son Gregorio being too ill of a fever to ride.

Sandridge lighted the camp lantern and read the letter. These were its words:

"Dear One: He has come. Hardly had you ridden away when he came out of the pear. When he first talked he said he would stay three days or more. Then as it grew later he was like a wolf or a fox, and walked about without rest, looking and listening. Soon he said he must leave before daylight when it is dark and stillest. And then he seemed to suspect that I be not true to him. He looked at me so strange that I am frightened. I swear to him that I love him, his own Tonia. Last of all he said I must prove to him I am true. He thinks that even now men are waiting to kill him as he rides from my house. To escape he says he will dress in my clothes, my red skirt and the blue waist I wear and the brown mantilla over the head, and thus ride away. But before that he says that I must put on his clothes, his pantalones and camisa and hat, and ride away on his horse from the jacal as far as the big road beyond the crossing and back again. This before he goes, so he can tell if I am true and if men are hidden to shoot him. It is a terrible thing. An hour before daybreak this is to be. Come, my dear one, and kill this man and take me for your Tonia. Do not try to take hold of him alive, but kill him quickly. Knowing all, you should do that. You must come long before the time and hide yourself in the little shed near the jacal where the wagon and saddles are kept. It is dark in there. He will wear my red skirt and blue waist and brown mantilla. I send you a hundred kisses. Come surely and shoot quickly and straight.

- Thine Own Tonia"

Sandridge quickly explained to his men the official part of the missive. The rangers protested against his going alone.

"I'll get him easy enough," said the lieutenant. "The girl's got him trapped. And don't even think he'll get the drop on me."

Sandridge saddled his horse and rode to the Lone Wolf Crossing. He tied his big dun in a clump of brush on the arroyo, took his Winchester from its scabbard, and carefully approached the Perez jacal.

There was only the half of a high moon drifted over by ragged, milk-white gulf clouds.

The wagon-shed was an excellent place for ambush; and the ranger got inside it safely. In the black shadow of the brush shelter in front of the jacal he could see a horse tied and hear him impatiently pawing the hard-trodden earth.

He waited almost an hour before two figures came out of the jacal. One, in man's clothes, quickly mounted the horse and galloped past the wagon-shed toward the crossing and village. And then the other figure, in skirt, waist, and mantilla over its head, stepped out into the faint moonlight, gazing after the rider. Sandridge thought he would take his chance then before Tonia rode back. He fancied she might not care to see it.

"Throw up your hands," he ordered loudly, stepping out of the wagon-shed with his Winchester at his shoulder.

There was a quick turn of the figure, but no movement to obey, so the ranger pumped in the bullets—one—two—three—and then twice more; for you never could be too sure of bringing down the Cisco Kid. There was no danger of missing at ten paces, even in that half moonlight.

The old ancestor, asleep on his blanket, was awakened by the shots. Listening further, he heard a great cry from some man in mortal distress or anguish, and rose up grumbling at the disturbing ways of moderns.

The tall, red ghost of a man burst into the jacal, reaching one hand, shaking like a tule reed, for the lantern hanging on its nail. The other spread a letter on the table.

"Look at this letter, Perez," cried the man. "Who wrote it?"

"Ah, Dios! it is Senor Sandridge," mumbled the old man, approaching. "Pues, senor, that letter was written by 'El Chivato,' as he is called—by the man of Tonia. They say he is a bad man; I do not know. While Tonia slept he wrote the letter and sent it by this old hand of mine to Domingo Sales to be brought to you. Is there anything wrong in the letter? I am very old; and I did not know. Valgame Dios! it is a very foolish world; and there is nothing in the house to drink— nothing to drink."

Just then all that Sandridge could think of to do was to go outside and throw himself face downward in the dust by the side of his humming-bird, of whom not a feather fluttered. He was not a caballero by instinct, and he could not understand the niceties of revenge.

A mile away the rider who had ridden past the wagon-shed struck up a harsh, untuneful song, the words of which began:

Don't you monkey with my Lulu girl
Or I'll tell you what I'll do—

6

A HANDFUL OF COWBOY SONGS

Cowboys and other Old Westerners enjoyed singing as much as any other culture does, and perhaps even more so when their only entertainment was the sound of their own voices while riding night-herd or sitting around a campfire.

Here are four traditional ballads, each chronicling an event that ends with a moral.

The Texas Ranger

Come, all ye Texas rangers, wherever you may be,
I'll tell ye of some trouble that happened unto me.
Come, all ye Texas rangers, I'm sure I wish you well,
My name is nothing extra, so that I will not tell.

When at the age of sixteen I joined the jolly band,
That marched from San Antonio down to the Rio Grande.

Our captain he informed us, I suppose he thought it right,
"Before you reach the Station, my boys, you'll have to fight."

We saw the Indians coming, we heard them give the yell;
My feelings at that moment, no human tongue can tell.
We saw the glittering lances, the arrows round me hailed;
My heart it sank within, my courage almost failed.

We fought them nine long hours before the strife was o'er,
And the like of dead and dying I never saw before.
Twelve of the noblest rangers that ever roamed the West,
Were buried with their comrades and sank in peace to rest.

Then I thought of my dear mother, who through tears to me did say,
"These men to you are strangers; with me you'd better stay."
But I thought her old and childish, the best she did not know,
For my mind was bent on rambling and rambling I did go.

Perhaps you have a mother, perhaps a sister, too;
Likewise you have a sweetheart to weep and moan for you.
If this be your condition and you're inclined to roam,
I'll tell you by experience you'd better stay at home.

Billy the Kid

I'll sing you a true song of Billy the Kid,
And tell of the desperate deeds that he did,
Out here in the West, boys, in New Mexico,
When a man's best friend was his old Forty-four.

When Billy the Kid was a very young lad,
In old Silver City, he went to be bad;
At twelve years of age the Kid killed his first man,
Then blazed a wide trail with a gun in each hand.

Fair Mexican maidens played soft on guitars
And sang of "Billito" their king 'neath the stars;
He was a brave lover, and proud of his fame,
And no man could stand 'gainst the Kid's deadly aim.

Now Billy ranged wide, his killings were vile;
He shot fast, and first, when his blood got a-rile,
And, 'fore his young manhood did reach its sad end,
His six-guns held notches for twenty-one men.

Then Gov'ner Lew Wallace sent word to the Kid
To ride in and talk, for a pardon to bid,
But Billy said: "I ain't a-feerd of the law;
There's no man a-livin' can beat me to the draw!"

The Gov'ner then sent for another fast man:
Pat Garrett, the sheriff, and told of a plan
To catch Billy napping at his gal's; so he said:
"We'll bring him to Justice: alive or plumb dead!"

"Twas on that same night, into town Billy rid,
And said: "Mis amigos, all hark to the Kid!
There's twenty-one men I have put bullets through
And Sheriff, Pat Garrett, must make twenty-two!"

Now this is how Billy the Kid met his fate:
The bright moon was shining, the hour was late;
To Pete Maxwell's place Billy went in all pride,
Not knowing the dark hid the Sheriff inside.

As Billy show'd plain in the moon-lighted door,
He fell in his tracks, and laid dead on the floor;
Shot down by Pat Garrett, who one was his friend,
Young Billy, the Outlaw, and his life did end!

There's many a young boy with fine face and air
That starts in his life with the chances all fair;
But, like young Billito, he wanders astray
And departs his life in the same hardful way!

Zebra Dun

We were camped on the bend
at the head of the Cimmarron,
When along come a stranger,
and he stopped to argue some,
Well, he looked so very foolish
we began to look around,
We thought he was a greenhorn,
just escaped from town.

He said he'd lost his job
upon the Sante Fe,
And was going cross the prairie
to strike the 7D,
He didn't say how come it,

some trouble with the boss,
And asked if he could borrow
a fat saddle horse.

This tickled all the boys to death,
they laughed right up their sleeves,
Oh, we will lend you a fine horse,
as fresh as fat as you please,
Then Shorty grabbed the lariat,
and he roped the Zebra Dun,
And he gave him to the stranger,
and waited for the fun.

Now old Dunny was an outlaw,
he had grown so very wild,
Well he could paw the moon down,
boys he could jump a mile,
Old Dunny stood right still,
as if he didn't know,
Until he was saddle
and a-ready for the go.

When the stranger hit the saddle,
well old Dunny quit the earth,
He traveled right straight upwards
for all that he was worth,
A bucking and a squealing,
and a having wall-eyed fits,
His hind feet perpendicular,
his front feet in the bits.

We could see the tops of the mountains
under Dunny's every jump,
The stranger he was growed there,
like the camel's hump,
The stranger sat upon him,
and he curled his black mustache,
Just like a summer boarder
who was waiting for his hash.

Well, he thumped him in the shoulders
and he spurred him when he whirled,
He hollered to the punchers,
"I'm the wolf of the world,"
And when he had dismounted
once more upon the ground,
We knew he was a thoroughbred
and not a gent from town.

Now the boss who was a standing around,
a watching of the show,
He walked up to the stranger,
and he said he needn't go,
If you can handle a lariat
like you rode the Zebra Dun,
You're the man that I've been looking
for since the year of one.

Well, there's one thing, and a sure thing,
I've learned since I've been born,
That every educated feller
ain't a plumb greenhorn.

Sweet Betsy from Pike

Did you ever hear tell of sweet Betsy from Pike
Who crossed the wide prairies with her lover Ike
With two yoke of cattle and a one-spotted hog
A tall Shanghai rooster and an old yellow dog

One evening quite early they camped on the Platte
Made down their blankets on a green shady flat
Where Betsy, sore-footed, lay down to repose
With wonder Ike gazed on his Pike County rose

Their wagons broke down with a terrible crash
And out on the prairie rolled all sorts of trash
A few little baby clothes, done up with care
'Twas rather suspicious, though all on the square

The Shanghai ran off and the cattle all died
That morning the last piece of bacon was fried
Poor Ike was discouraged, and Betsy got mad
The dog drooped his tail and looked wondrously sad

They soon reached the desert, where Betsy gave out
And down in the sand she lay rolling about
While Ike, half distracted, looked on with surprise
Saying "Betsy, get up, you'll get sand in your eyes"

Sweet Betsy got up in a great deal of pain
Declared she'd go back to Pike County again
But Ike heaved a sigh, and they fondly embraced
And they traveled along with his arm 'round her waist

They swam the wide rivers and climbed the tall peaks
And camped on the prairies for weeks upon weeks
Starvation and cholera, hard work and slaughter
They reached California spite of hell and high water

That morning they stood on a very high hill
And with wonder looked down into old Placerville
Ike shouted and said, as he cast his eyes down
"Sweet Betsy, my darling, we've got to Hangtown."

Long Ike and sweet Betsy attended a dance
Where Ike wore a pair of his Pike County pants
Sweet Betsy was covered with ribbons and rings
Said Ike "You're an angel, but where are your wings?"

This Pike County couple got married, of course
But Ike became jealous, obtained a divorce
And Betsy, well satisfied, said with a shout,
"Goodbye, you big lummox, I'm glad you backed out."

Streets of Laredo

As I walked out in the streets of Laredo
As I walked out in Laredo one day,
I spied a dear cowboy wrapped up in white linen
Wrapped up in white linen and cold as the clay.

"I see by your outfit that you are a cowboy,"
These words he did say as I boldly stepped by;
"Come sit down beside me and hear my sad story
I am shot in the breast and I know I must die.

"It was once in the saddle I used to go dashing
It was once in the saddle I used to go gay;
But I first took to drinkin' and then to card playin'
Got shot in the breast and I am dying today.

"Oh, beat the drum slowly and play the fife lowly
Play the dead march as you carry me along;
Take me to the green valley, there lay the sod o'er me
For I'm a young cowboy and I know I've done wrong.

"Get six jolly cowboys to carry my coffin
Get six pretty maidens to bear up my pall;
Put bunches of roses all over my coffin
Put roses to deaden the sods as they fall.

"Then swing your rope slowly and rattle your spurs lowly
And give a wild whoop as you carry me along;
And in the grave throw me and roll the sod o'er me
For I'm a young cowboy and I know I've done wrong.

"Go bring me a cup, a cup of cold water
To cool my parched lips," the cowboy then said;
Before I returned his soul had departed
And gone to the round-up, the cowboy was dead.

We beat the drum slowly and played the fife lowly
And bitterly wept as we bore him along;
For we all loved our comrade, so brave, young, and handsome
We all loved our comrade although he'd done wrong.

7

THE SUNSET TRAIL

BY ALFRED HENRY LEWIS

Old Western fiction was full of real-life characters who assumed legendary status via novels and short stories in which they appeared. Such was the case of Bat Masterson, whose elegant vocabulary and shrewd schemes were later reflected in the popular television series. How close it came to the truth is largely irrelevant, for to quote the newspaperman's line in the classic John Wayne movie "The Man Who Shot Liberty Valence," "when legend becomes fact, print the legend." Case in point: this 1905 novel The Sunset Trail.

HOW IT MIGHT HAVE BEEN DIFFERENT

His baptismal name was William Barclay, but before the corn-coloured pencilling on his upper lip had foretold the coming of a moustache, he was known throughout that wide-flung region lying between the Platte and the Rio Grande, the Missouri and the Mountains, as Bat. This honour fell to the boyish share of Mr. Masterson because his quick eye, steady hand, and stealthy foot rendered him invincible against bears and buffaloes and other animals, *ferae naturae*, and gray oldsters of the plains were thereby reminded of a Batiste Brown who had been celebrated as a hunter in the faraway heroic days of Chouteau, Sublette, Bridger, and St. Vrain.

There is no such season as boyhood on the plains, folk are children one day, men the next, and thus it befell with Mr. Masterson. He owned, while yet his cheek was as hairless as an egg, primeval gravities and silences, and neither asked nor answered questions, neither took nor gave advice. Among his companions of the range he gained the reputation of one who "attends strictly to his own business"; and this contributed to his vogue and standing, and laid the bedplates of a popular confidence in Mr. Masterson.

Also, Mr. Masterson, being few of years and not without a dash of the artistic, was in his way a swell. His spurs were of wrought steel traced with gold, the handkerchief—an arterial red for hue—knotted about his brown throat was silk, not cotton, while his gray sombrero had been enriched with a bullion band of braided gold and silver, made in the likeness of a rattlesnake, fanged and ruby-eyed. This latter device cost Mr. Masterson the price of one hundred buffalo robes, and existed a source of wondering admiration from Dodge to the Pueblos.

As a final expression of dandyism, Mr. Masterson wore a narrow crimson sash wound twice about his waist, the fringed ends descending gallantly down his left leg. The sash had come from Mexico, smuggled in with a waggon load of Chihuahua hats, and when Mr. Masterson donned it, being privily a-blush to find himself so garish, he explained the same as something wherewith he might hogtie steers when in the course of duty he must rope and throw them. Doubtless the sash, being of a soft, reluctant texture and calculated to tie very tight into knots that would not slip, was of the precise best material with which to hogtie steers; but since Mr. Masterson never wore it on the range and always in the dance halls, it is suspected that he viewed it wholly in the light of a decoration.

Mr. Masterson's saddle, as exhibiting still further his sumptuous nature, was of stamped leather; while his war-bags and leggings were faced with dogskin, the long black fell warranted to shed rain like a tin roof. The one thing wanting a least flourish of ornament was Mr. Masterson's heavy, eight-square buffalo gun—a Sharp's 50-calibre rifle.

And yet this absence of embellishment was not because of Mr. Masterson's want of respect for the weapon; rather he respected it too much. A rifle was a serious creature in the eyes of Mr. Masterson, and not to be regarded as jewelry; to mount it with silver or inlay its stock with gold would have been as unbecoming as to encrust a prayer-book with diamonds. Mr. Masterson's rifle's name was Marie; and when abroad on the range he made remarks to it, and took it into his confidence, apropos of events which transpired as part of the day's work.

When Mr. Dixon, for whom Mr. Masterson was killing buffaloes along the Canadian, told that young gentleman how his visiting sister and niece would pass a fortnight at the 'Dobe Walls, the better to realise a virgin wilderness in all its charms, Mr. Masterson made no comment. Behind his wordlessness, however, Mr. Masterson nourished a poor opinion of this social movement. At its best, the 'Dobe Walls, as well as the buffalo range of which it lived at once the centre and the ragged flower, was rude beyond description, and by no means calculated—so Mr. Masterson thought—to dovetail with the tastes of ladies fresh from Beacon Hill. Besides, Mr. Masterson was not satisfied as to the depth and breadth of what friendships were professed by certain

Cheyennes, who hunted buffaloes in the neighbourhood of the Canadian, for their paleface brothers and sisters.

Mr. Masterson's opinions on this point of Cheyenne friendship was not the offspring of surmise. Within the month, eight Cheyennes, supposed by the authorities in Washington to be profoundly peaceful, had come upon him while busy with both hands husking the hide from a buffalo bull. Full of the Washington impression of a Cheyenne peace, at least so far as deeds done of daylight and on the surface were concerned, Mr. Masterson paid no mighty heed to the visitors. Indeed, he paid none at all until one of them caught up his rifle from the grass, and smote him with it on the head. The Cheyenne, cocking the gun and aiming it, told him in English learned at Carlisle, and, with epithets learned at the agencies, to _vamos_ or he'd shoot him in two. With the blood running down his face, Mr. Masterson so far accepted the Cheyenne suggestion as to back slowly from the muzzle of the rifle until he reached the edge of a ravine, upon which he had had his mind's eye from the beginning. Then he suddenly vanished out of harm's way.

Once in the ravine, Mr. Masterson flew for his camp, distant not a quarter of a mile. Getting a second rifle, Mr. Masterson bushwhacked those vivacious Cheyennes at the mouth of Mitchell's Canyon, and killed four, among them the violent individual who had so smote upon him with his own personal gun. The lost rifle, which was as the honour of Mr. Masterson, was recovered; and inasmuch as the four scalps were worth one hundred dollars in Dodge—for which amount they were a lien upon funds heaped together by public generosity to encourage the collection of such mementoes—it might be said that Mr. Masterson was repaid for his wound. He thought so, and in the language of diplomacy regarded the incident as closed.

For all that, the business was so frankly hostile in its transaction that Mr. Masterson, young of years yet ripe of Western wisdom, went more than half convinced that the Panhandle, at the time when Mr. Dixon decided to have his fair relatives pay it a visit, did not offer those conditions of a civilised safe refinement for which ladies of culture would look as their due. Mr. Masterson was right. Mr. Dixon's approval of his sister and her daughter in their descent upon the 'Dobe Walls was weakly foolish. Still, neither Mr. Masterson nor any one else felt free to show this truth to Mr. Dixon, and preparations for the tender invasion went briskly forward.

As Mr. Masterson was buying cartridges in the outfitting store, which emporium was one of the mud structures that constituted the 'Dobe Walls, he observed that Mr. Wright was clearing away the furniture from the office, this latter being a small room to the rear of the store.

"Going to give it to Billy Dixon's sister and her girl," explained Mr. Wright. "When do they hit camp?" asked Mr. Masterson, mildly curious.

"Day after to-morrow, I reckon; they're coming over in a buckboard. Billy says there's a French party, a Count or something, who is coming with them. It looks like he's going to marry Billy's niece. If he shows up, he'll have to bunk in with you buffalo killers over in Hanrahan's saloon."

"Just so he don't talk French to us," said Mr. Masterson, "I won't care. I've put up with Mexican and Cheyenne, but I draw the line at French."

There were a score of men at the 'Dobe Walls, and Ruth Pemberton confessed to herself that Mr. Masterson was the Admirable Crichton of the array. She secretly admired his powerful shoulders, and compared him—graceful and limber and lithe as a mountain lion—with the tubby Count Banti to that patrician's disadvantage. Also, Mr. Masterson's hands and feet were smaller than those of Count Banti.

Ruth Pemberton and Count Banti made brief saddle excursions up and down the banks of the Canadian. Mr. Wright, using sundry ingenious devices to that end, had trained one of the more sedate of the 'Dobe Walls' ponies to carry a lady without going insane. The training was successful, and the bronco thus taught to defy the dread mysteries of skirts and sidesaddle, had been presented to Ruth Pemberton. While Ruth Pemberton and Count Banti rode abroad, Madam Pemberton uplifted herself with George Eliot's novels, and the sermons of Theodore Parker.

Ruth Pemberton and her noble escort never traveled far from camp, for Mr. Wright had convinced them that Cheyennes were not to be trusted. The several specimens of this interesting sept whom they saw about the 'Dobe Walls, trading robes for calico and cartridges, served by their appearance to confirm the warnings of Mr. Wright.

When not abroad in the saddle, Ruth Pemberton developed a surprising passion to know intimately the West and its methods, rude and rough. She asked Mr. Masterson if she might go to school to him in this study so near her pretty heart. That young gentleman, looking innocently into her slumberous brown eyes, said "Yes" directly. Or rather Mr. Masterson, lapsing into the Panhandle idiom, said, "Shore!"

Being thus permitted, Ruth Pemberton, when Mr. Masterson galloped in from his buffalo killing and the Mexican skinners had brought home the hides in a waggon, would repair to the curing grounds, the latter being a flat, grassy stretch within two hundred yards of Mr. Wright's store. Once there, she looked on while Mr. Masterson pegged out the green hides. It interested her to see him sprinkle them, and the nearby grass, with poisoned water to keep off hidebugs. The hidebug, according to Mr. Masterson, must have been an insect cousin of the buffalo, for he came and went with the robe-hunters, and lived but to spoil hides with the holes that he bored in them.

Ruth Pemberton asked Mr. Masterson questions, to which he replied in one syllable. Also she did not pay sufficient attention to Count Banti—giving her whole bright-eyed time to Mr. Masterson. Whereat Count Banti sulked; and presently deserting Ruth Pemberton he withdrew to Mr. Hanrahan's saloon, where he was taught draw-poker to his detriment. Count Banti, when he left Ruth Pemberton, expected that she would call him back; she did not, and the oversight made him savage. One morning, while they were riding among the riverside cottonwoods, Count Banti became hysterical in his reproaches; he averred that Ruth Pemberton tortured in order to try his love. Proceeding to extremes, he said that, should she drive him desperate, he would destroy Mr. Masterson. At this, Ruth Pemberton's rice-white teeth showed between roseleaf lips; she smiled in half admiration upon Count Banti. "Oh!" thought Ruth Pemberton, "if only he would kill somebody I might love him from my heart!"

The soul of Ruth Pemberton of Beacon Hill and Vassar, having been west of the Missouri one month and at the 'Dobe Walls two days, was slipping into savagery—so friendly is retrogression, so easy comes reversion to type! She had supposed she loved Count Banti; and here was her soul going out to Mr. Masterson! How she dwelt upon him, when, bronzed of brow, cool of eye, alert, indomitable, he rode in from the day's kill! The rattle of his spurs as he swung from the saddle was like a tune of music!

Not that Ruth Pemberton wore these thoughts on her face. She hid them from others, she even concealed them from herself. Had one told her that she was beginning to love Mr. Masterson, she would have stared. Count Banti himself never thought of so hideous a possibility; his jealous petulance arose solely from her calm neglect of himself.

Ruth Pemberton asked Mr. Masterson how old he was, and it pleased her to hear that he was several months her superior.

Civilisation is a disguise, and in travel one loses one's mask. One's nature comes out and basks openly in new suns. This is so true that the West, when a compliment is intended, says of a man: "He'll do to cross the plains with." What the West means is that on such an expedition, what is treacherous or selfish or cowardly in a man will appear. Wherefore, to say of one that he will do to cross the plains with, is a most emphatic declaration that the one thus exalted is unmarked of vices.

Ruth Pemberton, who on Beacon Hill would have paled at a pin-prick and the red bead of blood it provoked, now thought kindly of mere slaughter, and insisted on riding ten miles with Mr. Masterson to the buffalo grounds to witness the day's work.

"But, my child!" cried Madam Pemberton.

"It's the only chance, mamma, I'll ever have to see a buffalo killed."

Madam Pemberton was not a deep mind, but exceeding shallow; to say that any chance was an only chance struck her as a reason for embracing it.

Ruth Pemberton was to journey to the buffalo grounds in the buckboard; Count Banti might accompany her, a Mexican would drive. Mr. Masterson, when told of the good company he would have on his next day's hunt, made no objection. To the direct question as to whether the country were possible for buckboards, he said it was.

"What do you think yourself, Bob?" asked Mr. Masterson, when that evening he met Mr. Wright in Mr. Hanrahan's bar, and they discussed this feminine eagerness to see dead buffaloes. "If we cross up with a bunch of Cheyennes, there may be trouble. It's a chance they'd try to capture the girl. Besides, they've got it in for me about that hair on my bridle."

"There's no Cheyennes about," said Mr. Wright. "When they drift within twenty miles of us, they are sure to show up at the store, and I haven't seen an Indian for two days."

Count Banti took a Winchester rifle with him. There were two seats in the buckboard; Ruth Pemberton and Count Banti occupied the rear seat, the front seat being given over to the Mexican, and a basket flowing with a refection prepared by Mr. Hanrahan's darky cook. Mr. Masterson, on his buckskin pony, Houston, rode by Ruth Pemberton's side of the buckboard. Madam Pemberton remained behind with *The Mill on the Floss*.

The expedition skirted the suburbs of a prairie dog village, and the shrill citizens were set a-flutter, or pretended to be, and dived into their houses. The polite diminutive owls, the prairie dogs' companions, stood their ground and made obeisances. Ruth Pemberton's cheek flushed with an odd interest as she gazed at the prairie dogs and the little polite ground owls.

Off to one side a dozen coyotes loafed along, not unlike a dozen loafing dogs, keeping abreast of the buckboard. Ruth Pemberton pointed to them:

"Isn't it strange," she asked, "that they should accompany us?"

There was the emphasis of a half alarm in her tones; a coyote was not, to her eyes, without formidable characteristics. Mr. Masterson explained.

"They go with us to the kill. When we leave, there will be a battle royal between them and the buzzards for the beef."

Mr. Masterson pushed forward to show the buckboard Mexican his way across a piece of broken ground. Count Banti took note of the parted lips, and that soft sparkle of the brown eyes, as Ruth Pemberton followed him with her glances. Count Banti made no criticism of these dulcet phenomena; he was too much of a gentleman and she too much of an heiress.

Count Banti, moved of a purpose to recall Ruth Pemberton from her train of fancy, did say that since a waggon, with the skinners, must go and come every day to bring in the buffalo hides, he was surprised that Mr. Masterson didn't ride in that waggon. It was superfluous, nay foolish, to saddle a pony under such waggon circumstances.

This idiotic conversation earned the commentator on buffalo hunters and their ways immediate grief. Ruth Pemberton wheeled upon Count Banti like a little lioness, that is, a little lioness subdued of Vassar and Beacon Hill. Ruth Pemberton said that she had never been treated to a more preposterous remark! It was unworthy, Count Banti! Mr. Masterson in a waggon! One might as easily conceive of Sir Launcelot or Richard the Lion Heart in a waggon.

When Mr. Masterson returned to the buckboard, Ruth Pemberton deftly lost her handkerchief overboard. Mr. Masterson brought Houston to the right about, and riding back stooped from the saddle and swept up the scrap of cambric from the short grass.

Because you are so good," said Ruth Pemberton, with a smile, "you may keep it for your reward."

Count Banti ground his teeth; he expected that Mr. Masterson would bind the sweet trophy in his sombrero. Count Banti gasped; instead of tucking the dainty guerdon behind that gold and silver rattlesnake, the favoured dull one continued to offer it to Ruth Pemberton.

"I've no place for it," said Mr. Masterson; "I'd lose it."

Ruth Pemberton's brow was red as she received her property; for one wrathful moment a flame showed in the brown eye like a fire in a forest. Mr. Masterson's own eye was as guileless as an antelope's. Was he a fool? Was he deriding her? Ruth Pemberton decided that he was merely a white Indian. She appeased her vanity by turning her shoulder on the criminal and giving her conversation to Count Banti. Under these direct rays of the sun, our Frenchman's noble soul expanded like a flower; as the fruit of that blossoming he began to brag like a Sioux.

Having caught some glint of the lady's spirit, Count Banti told of adventures in India and Africa. He was a hero; he had haunted water-holes by night and killed black-maned lions; he had stalked tigers on foot; he had butchered Zulus who, moved of a tropical venom, assailed him with battle axes.

Count Banti, pressing forward, set forth that he had been sustained as he crossed the Atlantic by a hope that he might war with America's red natives. Alas, they were broken and cowed; their spirit had been beaten down! He must return wrapped in disappointment.

Still—and now Count Banti became tender—it had been the most fortunate journey of his career. If not Mars then Venus! Count Banti had found the most lovely and most lovable woman in the world! And, by the way, would Ruth Pemberton make Count Banti delirious with joy by presenting him the handkerchief which the aborigine on the pony had had neither the wit nor the gentle fineness to accept?

For reply, Ruth Pemberton furtively wadded the poor rejected cambric into a ball about the size of a buckshot, and dropped it overboard again. And, because neither Mr. Masterson nor Count Banti saw its fall, there it lies among the buffalo grasses on the flat banks of the Canadian to this day.

Count Banti repeated his request and backed it with a sigh. There-upon Ruth Pemberton opened both small hands to show how that desirable cambric had disappeared. Count Banti made rueful eyes rear-ward as though contemplating a search.

Mr. Masterson halted the buckboard; they had arrived within a mile of the buffaloes; he pointed where hundreds of them were grazing or reposing about the base of a gently sloping hill. The heavy dust-coloured creatures looked like farm cattle to the untaught Ruth Pemberton.

There was a bowl-like depression a few yards from where the buckboard came to a stop. It was grassed and regular, and one might have imagined that it had been shaped and sodded by a gardener. Mr. Masterson defined it as a buffalo wallow; he tried to make clear how, pivoting on one horn, a buffalo bull, shoulder to the ground, had excavated the cup-fashioned hollow they beheld.

While the Mexican was slipping free the team's traces, and making the few camp arrangements required for their stay, Count Banti began a lively talk with Mr. Masterson.

How long would it take Mr. Masterson to complete his day's kill?

Mr. Masterson, it seems, would kill thirty buffaloes; that would take an hour.

And then they would return? Yes; or if the visitors tired, they might hook up and start at any moment. It was not worth while to sit through the slaughter of thirty buffaloes. The killing of one would be as the killing of another; to see the first was to see all.

Ruth Pemberton interposed; she would wait and return with Mr. Masterson.

Count Banti said he could see that killing buffaloes was slow, insipid sport. Now there might be a gallant thrill in fighting Indians—painted and perilous! Count Banti would have summoned up an interest for Indians. Had Mr. Masterson ever slain an Indian? Probably not; Mr. Masterson was a young man.

Mr. Masterson bent a cold eye upon Count Banti. Saying never a word, he sauntered over to Houston, and began twisting a pair of rawhide hopples about his fetlocks, for Mr. Masterson, like all professional buffalo hunters, killed his game on foot. As Count Banti was ruffling over Mr. Masterson's want of courtesy, the Mexican plucked him by the sleeve.

"See!" said the Mexican, pointing to the four braids of black hair hanging from Mr. Masterson's bridle. "Cheyenne skelps; four!" And the Mexican held up four fingers.

"Scalps!" returned Count Banti, the burgundy colour deserting his heavy face. "Where did he get them?" "Killed 'em here—anywhere!" vouchsafed the Mexican, waving a vague paw. "Killed 'em twelve weeks ago—mebby eight—no?" What Count Banti might have thought concerning the sinister character of the region into which he had stumbled, he was given no chance to divulge, for Mr. Masterson came up, rifle in hand, and speaking to Ruth Pemberton, said:

"Make yourself comfortable; you will be able to follow all that goes on, should you be interested in it, from the buckboard. You've brought a pair of field glasses, I see. Lucky we're down the wind! I can go straight to them."

As the ground between him and the buffaloes on the slope lay flat and open, with not so much as a bush to act as a screen, Mr. Masterson's remark about going straight to his quarry appeared a bit optimistic. However, Mr. Masterson did not think so, but seemed the sublimation of certainty; he started off at a slow, careless walk directly towards the herd.

Mr. Masterson had covered half the distance, that is to say, he had approached within a half mile of his game, before the buffaloes displayed a least excitement. When he had travelled thus far, however, those nearest began to exhibit a slow, angry alarm. They would paw the grass and toss a threatening horn; at times one would throw up his nose and sniff the air. The wind being from the buffaloes to Mr. Masterson, these nose experiments went without reward.

Yielding to the restless timidity of the perturbed ones, who if set running would infallibly stampede the herd, Mr. Masterson threw himself on his face and began to creep. His brown right hand gripped the stock of his rifle, and he dragged it over the grass, muzzle to the rear. Also, he was careful to keep his face hidden from the buffaloes behind the wide brim of his sombrero.

The herd's interest was sensibly abated when Mr. Masterson forsook the perpendicular. So long as they were granted no terrifying glimpses of his face, the buffaloes would believe him some novel form of wolf, and nobody to fly from. Acting upon this wolf theory, they watched the creeping Mr. Masterson curiously; they stood their ground, and some even walked towards him in a threatening mood, disposed to bully.

As Mr. Masterson, eyes to the grass, crept slowly forward, a dry "Bzz-z-z-z!" broke on his ear from a little distance in advance. Cautiously he lifted his eyes; the rattlesnake lay, coiled and open-mouthed, in his path. Mr. Masterson pushed the Sharp's towards the reptile; at that it uncoiled and crawled aside. For twenty minutes Mr. Masterson continued his slow, creeping advance. When he was within four hundred yards of the herd he rose on one knee. There was a big bull, evidently an individual of consequence, who, broadside on, stood furthest up the wind. Deliberately and without excitement, the Sharp's came to Mr. Masterson's shoulder and his steady eye brought the sights to bear upon a spot twelve inches square, just behind the foreshoulder.

For the sliver of a second Mr. Masterson hung on the aim; then the heavy buffalo gun, burning one hundred and twenty grains of powder and throwing a bullet eight to the pound, roared, and the bull leaped heavily forward, shot through the lungs. With forefeet spread wide, blood pumping from both nostrils, the buffalo fought desperately for breath and for strength to stand. The battle was against him; he staggered, caught himself, tottered, stumbled, and then with a sigh of despair sank forward on his knees to roll at last upon his side—dead.

At the roar of the buffalo gun, the herd, fear at their hearts' roots, began to run. Instantly a change came over them. The dying bull was to windward gushing blood, and the scent of that blood swept down upon them in a kind of madness. Their wits forsook them; they forgot their peril in the blood-frenzy that possessed them, and charged ferociously upon their dying comrade. When he fell, they gored him with crazy horns—a herd of humped, four-legged, shaggy, senseless, bellowing lunatics!

"Bang!" from the big buffalo gun, and another bull stood bleeding out his life. The herd, wild and frantic, fell upon him.

"Bang!" spoke the buffalo gun; a third, shot through and through, became the object of the herd's crazy rage.

Killing always to windward, Mr. Masterson might have stood in his tracks and slain a dozen score; the scent of the new blood would hold the fury-bitten buffaloes like a spell.

Knowing this to be the nature of buffaloes, Mr. Masterson felt profound surprise when after his third fire, and while still the last stricken bleeding buffalo was on his feet, the whole band seemed suddenly restored to their senses, and went lumbering off at a right angle.

"Cheyennes!" exclaimed the sophisticated Mr. Masterson; "they are over the brow of the hill!" Then he turned, and started for Ruth Pemberton and the others at a sharp trot.

While Mr. Masterson was creeping on the buffaloes, Ruth Pemberton from her buckboard perch, followed him through the field glasses. She saw him pause, and push forward with his rifle at the rattlesnake; while she could not see the reptile, by some instinct she realised it— coiled and fanged and venomous—and shuddered. She drew a breath of relief as Mr. Masterson re-began his stalk. She saw him when he rose to his knee; then came the straight, streaky puff of white smoke, and the dying bull stood staggering and bleeding. Next there drifted to her on the loitering breeze the boom of the buffalo gun, blunted by distance and direction. Her glasses covered the herd when in its blood-rage it held furious wake about the dying ones.

And, what was most strange, Ruth Pemberton took a primal joy therein. She was conscious of the free, original sweep of the plains about her, with the white shimmer of the Canadian beyond. And sensations claimed her, to flow in her veins and race along her nerves, which archery and tennis had never called up. There abode a glow in her blood that was like a brightness and a new joy. If the handkerchief-declining Mr. Masterson were a white Indian, what now was she? Only she never once thought on that.

Mr. Masterson came up at top speed, and said something in Spanish to the Mexican. That hare-heart became pale as paper; instead of bringing in his team, as Mr. Masterson had commanded, he cut the hopples of the nearest horse, and went powdering away towards the 'Dobe Walls. Mr. Masterson tossed up his Sharp's with a half-notion of stopping him; then he shook his head cynically.

"He's only a Mexican," said he. Helping Ruth Pemberton from the buckboard, where she sat in startled ignorance, he remarked: "Get into the buffalo wallow; you'll be safer there."

"Safe?" whispered Ruth Pemberton.

Mr. Masterson pointed to eleven Cheyennes on the far crest of the hill. Then he led Ruth Pemberton to the buffalo wallow, where Count Banti was already crouching.

"You've left your Winchester on the buckboard," said Mr. Masterson.

Count Banti stared glassily, the purple of his face a dingy gray. The man was helpless; the nearness of death had paralyzed him.

Mr. Masterson shifted his glance to Ruth Pemberton. Her eyes, shining like strange jewels, met him squarely look for look; there was a heave to her bosom and a red in her cheek. His own eyes were jade, and his brows had come sternly forward, masking his face with the very spirit of war. The two looked upon one another—the boy and the girl whose rearings had been so far apart and whose natures were so close together.

"I'll get it," she said, meaning the Winchester.

Mr. Masterson made her crouch down in the bottom of the buffalo wallow, where neither bullet nor arrow might reach her. Then, walking to the buckboard, he got the Winchester and the cartridge belt that belonged with it.

"It's Baldy Smith's," remarked Mr. Masterson, as though Ruth Pemberton might be interested in the news. "It's a good gun—for a Winchester."

One of the Cheyennes, glimpsing the recreant Mexican, started in pursuit; the others rode down the slope for a closer survey of the trio in the buffalo wallow. Mr. Masterson threw the loop of a lariat over the head of Houston and fastened him, hopples and all, to the buckboard.

Understanding that no surprise was possible, the Cheyennes began at a sweeping gallop to circle the garrison in the buffalo wallow, their dainty little war ponies a-flutter of eagle feathers and strips of red cloth. As they circled, they closed in nearer and nearer; at less than six hundred yards they opened fire.

Each attacking buck kept his pony between himself and Mr. Masterson, firing from beneath the pony's neck. The shooting was bad; the bullets struck the grass and kicked up puffs of dirt one hundred yards in front, and then came singing forty feet overhead. Count Banti heard the zip! zip! zip! and groaned as he lay on his face.

Mr. Masterson, who—being on his feet—was head and shoulders above the level of the flat, paid no heed to the terror-ridden Count Banti. Once he cast a look at Ruth Pemberton, making sure she was below the danger level. She, for her side, watched his expression as he stood, rifle in hand, observing the attack. She felt no fear, felt nothing only a sweep and choke of exultation. It was as though she were the prize for which a battle was being fought—a battle, one against ten! Also, she could read in the falconed frown of Mr. Masterson somewhat of that temper wherewith he had harvested those scalps on his bridle.

While Ruth Pemberton gazed in a kind of fondness without fear, the heavy Sharp's came to the sudden shoulder of Mr. Masterson. The roar of it fell upon her so close and loud that it was like a fog to her senses. Mr. Masterson threw open his gun, and clipped in a second cartridge. The brass shell flirted over his shoulder by the extractor, struck Count Banti's face. That hero—who had hunted lions by night and tigers on foot—gave a little scream, and then lay mute.

"It was this!" said Ruth Pemberton, holding up the empty shell to Mr. Masterson.

Mr. Masterson's bullet had gone through pony and rider as though they were papier-mâché. What life might have been left in the latter was crushed out by the falling pony who smashed chest and ribs beneath his heavy shoulder.

The nine other circling bucks gathered about the one who had died. Clustered as they were, there could be no thought of missing, and Mr. Masterson emptied another saddle. With that, the others swooped on the slain and bore them off beyond the hill.

As they did so, far away to the right a single Cheyenne came riding; he was yelping like twenty wolves at once, and tossing something and catching it in his hand. The single Cheyenne was he who had followed the craven Mexican, and the thing he tossed and played with was the Mexican's scalp. When he had joined the others, and they had laid their dead in a safe place, the whole party again came riding—open order—down the long slope towards the fatal buffalo wallow.

Mr. Masterson picked up the Winchester and forced cartridges into the magazine until it would hold no more.

"They're going to charge," said Mr. Masterson, apologising for the Winchester. "It'll come handy to back up my Sharp's in a case of quick work. There won't be time to load, and a Sharp's is only a single-shot gun, you know."

Ruth Pemberton did not know, and her mind was running on other matters than guns, single-shot or magazine.

"They're going to charge?" she asked.

"Yes; but don't lose your nerve. They'll make a heap of hubbub, but it's two for one I stand them off."

The assurance came as coolly as though Mr. Masterson considered the possibilities of a shower, and was confident of the integrity of Ruth Pemberton's umbrella.

"One thing!" said Ruth Pemberton wistfully.

"Yes?" said Mr. Masterson, his eye on the Cheyennes, his ear on Ruth Pemberton.

"Don't let them take me! Kill me first!"

"I've intended to from the beginning," said Mr. Masterson steadily. "First you, then me! You know the Western saying for an Indian fight: Always save your last shot for yourself!"

There was nothing of despair or lack of resolution; he spoke as speaks one who but gives a promise to one who has reason to receive it. He offered it without fear to one who accepted it without fear, and when he had spoken Ruth Pemberton felt as cheerfully light as a bird. She had a desire to seize on the Winchester and take her stand with

Mr. Masterson. But her ignorance of Winchesters was there to baffle her; moreover Mr. Masterson, as though he read her impulse, interfered.

"Stay where you are!" he commanded. From where she crouched in the buffalo wallow, Ruth Pemberton heard a whirl of yells, and the grass-muffled drumming of many hoofs; and the yells and the hoof-beats were bearing down upon her with the rush of a tempest. There came a rattle of rifles, and the chuck! chuck! of bullets into the soft earth. In the midst of the din and the clamour she heard the bold roar of the buffalo gun. Then she saw Mr. Masterson snatch up the Winchester, and spring clear of the buffalo wallow to the flat, grassy ground in front. Feeling nothing, knowing nothing beyond a resolution to be near him, live or die, she was out of the buffalo wallow as soon as was he, and on her knees at his feet. She could seize on no one element as distinct and separate from a whirling whole, made up of blur and smoke and yell and rifle crash, with feathers dancing and little ponies charging like meteors! She was sure only of the rock-bound fact to which she clung that Mr. Masterson never moved from where he stood. She heard the spitting, whip-like crack of the Winchester, so different from the menacing voice of the buffalo gun, as working it with the rapidity of a bell-punch he fired it faster than she could count.

The thing was on and by and over in a moment; the charging Cheyennes went to right and left, unable to ride up against that tide of death which set so fiercely in their faces. Nine Cheyennes made that charge upon the buffalo wallow; Ruth Pemberton counted but four to flash to the rear at the close. The four never paused; their hearts had turned weak, and they kept on along the river's bank, until at a low place they rode in and went squattering across. Five riderless ponies, running wild and lost, gave chase with neighs of protest at being left behind.

Out in front, one of the five Cheyennes who had been shot from his saddle in the charge raised himself, wounded, on his elbow. Mr. Masterson, who had recovered his Sharp's, sent a bullet into his head. Ruth Pemberton, even through the tingling trance of battle that still wrapped her close, turned cold.

"What else?" inquired Mr. Masterson. "We don't run any Red-Cross outfit in the Panhandle."

Ruth Pemberton made no reply: her fascinated eyes saw where a trickle of blood guttered the cheek of Mr. Masterson. She thought no more on dead or living Cheyennes, but with a great sob of horror came towards him, eyeing the blood.

"Only a nick," said he. "You can't fight all day without a scratch or two."

Count Banti began to stir. He sat up in a foolish way and looked at Ruth Pemberton. She turned from him, ashamed, and let her gaze rove to where the Cheyennes, far beyond the river, were rounding the corner of a hill. There was nothing she could say to Count Banti.

Mr. Masterson loosened and mounted Houston, which seasoned pony had comported himself throughout the mêlée with the steadiness which should go with his name. Presently he rode back to the buffalo wallow, and instead of four, there were eleven scalps on his bridle rein.

"A man should count his *coups*," he vouchsafed in explanation.

There was no need of defence; Ruth Pemberton, without understanding the argument which convinced her own breast, looked upon those scalps as the fitting finale of the morning's work.

Mr. Masterson caught up the buckboard horse, mate to the one upon which the Mexican had fled, and strapped a blanket on its back for the use and behoof of Count Banti—still speechless, nerves a-tangle. Then Mr. Masterson, taking a spare cinch from his war-bags, to the disgust of Houston, proceeded with more blankets to construct a pillion upon which Ruth Pemberton might ride behind him. Houston, as he felt the cinch drawing, pointed his ears resentfully.

"Well?" threatened Mr. Masterson.

Houston relaxed the resentful ears and acquiesced with grace, fearing worse. Mr. Masterson from the saddle held out his hand; Ruth Pemberton took it and, making a step of the stirrup which he tendered, sprang to the pillion.

"You can hold on by my belt," quoth Mr. Masterson.

And so they came back to the 'Dobe Walls; Ruth Pemberton's arms about Mr. Masterson, her cheek against his shoulder, while her soul wandered up and down in a world of strange happinesses, as one might walk among trees and flowers, with birds singing overhead.

Four days; and the buckboard bearing Ruth Pemberton, Madam Pemberton and Count Banti drew away for the North. A lieutenant with ten cavalrymen, going from Fort Elliot to Dodge, accompanied them by way of escort.

"And so you hate the East?" Ruth Pemberton had asked Mr. Masterson that morning before the start, her eyes dim, and her cheeks much too pale for so innocent a question.

"No, not hate," returned Mr. Masterson, "but my life is in the West."

As the buckboard reached the ridge from which would come the last glimpse of the Canadian, off to the south and west, outlined against the sky, stood a pony and rider. The rider waved his sombrero in farewell. Ruth Pemberton gazed and still gazed; the hunger of the brown eyes was as though her love lay starving. The trail sloped sharply downward, and the picture of the statue horseman on the hill was snatched away. With that—her life turned drab and desolate—Ruth Pemberton slipped to the floor of the buckboard, and buried her face in her mother's kindly lap.

THE STRATEGY OF MR. MASTERSON

This came long after the battle at the 'Dobe Walls, and was of the year next before Dull Knife, that Red Richard of the Cheyennes, with one hundred and forty-eight followers, two-thirds of whom were squaws and pappooses, broke from the soldiers and fought his way to his old home in the North, whipping the cavalry once, twice, thrice; yielding only and at last to the lying treachery of Red Cloud and his Sioux police. It was a great trail that last long running fight of Dull Knife, and proved his heart good and his "medicine" strong. Some one some day ought to write the story high among the gallant deeds of men. However, here is not the place nor this the time; for what comes after is to be a tale of stratagem, not battle; politics, not war.

Commonly the face of Dodge was as open and frank and care-free as the face of a Waterbury watch. On the occasion in hand it wore a look of occupation and serious business. This business expression was fairly founded; a sheriff for Ford County must be selected, the gentleman who had filled that post of trust being undeniably dead.

The passing of that sheriff was curious. One morning he rode forth, and fording the Arkansas at the Cimarron Crossing, made south and west for Sand Creek. And thereafter he never rode back. It was understood that he bore official papers to serve upon a certain miscreant who dwelt on Sand Creek. The Sand Creek miscreant having bought goods of Mr. Wright, later jeered at the suggestion that he pay, and Mr. Wright had been driven to ask aid of the law.

Three days after the sheriff splashed through the Cimarron Crossing his pony was picked up by cow people, saddled, bridled, and in the best of spirits, close by the river where the lush grass grows most to a pony's taste. It did not escape experienced eyes that, when the pony was thus recovered, the bridle reins were properly upon its neck and had not been lifted over its head, to hang by the bits and drag about its hoofs. Later, the missing one's six-shooter and belt, the latter tooth-marked, together with shreds of clothing, scraps of leather leggings, and sundry bones gnawed white, were found an hour's ride out on the trail. The pistol possessed a full furnishment of six unexploded cartridges. Also, the tooth-marked belt and those fragmentary reminders, scattered here and there and all about for the round area of a mile, offered much to support a belief that the late officer, in his final expression, had become of gustatory moment to coyotes, which grey beggarmen of the plains were many and hungry in those parts.

When the evidence recounted was all in, the wisdom of Dodge made divers deductions. These found setting forth in the remarks of Mr. Wright, the same being delivered to Mr. Short and others in the Long Branch saloon.

"Those bridle reins on the pony's neck," observed Mr. Wright, inspired to the explanation by Old Jordan and a local curiosity which appealed to him as among the best intelligences in camp, "those bridle reins on the pony's neck shows that Dave went out o' the saddle a heap sudden. If Dave had swung to the grass of his own will he'd have lifted the reins over the pony's head, so's to keep that equine standin' patient to his call."

"Don't you reckon, Bob," broke in Mr. Short, "your Sand Creek bankrupt bushwhacks Dave?"

"No; Dave wasn't shot out o' the saddle, the six loads in his gun bein' plenty on that point. It's preposterous that an old hand like Dave, in an open country, too, could have been rubbed out, an' never get a shot. Dave wasn't that easy. Besides, if the Sand Creek hold-up had bumped Dave off, he'd have cinched the pony. Gents, the idea I entertain is that Dave, in a fit of abstraction, permits himself to be bucked off. Landin' on his head that a-way, his neck naturally gets broke."

The Wright theory having been adopted, Dodge, in addition to the serious business look, took on an atmosphere of disappointment which trenched upon the mournful. Not that the late sheriff's death preyed upon Dodge. Dodge was aware of sheriffs in their evanescence. They were as grass; they came up like the flowers to be cut down. What discouraged Dodge was the commonplace character of that officer's exit, as so convincingly explained by Mr. Wright. Nothing had been left wherewith to gild a story and tantalize the envious ears of rivalry. To be chucked from a careless saddle to the dislocation of an equally careless neck was not a proud demise.

By Western tenets the only honourable departure would have been the one usual and official. The sheriff who would quit his constituents under noblest conditions must perish in the smoke of conflict, defending communal order and the threatened peace of men. Obviously he must not be pitched from his own pony to fatten coyotes.

"For," as Cimarron Bill was moved to observe, "to be bucked into a better life, inadvertent, is as unromatic as bein' kicked to glory by an ambulance mule."

Had the late sheriff gone down before the lawless muzzle of some desperate personage, bent, as runs the phrase, on "standing Dodge on its head," what exhilarating ceremonies would have been the fruit! The desperate personage, on the hocks of that snuffing out, would have been earnestly lynched. The slain sheriff, his head pillowed in his saddle, his guns by his side, would have lain in state. Dodge, crape on its sombrero and with bowed head, would have followed the catafalque, while a brass band boomed the dead march; the rites, conducted in a mood of gloomy elevation, would have aroused the admiration of an entire border. All these good advantages were denied Dodge, and it was that funeral loss which clouded the public brow. The possibilities would now be exhausted when the fate of the once sheriff was officially noticed, and the vacancy thus arranged had been filled.

And now a new sheriff must be chosen. Dodge, politically speaking, was all there was of Ford County. Politics, in the sinister sense of party, had never reared its viper head in Dodge; there existed no such commodity of misrule. Also, the station of sheriff was of responsible gravity. Thus, indeed, thought Dodge; and went upon that sheriff-mongering with care.

"My idea of a sheriff," vouchsafed Mr. Short, "is one who, while he does not wear his six-shooters for ornament, can be relied on not to go shootin' too promiscuous. The prosperity of Dodge swings and rattles on the boys who drive the herds. It isn't commercially expedient to put a crimp in one of 'em for trivial cause. Of course, should the most free-handed consumer that ever tossed his *dinero* across a counter pull his hardware for blood, it is obvious that he must be downed. The demand of the hour is for a sheriff who can discriminate on the lines I've laid down."

This and more was said. When discussion had been exhausted Mr. Trask, with a view of focussing suggestion, advanced the name of Mr. Masterson. Mr. Wright, as well as Mr. Short, was prompt with his support.

"For," said Mr. Wright, "where can you find a cooler head or a quicker gun than Bat's?"

"But Bat ain't here none," explained Cimarron Bill. "He's down on the Medicine Lodge, killin' buffalo; his camp's in Walker's Timber."

It was apparent that the better element, that is to say, the better shots, favoured Mr. Masterson. An informal count displayed among his supporters such popular towers as Mr. Wright, Mr. Trask, Mr. Short, and Mr. Kelly. Mr. Short was emphatic in his partisanship.

"Not only," explained Mr. Short, "is Bat cool an' steady, but, bar Mike Sutton, he's the best educated sharp in Dodge."

Cimarron Bill, who seemed born to ride bad ponies, saddled a bronco whose studied villainy of disposition was half atoned for by an ability to put one hundred miles between himself and his last feed. Cimarron Bill had been directed to bring in Mr. Masterson.

"An' don't tell him what's in the wind," warned Mr. Wright. "Bat's modest, an' if you spring this on him plumb abrupt it might shock him so he wouldn't come."

"What'll I tell him, then?" demanded Cimarron Bill. "I shore can't rope up Bat without a word an' drag him yere with my pony."

"Here's what you do," said Mr. Short. "Tell him I'm goin' to run, with Updegraffe up for the opp'sition. Tell him that Walker of the Cross K, an' Bear Creek Johnson are ag'in me. That would fetch Bat from the Rio Grande."

On the south bank of the Medicine Lodge was a horseshoe bend, and the enclosed forty acres, thick-sown of trees, were known as Walker's Timber. Here was pitched the buffalo camp of Mr. Masterson, and therefrom, aided and abetted by his brother Ed and Mr. Tighlman, he issued forth against the buffaloes, slaying them serenely, to his profit and the full-fed joy of sundry coyotes and ravens that attended faithfully his hunting.

It was in the earlier darkness of the evening, and Mr. Masterson was sitting by his campfire, peering into a little memorandum book by the dancing light of the flames. In this book, with a stubby pencil, he soberly jotted down a record of the day's kill.

"We've made eight hundred and thirty-three robes, Billy," observed Mr. Masterson to Mr. Tighlman, who was busy over a bake-kettle containing all that was mortal of two hen turkeys—wild and young and lively the night before. "And," concluded Mr. Masterson, with just a shade of pride in his tones, "I fetched them with precisely eight hundred and thirty-three cartridges, the nearest bull four hundred yards away."

Mr. Tighlman grunted applause of the rifle accuracy of Mr. Masterson. Mr. Tighlman was the camp's cook, having a mysterious genius for biscuits, and knowing to a pinch what baking-powder was required for a best biscuit result.

Mr. Tighlman presently announced supper by beating the side of the bake-kettle with the back of a butcher-knife. The challenge brought Ed Masterson from the drying-grounds, where he had been staking out and scraping, with an instrument that resembled a short-handed adz, the fresh hides of that day's hunt. Mr. Masterson put away his roster of buffalo dead and made ready to compliment Mr. Tighlman in the way in which cooks like best to be praised.

Suddenly there came a sound as of some one crossing the little river. Each of the three seized his rifle and rolled outside the circle of firelight. It was as one hundred to one there abode no danger; the Cheyennes had not yet recovered from the calmative influences of the Black Kettle war. Still, it was the careful practice of the plains to distrust all things after dark.

"Go back to your fire," shouted a voice from out the shadows. "Do you-all prairie dogs reckon that, if I was goin' to jump your camp, I'd come walloppin' across in this egregious style?"

"It's Cimarron Bill," exclaimed Mr. Masterson, discarding his rifle in favour of renewed turkey.

Cimarron Bill tore the saddle off the malevolent bronco and hobbled him. "Whoopee!" he shouted softly, as he pushed in by the fire and pulled the bake-kettle towards him, "I'm hungry enough to eat a saddle cover."

Cimarron Bill, being exhaustively fed, laid forth his mission mendaciously. He related the vacancy in the office of sheriff, and said that it was proposed to fill the same with Mr. Short. Cimarron Bill, seeing a chance to tell a little truth, explained that the opposition would put up Mr. Updegraffe.

"Who's behind Updegraffe?" asked Mr. Masterson.

The veracious Cimarron Bill enumerated Mr. Webster of the Alamo, Mr. Peacock of the Dance Hall, Mr. Walker of the Cross-K, and Bear Creek Johnson.

This set Mr. Masterson on edge.

"We'll start by sun-up," quoth Mr. Masterson. "Ed and Billy can pick up the camp."

When Mr. Masterson discovered how he had been defrauded into Dodge, and learned of those honours designed for him, his modesty took alarm.

"I didn't think, Cimarron," said Mr. Masterson, in tones of reproach, "that you'd cap me up against a game like this!" Then he refused squarely to consider himself a candidate.

"But it's too late, Bat," explained Mr. Short. "You've already been in the field two days, with Updegraffe in opposition. If you refuse to run they'll say you crawfished."

Mr. Short spoke with sly triumph, for it was his chicane which had announced Mr. Masterson as a candidate. He had foreseen its value as an argument.

The sagacity of Mr. Short was justified; Mr. Masterson was plainly staggered. His name had been used; his opponent was in the field; Mr. Masterson could find no avenue of retreat. It was settled; Mr. Masterson must be a candidate for sheriff of Ford.

The great contest of Masterson against Updegraffe had occupied the public four days when Mr. Peacock, Mr. Webster and Mr. Walker, acting for Mr. Updegraffe, waited upon Mr. Wright, Mr. Kelly and Mr. Short, who received them on behalf of Mr. Masterson. Mr. Peacock, for the Updegraffe three, made primary explanation. He and his fellow commissioners had observed a falling off in trade. The Alamo was not taking in one-half its normal profits; the same was true of the Dance Hall. The Updegraffe committee asked Mr. Short if an abatement of prosperity had not occurred at the Long Branch, and put the same question concerning the Alhambra to Mr. Kelly. Mr. Kelly and Mr. Short, being appealed to, confessed a business slackness.

"But you know," observed Mr. Kelly, philosophically, "how it is in business; it's a case of come-an'-go, like the old woman's soap."

Mr. Webster believed the falling off due to an election interest which engulfed the souls of folk.

"It takes their minds off such amusements as roulette an' farobank an' rum," explained Mr. Webster. "Besides, the people of Dodge are a mighty cautious outfit. Dodge won't take chances; an' at a ticklish time like this Dodge sobers up."

"There may be something in that," mused Mr. Short. "But, coming down to the turn, what was it you jack-rabbits wanted to say?"

"This is the proposition," said Mr. Webster, "an' we make it for the purpose of gettin' the racket over without delay. Our idea is to set the time for a week from now, round up the votin' population in the Plaza, say at eight o'clock in the evenin', an' count noses, Masterson ag'in Updegraffe, high man win. That's the offer we make. You gents will need an hour to look it over, an' we'll return at the end of that time an' get your answer."

"How do you figure this?" asked Mr. Wright of his fellow committeemen when the Updegraffe delegation had departed. "Is it a deadfall?"

"Strange as it may sound," responded Mr. Short, "considerin' what liars that outfit is, I'm obliged to admit that for once they're on the squar'."

Mr. Kelly coincided with Mr. Short, and it was finally agreed that the proffer of the Updegraffe contingent should be accepted.

"We're with you," said Mr. Short when Mr. Webster and the others returned, "but not on selfish grounds. We base our action on the bluff that the peace of Dodge requires protection, an' that the office of sheriff, now vacant, should be promptly filled."

"Then the election is settled," said Mr. Webster, who was a practical man, "for eight o'clock in the evenin', one week from to-day, to be pulled off in the Plaza?"

"That's the caper," retorted Mr. Short, and the commissions adjourned.

The canvass went forward in lively vein, albeit, as Mr. Webster had complained, there was a notable falling away in the local appetite for rum. Plainly, Dodge had turned wary in a day that wore a six-shooter, and under circumstances which tested the tempers of men. Evidently, it had determined that while this election crisis lasted, its hand should remain steady and its head cool.

It was five days before the one appointed for, as Mr. Webster called it, "a count of noses" in the Plaza. The friends of Mr. Masterson developed an irritating fact. There were, man added to man, four hundred and twelve votes in Dodge; of these a careful canvass betrayed two hundred and twelve as being for Mr. Updegraffe—a round majority of twelve.

This disquieting popular condition was chiefly the work of Bear Creek Johnson. The malign influence of that disreputable person controlled full forty votes, being the baser spirits; and these now threatened the defeat of Mr. Masterson.

Cimarron Bill, when he grasped the truth, was for cleansing Dodge of Bear Creek with a Colt's-45. These sanitary steps, however, were forbidden by Mr. Masterson; at that the worthy Cimarron tendered a compromise. He would agree to do no more than mildly wing the offensive Bear Creek.

"No," said Mr. Masterson, "don't lay hand to gun. I'm not going to have Abilene and Hays pointing fingers of scorn at Dodge as being unable to elect a peace officer of the county without somebody getting shot. Besides, it isn't necessary; I'll beat 'em by strategy."

Cimarron Bill, withheld from that direct aid to Mr. Masterson which his simple nature suggested, groaned in his soul. Observing his grief, Mr. Masterson detailed Mr. Tighlman to be ever at Cimarron Bill's elbow, ready to repress that volatile recruit in case his feelings got beyond control and sought relief in some sudden bombardment of the felon Bear Creek.

That profligate, thus protected, pursued his election efforts in behalf of Mr. Updegraffe cunningly, being all unchecked. His methods were not unmarked of talent; this should be a specimen:

"What party be you for?" Bear Creek demanded of an Ishmael who lived precariously by chuck-a-luck. The one addressed was of so low a caste that he would accept a wager of ten cents. This put him beneath the notice of such as Mr. Short, whose limit was one hundred and two hundred, and in whose temple of fortune, the Long Branch, white chips were rated at fifty dollars a stack. "Which is it? Masterson or Updegraffe?"

"Well," returned the Ishmael of chuck-a-luck, doubtfully, "I sort o' allow that Bat Masterson's the best man."

"You do!" retorted the abandoned Bear Creek, disgustedly. "Now listen to me. What does a ten-cent hold-up like you want of the best man? You want the worst man, an' so I tell you! Make it Updegraffe," concluded Bear Creek, convincingly, "an' you stay in Dodge. Make it Masterson, an' he'll make you an' every other tinhorn hard to find."

It was in that fashion the industrious Bear Creek piled up the majority of twelve. Unless something was done Mr. Masterson would sup disaster, and even the conservative Mr. Kelly whispered that he really thought the plan of Cimarron Bill, for the abatement of Bear Creek, possessed a merit.

"Let me think this over a bit," said Mr. Masterson to Mr. Kelly.

That night Mr. Masterson met Mr. Kelly, Mr. Wright and Mr. Short at the Long Branch and laid bare a plan. Its simplicity impressed Mr. Masterson's hearers; Mr. Wright even waxed enthusiastic.

"It'll win!" he cried, smiting the poker table about which the four were gathered.

"It shore looks it," coincided Mr. Short. "In any event we lose nothin'; we can always fall back on the guns."

At the latter intimation Mr. Kelly nodded solemnly. While not mercurial, Mr. Kelly was in many of his characteristics one with Cimarron Bill. There were questions over which their honest natures met and sympathised.

Acting on the plan of Mr. Masterson, Mr. Wright and Mr. Short and Mr. Kelly craved in their turn a conference with the Updegraffe three.

"It is this, gents, that troubles us," began Mr. Wright, when the committees found themselves together for the second time. "There are hot and headlong sports on our side as there are on yours. If we convene in the Plaza, as we've arranged, there'll be bloodshed. I'm afraid we couldn't restrain some of the more violent among us; indeed, to be entirely frank, I'm afraid I couldn't even restrain myself. And yet, there's a way, gents, in which danger may be avoided. Let us abandon that clause which provides for a count of noses in the Plaza.

The end in view can be attained by having it understood that at eight o'clock the Masterson forces are to rally in the Long Branch, and the Updegraffe people in Mr. Peacock's Dance Hall. Thus the two sides may be counted separately and the chance of deadly collision eliminated. We will set our watches together so that the count shall occur at eight o'clock sharp. Mr. Kelly for our side will be at the Dance Hall to act with Mr. Peacock in a count of the Updegraffe votes, while Mr. Webster for your interests is welcome to come to the Long Branch to aid Mr. Short in a round-up of the strength of Mr. Masterson. The two forces being out of gunshot of each other, the attendance will be freer and more untrammelled. Following the count Mr. Short and Mr. Kelly, Mr. Webster and Mr. Peacock will come together and declare the result. There of course will be no appeal, unless those appealing aim at civil war."

As Mr. Wright talked on, suavely, smoothly, laying down each feature of his design, a slow look of relief stole into the faces of Mr. Webster and Mr. Peacock. Even the more hardy features of Mr. Walker were not untouched.

There had been doubts tugging at the Updegraffe three. True, the majority of twelve was theirs, but the weight of valour stood overwhelmingly with Mr. Masterson. The offer of a safe separation of forces was a relief, and Mr. Peacock, Mr. Walker and Mr. Webster lost no time in accepting. Notices were posted proclaiming an election after the scheme laid down by Mr. Wright.

It was election night; only the enterprising and those with votes and guns were abroad in Dodge. The rival clans of Masterson and Updegraffe began to gather, respectively, at the Long Branch and the Dance Hall. There was never a ripple of disorder; nothing could be finer than that peace which was. Ten minutes before eight o'clock, the hour fixed for the count, the strength of each had convened.

The Updegraffe people were jubilant; every man belonging to them being in the Dance Hall, that majority of twelve was sure. The minutes went ticking themselves into eternity, and the watches of Mr. Kelly and Mr. Peacock registered one minute before eight. In sixty seconds the count in the Dance Hall would take place.

At the Long Branch, where the followers of Mr. Masterson filled the rooms, conditions were much the same. There Mr. Webster and Mr. Short would make the tally. Watch in hand they stood waiting for the moment.

It was at this crisis that Mr. Tighlman pulled his pistol and fired through the Long Branch floor. The report was as a joyful signal. Instantly one hundred shots rang out. Indeed, it was a noble din! The room filled with smoke; excitement mounted! Cimarron Bill, a six-shooter in each faithful hand, was in the midst of the hubbub, blazing like a piece of fireworks, whooping like a Comanche.

The night breeze carried the stirring story of riot and uproar to the waiting multitude in the Dance Hall. Those waiting ones looked first their amazement, then their delight. As by one impulse they tore through the door and made, hotfoot, for the Long Branch. By conservative estimates, founded upon the whole number of shots, there should be at least five dead and fifteen wounded.

As the advance guard arrived at the Long Branch they found Mr. Short outside.

"Bat's downed Bob Wright," remarked Mr. Short, "plugged him plumb center."

Inside went the hilarious Dance Hallers. The astute Mr. Short followed, closed the door and set his back against it.

"It's eight o'clock, Mr. Webster," remarked Mr. Short. "We must begin to count." It was observable that in the hand that did not hold the watch Mr. Short held a six-shooter.

Mr. Webster was in a flutter of nerves; he had been the only one in the Long Branch who did not understand and had not anticipated those frantic excesses of Mr. Tighlman, Cimarron Bill and others of that heroic firing party. Mr. Webster was in no wise clear as to what had happened. Borne upon by a feeling of something wrong he made a protest.

"Stop!" he cried, "there's a lot of Updegraffe men in here."

"No, sir," responded Mr. Short, coldly, while a gray glimmer, a kind of danger signal it was, began to show in his eye. "Every gent inside the Long Branch is for Bat Masterson or he wouldn't be here. Also, to suggest fraud," concluded Mr. Short, as Mr. Webster seemed about to speak, "would be an attack upon my honour, me ownin' the joint."

Now the honour of Mr. Short, next to Mr. Short's six-shooter, was the most feverish thing in Dodge. The mere mention of it sent a shiver through Mr. Webster. Without parley he surrendered tamely, and the count at the Long Branch began. The total proved satisfactory; the returns gave Mr. Masterson two hundred and sixty votes.

"Let us go over to the Dance Hall," said Mr. Wright, "and see what Kelly and Peacock have to report."

They were saved the journey; Mr. Kelly and Mr. Peacock, the latter bewildered and fear-ridden in the face of the unknown, just then came into the Long Branch. "Only thirty-three for Updegraffe," said Mr. Kelly. "That's correct, ain't it, Peacock?"

Mr. Peacock gasped, but seemed to nod assent.

"Mr. Masterson, it would appear, is elected," observed Mr. Wright, benignantly, "by a majority of two hundred and twenty-seven. It is a tribute to his popularity. The whole vote, however, is much smaller than I looked for," and Mr. Wright beamed.

"I think," said Mr. Kelly, judgmatically, "that thar's a passel of Updegraffe people stampedin' about the streets. But, of course, since they weren't in the Dance Hall, me an' Peacock had no authority to incloode 'em; did we, Peacock?"

Mr. Peacock mopped his moonlike countenance and shook his head in forlornest fashion. He was too much cast down to oppose the word of Mr. Kelly.

Bear Creek Johnson, eye aflame, a-bristle for trouble, pushed through. Cimarron Bill, who was the soul of business at a time like this, met the outraged Bear Creek in the door.

"Whatever do you reckon you're after?" queried Cimarron Bill, maintaining the while a dangerous eye.

Bear Creek Johnson surveyed Cimarron Bill, running him up and down with an uneasy, prudent glance. He smelled disaster off him as folk smell fire in a house.

"Me?" he returned, mildly. "Which I simply comes pirootin' over to move we make the 'lection of Bat Masterson yoonanimous."

Thus did the *ruse de guerre* of Mr. Masterson result in victory; thus was he made sheriff of Dodge.

8

THE DEPUTY SHERIFF OF COMANCHE COUNTY

BY EDGAR RICE BURROUGHS

Although far better known for his Tarzan the Ape Man *and* John Carter of Mars, *Edgar Rice Burroughs tried his hand at Western writing. Here are the first two chapters of a 1940 novel,* The Deputy Sheriff of Comanche County, *that establish the plot. We know Buck Mason will exonerate himself by solving the mystery, but the question becomes how?*

A lone rider drew rein before a gate consisting of three poles cut from straight pine saplings. He leaned from the saddle and dropped one end of each of the two upper bars to the ground, stepped his horse over the remaining bar and, stooping again, replaced the others. Then he rode slowly along a dirt road that showed little signs of travel.

As he rode he seemed but an animated part of the surrounding landscape, so perfectly did he harmonize from the crown of his Stetson to the light shod hoofs of his pony.

Everything that he wore seemed a part of him, as he seemed a part of his horse. His well worn chaps, his cartridge belt and holster, his shirt and bandana, like the leather of his horse trappings, were toned and mellowed by age and usage; yet they carried the same suggestion of strength and freshness and efficiency as did his bronzed face and his clear, gray eyes.

His mount moved at an easy, shuffling gait that some horsemen might call a rack, but which the young man would have described as a pace.

The horse was that homeliest of all horse colors, a blue roan, the only point of distinction in his appearance being a circular white spot, about the size of a saucer, that encircled his right eye, a marking which could not be said to greatly enhance his beauty, though it had served another and excellent purpose in suggesting his name—Bull's Eye.

At first glance the young man might have been found as little remarkable as his horse. In New Mexico there are probably thousands of other young men who look very much like him. His one personal adornment, in which he took a quiet, secret pride, was a flowing, brown mustache with drooping ends, which accomplished little more than to collect alkali dust and hide an otherwise strong and handsome mouth, while the low drawn brim of his Stetson almost accomplished the same result for the man's finest features—a pair of unusually arresting gray eyes.

The road wound through low rolling hills covered with stunted cedars, beyond which rose a range of mountains, whose sides were clothed with pine, the dark green of which was broken occasionally by irregular patches of quaking aspens, the whole mellowed and softened and mysterized by an enveloping purple haze.

The road, whose parallel twin paths suggested wheels of traffic, but in whose dust appeared only the spoor of hoofed animals, wound around the shoulder of a hill and debouched into a small valley, in the center of which stood a dilapidated log house.

"This here," said the young man to his pony, "is where we were headed fer. I hope the old man's in," and as though to assure him of the fulfillment of his wish, the door of the cabin opened and a large, droop-shouldered, gray haired man emerged.

"Ev'nen, Ole," said the rider.

"Ev'nen," said the older man, rather shortly, as the other stopped his horse and swung from the saddle. "What you doin' here?"

"I come to see you about that line fence, Ole," said the young man.

"Gol durned if you aint as bad as your pa," said the older man. "I aint heared nuthin' else but that durned line fence fer the last twenty years."

"You and the old man fit over that fence for eighteen years up to the very day he died, but I'll be doggoned if I want to scrap about it."

"Then what you doin' up here about it?" demanded the other.

"I aint up here to scrap with you, Ole. I just come up to tell you."

"Tell me what?"

"You aint doin' nuthin' with that land. You aint never done nuthin' with it. You can't get water on to it. I can and there's about a hundred acres of it that lies right for alfalfa and joins right on to the patch I put in last year."

"Well what you goin' to do about it? It's my land. You sure can't put alfalfa on my land."

"It aint your land, Ole, and you know it. You put your line fence in the wrong place. Maybe you did it accidental at first, but you know well enough that you aint got no title to that land."

"Well I got it fenced and I have had it fenced for twenty years. That's title enough for me," growled Gunderstrom.

"Now listen, Ole; I said I didn't come up here figurin' on quarrelin' with you and I aint a goin' to. I'm just tellin' you, I'm goin' to move that fence and put in alfalfa."

Olaf Gunderstrom's voice trembled with suppressed anger as he replied. "If ye lay a hand on that fence of mine, Buck Mason, I'll kill you."

"Now don't make me quarrel with you, Ole," said the young man, "cause I don't want to do nuthin' like that. I'm gonna move the fence, and I'm gonna say here that if anybody gets shot, it aint me. Now let's don't chaw any more fat over that. What do you hear from Olga?"

"None of your durn business," snapped Gunderstrom.

Mason grinned. "Well, Olga and I grew up together as kids," he reminded the older man, "and I'm just naturally interested in her."

"Well, I'll thank you to mind your own business, Buck Mason," said Gunderstrom surlily. "My girl aint fer no low down cowman. Me and her maw was nuthin' but trash. We seen it once when we went to Frisco and I aint never been nowhere since, but I made up my mind that my girl was gonna be able to herd with the best of 'em. That's why I sent her East to school—to keep her away from trash like you and the rest of the slab-sided longhorns that range in Comanche County.

"My girl aint gonna know the dirt and sweat and greasy pots in no cowman's kitchen. She aint gonna have no swells high hattin' her. She's goin' to be in a position to do the high hattin' herself. God and her mother give her the looks; the schools back in the states can give her the education, and I can give her the money; so she can herd with the best of 'em. My girl's gonna marry a swell; so you needn't waste your time asking no more questions about her. You aint never goin' to see her again, and if you do she won't even know you."

"Come, come, Ole," said Mason, "don't get so excited. I wasn't aimin' on bitin' Olga. She was a good kid; and we used to have a lot of fun together; and, say, if Olga marries a duke she wouldn't never high hat none of her old friends."

"She won't never get a chance while I'm alive," said Gunderstrom. "She aint never comin' back here."

"That's your business and hers," said Mason. "It aint none o'mine." He swung easily into the saddle. "I'll be moseyin' along, Ole. So long!"

"Listen," cried the older man as Mason wheeled his horse to move away. "Remember what I said about that line fence. If you lay a hand on it I'll kill you."

Buck Mason reined in his pony and turned in his saddle. "I hope there aint nobody goin' to be killed, Ole," he said quietly; "but if there is it aint goin' to be me. Come on, Bull's Eye, it's a long way back to town."

But Buck Mason did not ride to town. Instead he stopped at his own lonely ranch house, cooked his supper and afterward sat beneath an oil lamp and read.

The book that he was reading he had taken from a cupboard, the door of which was secured by a padlock, for the sad truth was that Mason was ashamed of his library and of his reading. He would have hated to have had any of his cronies discover his weakness, for the things that he read were not of the cow country. They included a correspondence course in English, a number of the classics which the course had recommended, magazines devoted to golf, polo, yachting, and a voluminous book on etiquette; but perhaps the thing that caused him the greatest mental perturbation in anticipation of its discovery by his candid, joke-loving friends was a file of the magazine *Vogue*.

No one knew that Buck Mason pored over these books and magazines whenever he had a leisure moment; in fact, no one suspected that he possessed them; and he would have died rather than to have explained why he did so.

He had led rather a lonely life, even before his father had died two years previously; but perhaps the greatest blow he had ever suffered had been the departure of Olga Gunderstrom for the East, nearly six years before.

She was sixteen then, and he eighteen. They had never spoken of love; perhaps neither one of them had thought of love; but she was the only girl that he had ever known well. When she had gone and he had commenced to realize how much he missed her, and then gradually to understand the barrier that her education was destined to raise between them, he began to believe that he loved her and that life without her would be a drab and monotonous waste.

Perhaps it was because he was a little bashful with women and guessed that he would never be well enough acquainted with any other girl to ask her to be his wife. He knew that he and Olga would get along well together. He knew that he would always be happy with her, and he thought that this belief constituted love; so he determined to fit himself as best he might to appear well in the society that he believed her superior education destined her to enter, that she might not ever have cause to be ashamed of him.

It was a pathetic little weakness. He did not think of it as pathetic but only as a weakness, and he was very much ashamed of it. Like most quiet men, he had a horror of ridicule; and so he always kept his books and his magazines locked in his cupboard, nor ever took one out unless he was alone, except that when he took one of those long, lonely trips, which were sometimes made necessary in pursuance of his office as deputy sheriff of Comanche County, he would carry one of his books along with him; but never the book of etiquette or a copy of *Vogue*, each of which he considered a reflection upon his manhood.

~~~~~~

In another lonely cabin, several miles away, Olaf Gunderstrom had cooked his own frugal meal, washed his dishes and gone to bed.

He was an eccentric old man, and he had permitted his eccentricities to become more and more marked after the death of his wife and the departure of his daughter for the East.

Possibly the wealthiest man in the county, he lived in the meanest of cabins, notwithstanding the fact that he had a comfortable, if not luxurious home in the county seat; and always he lived alone. His ranch and cow hands had their headquarters on another one of his ranches, several miles from Gunderstrom's shack. He rode there every day, and sometimes he ate dinner with them; but he always returned to his lonely cabin for his supper.

His only pleasures in life were directing his business, computing his profits and dreaming of the future of his daughter; and, before he fell asleep this night, his mind thus occupied with his daughter, he was reminded of the visit of Buck Mason in the afternoon.

"Always a askin' about Olga," he soliloquized grumblingly. "Never see that fellah that he aint askin' me about Olga. Guess he thinks I can't see right through him like a ladder. He'd like to marry Ole Gunderstrom's daughter. That's what he'd like to do and get his paws on all my land and cattle; but he aint aggona get Olga, and he aint even goin' to get that quarter section. I've had a fence around that for more'n twenty years now; and I guess if that don't give me no title, nuthin' else does. Buck Mason! Huh!" he snorted in disgust, and with Mason still in his thoughts he fell asleep.

WHO KILLED GUNDERSTROM?

The night wore on, its silence broken once by the hoot of an owl and again by the distant yapping of a coyote, and Olaf Gunderstrom slept.

Toward midnight subdued sounds floated up from the twin trails that wound in from the highway—the mellowed creaking of old leather, mingled with the breathing of horses—and then darker shadows moved beneath the moonless sky, slowly taking form and shape until they became distinguishable as five horsemen.

In silence they rode to the shack and dismounted where a long tie rail paralleled the front of the building. They moved very softly, making no noise in dismounting, nor speaking any words. They tied their horses to the tie rail and approached the door of the cabin. To the mystery of their silent approach there was added a sinister note by the handkerchiefs tied across their faces just below their eyes. Men come not thus at night in friendliness or well meaning.

Gently the leader pushed open the door, which was as innocent of bar and lock as are most cabin doors behind which no woman dwells.

Silently the five entered the single room of the cabin. The leader approached the wooden cot, roughly built against one of the cabin walls, where Gunderstrom lay asleep. It was dark within the cabin, but not so dark but that one familiar with the interior could locate the cot and the form of the sleeper. In the hand of the man crossing the room so stealthily was a long-barreled Colt.

The silent intruder could see the cot and the outlines of the blur that was the sleeper upon it; but he did not see one of Gunderstrom's boots that lay directly in his path, and he stepped partially upon it and half stumbled and as he did so, Gunderstrom awoke and sat up. "Buck Mason!" he exclaimed. "What do you want here?" and at the same time he reached for the gun that lay always beside him.

There was a flash in the dark, the silence was split by the report of a pistol and Olaf Gunderstrom slumped back upon his blanket, a bullet in his brain.

For a few moments the killer stood above his prey, seeking perhaps to assure himself that his work has been well done. He did not move, nor did his companions, nor did the dead man upon the cot. Presently the killer leaned low and placed his ear upon the breast of Gunderstrom. When he straightened up he turned back toward the doorway.

"We'd better be on our way," he said, and as the five men filed out of the cabin and mounted their horses, no other words were spoken. As silently as they had come they disappeared along the twin trails that led down to the highway.

It was nine o'clock in the morning. The sheriff of Comanche County sat in his office. He had read his mail and was now immersed in a newspaper.

An old man, leaning in the doorway, spit dexterously across the wooden porch into the dust of the road and shifted his quid. He, too, was reading a newspaper.

"Seems mighty strange to me," he said, "that nobody aint caught these fellers yet."

"There don't nobody know who they be," said the sheriff.

"I see by the papers," said the old man, "that they think they got a line on 'em."

"They aint got nuthin' on 'em," snapped the sheriff. "They don't even know that it's the same gang."

"No, that's right," assented the old man, "but it sure does look suspicious. Robbin' and murderin' and rustlin' breakin' out all of a sudden in towns here where we aint had none o' it for years. Why say, in the last year there's been more Hell goin' on around in this neck of the woods and over into Arizony than I've saw all put together for ten year before."

At this juncture the telephone bell rang and the sheriff rose and walked to the instrument, where it hung against the wall.

"Hello," he said as he put the receiver to his ear, and then, "The hell you say!" He listened for a moment longer. "Don't touch nuthin' leave everything as it is. I'll notify the Coroner and then I'll be out as soon as I can."

He hung up the receiver and as he turned away from the instrument Buck Mason entered the office. "Mornin', sheriff!" he said.

"Good morning, Buck!" returned the sheriff.

"Who's killed now?" demanded old man Cage, who, having heard half the conversation and scenting excitement, had abandoned his post in the doorway and entered the room.

Buck Mason looked inquiringly at the sheriff. "Somebody killed?" he asked.

The sheriff nodded. "Tom Kidder just called me up from the Circle G home ranch. He says they found old man Gunderstrom shot to death in his shack over on Spring Creek."

"Gunderstrom?" he exclaimed. "Why I see—," he hesitated. "Do they know who done it?" The sheriff shook his head. "Perhaps I better get right over there," continued Mason.

"I wish you would, Buck," said the sheriff. "Got your horse?"

"Yes."

"I got to pick up Doc Bellows; and you can be there, if you cut across the hills, long before I can shag Lizzie around by the roads."

"I'll be gettin' along then," said Mason, and as he left the office and mounted his horse the sheriff strapped on his gun and prepared to go after the coroner.

"Looks to me like that hit Buck pretty hard," said old man Cage. "Warnt he kinda soft on that Gunderstrom heifer?"

Bull's Eye carried his master at an easy lope across the flat toward the hills, where there was a stiff and rocky climb to the summit and an equally precipitous drop into Spring Valley, where Gunderstrom's shack lay a scant five miles from town by trail.

Uncle Billy Cage had resumed his position in the doorway of the office as the sheriff departed to look for the coroner. Half way to his car, the officer stopped and turned back. "If you aint got nuthin' else to do, sorta hang around the office until I get back, Uncle Billy. Will you?" he asked.

"I'll stay here as long as I can, sheriff," replied the old man. "Maybe I better go and fetch my bed."

"Shucks. I won't be gone long," the sheriff assured him.

"I don't know about that," replied Cage. "It's twenty mile of rough road from here to Gunderstrom's shack, and Lizzie aint what she used to be."

"Shucks. I could take her over the horse trail, Uncle Billy, if I wasn't afraid of scaring Doc Bellows," replied the sheriff with a grin.

~~~~~~

As Buck Mason rode up to the Gunderstrom shack he was greeted by Tom Kidder, foreman of the Circle G outfit, and two of the cowhands. The three men were squatting on their heels in the shade of a tree near the shack; and as Mason approached, Kidder rose. "Hello, Buck!" he said.

"Hello, Tom!" replied Mason. "How's everything?"

"Oh, so so," replied the foreman. "I reckon the sheriff told you."

"Yeah, that's why I'm here. You fellers aint been messin' around here none, have you?"

"No," replied Kidder. "When the old man didn't show up at the home ranch this morning, I rode over. I went in the shack, and when I seen there wasn't nuthin' to be done for him I rode back to the ranch and called up the sheriff. There aint been nobody in the shack since."

"Got any idea who done it?" asked Mason.

"No," replied the foreman. "There's been horses in and out from the highway recently. You could see that plain in the dirt; and there were horses tied up to his hitchin' rail last night, but I didn't mess around here any after what the sheriff told me. So everything's about like it was after the old man croaked."

"I'll take a look around," said Mason, who had dismounted.

Dropping his reins to the ground, he approached the shack. He moved slowly and deliberately, his keen eyes searching for any sign that the soft earth might give back to him. For several minutes he scrutinized the ground about the hitching rail, and then he entered the shack.

Inside he disturbed nothing, but examined everything minutely. For a brief moment he paused at the side of the cot, looking down into the upturned face of the dead man, the ghastliness of which was accentuated by the wound in the center of the pallid forehead.

Whatever thoughts the sight engendered in the mind of Buck Mason were not reflected in his calm, inscrutable gaze.

At Mason's feet lay the boot upon which the murderer had stepped and stumbled; and to it the eyes of the deputy dropped, casually at first and then with aroused interest. He stooped down then and examined it closely, but he did not touch it. After a moment he straightened up and left the shack, pausing again to make another examination of the ground about the hitching rail.

As he joined the men beneath the tree they looked at him inquiringly. "Well," asked Kidder, "what do you make of it?"

Mason squatted down upon his heels, his eyes upon the ground. "Well," he said, "there were five of them. At least there were five horses tied to the hitching rail last night, and that's about all we have to go on."

"About all? What do you mean?"

"There aint much more except that it don't look like a case of robbery. As far as I can see there wasn't nuthin' touched in the shack."

"A lot of folks thought the old man kept money hidden here," said Kidder.

"Yes, I know that," replied Mason, "and I expected to find the shack all torn to pieces where they searched for it."

"Mebbe he give it to 'em," suggested one of the cowhands.

"I reckon you didn't know old man Gunderstrom very well then," said the foreman. "In the first place he never kept no money here, and in the second place he wouldn't have told them where it was if he had."

"I think he had started to reach for his gun," said Mason.

"Mebbe that's why they bored him," suggested the cowhand.

"Maybe," assented Mason.

"This'll be tough on the girl," said Kidder.

Mason made no comment. His eyes were searching the ground all about the three men, though they did not know it.

"I reckon she'll live through it," said the cowhand, "especially after she gets a slant at her bank balance. She'll be the richest gal in a dozen counties."

"There'll be plenty hombres campin' on her trail now," said the foreman, shooting a quick, shrewd glance at Mason.

"Did the old man have any squabbles with anybody lately?" asked the deputy sheriff.

"He was a hard man to do business with," replied Kidder; "and there's lots of folks around here that didn't have much use for him, but there aint no one that I know of that had any call to kill him."

"Did he have any new business deals on with anyone that you know of?"

"I didn't know nuthin' about his business," replied Kidder; "he kept that to himself. But I've seen signs around the shack before that there'd been fellers up here at night. I don't know who they was or what they come for, and I never seen 'em. I just seen horse tracks around once in a while; and I knew fellers had been here, but it was none of my business, and I kept my mouth shut."

"Here comes a car," said the cowhand.

"That'll be the sheriff and the coroner," said Mason.

"Lizzie made pretty good time," said Kidder. "They must have packed her on their shoulders and run."

"She's hittin' on two and a half," said the cowhand, "which is better than I ever seen her do before."

As the car wheezed to a stop, the fat and jovial Doc Bellows lowered himself ponderously to the ground; and after the brief greetings of the cow country he asked a few questions.

"When you go in the shack," said Mason, "I wish you'd both notice that boot of Ole's that's lying in front of the cot. You seen it, didn't you, Kidder?" The foreman nodded. "Well," continued Mason, "guess all of you'll remember where you seen it; and then, sheriff, I wish you'd take care of it and not let nobody touch it."

"Is that a clue?" demanded the sheriff.

"I don't know that it amounts to nuthin'" replied Mason, "but I'd like to have the chance to follow it up."

"Sure," said the sheriff.

"All right then, I'll be gettin' along," replied the deputy. "There aint nuthin' more I can do here," and as the other men entered the shack he mounted and turned Bull's Eye's nose down the road toward the main highway.

It was late when the sheriff returned to his office, but Uncle Billy Cage was still there.

"There weren't no call for you to stay all night, Uncle Billy," said the sheriff.

"I wanted to see you," said the old man. "I got some important news for you, but by gum I don't believe it."

"What is it?" demanded the sheriff.

"About an hour after you left the telephone rung and some feller at the other end that talked like he had a harelip said, 'Is this the sheriff's office?' and I said, 'Yes'; and he said, 'Do you want to know who killed Gunderstrom?' and I said, 'Sure'; and he said, 'Well, it was Buck Mason,' and then he hung up."

"I don't believe it," said the sheriff.

"Neither do I," said Uncle Billy Cage.

9

A VOICE IN THE WILDERNESS, CHAPTER 1

BY GRACE LIVINGSTON HILL

Grace Livingston Hill, whose novel-writing career spanned the end of the nineteenth well into the twentieth century, published hundreds of inspirational novels and short stories, often featuring young female characters faced with dramatic turning points. This 1916 novel focused on one such naïve and devout heroine whose job as a schoolteacher takes her into the religious life of an isolated Western town, where she befriends cowboys including one very special young man.

With a lurch the train came to a dead stop and Margaret Earle, hastily gathering up her belongings, hurried down the aisle and got out into the night.

It occurred to her, as she swung her heavy suit-case down the rather long step to the ground, and then carefully swung herself after it, that it was strange that neither conductor, brakeman, nor porter had come to help her off the train, when all three had taken the trouble to tell her that hers was the next station; but she could hear voices up ahead. Perhaps something was the matter with the engine that detained them and they had forgotten her for the moment.

The ground was rough where she stood, and there seemed no sign of a platform. Did they not have platforms in this wild Western land, or was the train so long that her car had stopped before reaching it?

She strained her eyes into the darkness, and tried to make out things from the two or three specks of light that danced about like fireflies in the distance. She could dimly see moving figures away up near the engine, and each one evidently carried a lantern. The train was tremendously long. A sudden feeling of isolation took possession of her. Perhaps she ought not to have got out until some one came to help her. Perhaps the train had not pulled into the station yet and she ought to get back on it and wait. Yet if the train started before she found the conductor she might be carried on somewhere and he justly blame her for a fool.

There did not seem to be any building on that side of the track. It was probably on the other, but she was standing too near the cars to see over. She tried to move back to look, but the ground sloped and she slipped and fell in the cinders, bruising her knee and cutting her wrist.

In sudden panic she arose. She would get back into the train, no matter what the consequences. They had no right to put her out here, away off from the station, at night, in a strange country. If the train started before she could find the conductor she would tell him that he must back it up again and let her off. He certainly could not expect her to get out like this.

She lifted the heavy suit-case up the high step that was even farther from the ground than it had been when she came down, because her fall had loosened some of the earth and caused it to slide away from the track. Then, reaching to the rail of the step, she tried to pull herself up, but as she did so the engine gave a long snort and the whole train, as if it were in league against her, lurched forward crazily, shaking off her hold. She slipped to her knees again, the suit-case, toppled from the lower step, descending upon her, and together they slid and rolled down the short bank, while the train, like an irresponsible nurse who had slapped her charge and left it to its fate, ran giddily off into the night.

The horror of being deserted helped the girl to rise in spite of bruises and shock. She lifted imploring hands to the unresponsive cars as they hurried by her—one, two, three, with bright windows, each showing a passenger, comfortable and safe inside, unconscious of her need.

A moment of useless screaming, running, trying to attract some one's attention, a sickening sense of terror and failure, and the last car slatted itself past with a mocking clatter, as if it enjoyed her discomfort.

Margaret stood dazed, reaching out helpless hands, then dropped them at her sides and gazed after the fast-retreating train, the light on its last car swinging tauntingly, blinking now and then with a leer in its eye, rapidly vanishing from her sight into the depth of the night.

She gasped and looked about her for the station that but a short moment before had been so real to her mind; and, lo! on this side and on that there was none!

The night was wide like a great floor shut in by a low, vast dome of curving blue set with the largest, most wonderful stars she had ever seen. Heavy shadows of purple-green, smoke-like, hovered over earth darker and more intense than the unfathomable blue of the night sky. It seemed like the secret nesting-place of mysteries wherein no human foot might dare intrude. It was incredible that such could be but common sage-brush, sand, and greasewood wrapped about with the beauty of the lonely night.

No building broke the inky outlines of the plain, nor friendly light streamed out to cheer her heart. Not even a tree was in sight, except on the far horizon, where a heavy line of deeper darkness might mean a forest. Nothing, absolutely nothing, in the blue, deep, starry dome above and the bluer darkness of the earth below save one sharp shaft ahead like a black mast throwing out a dark arm across the track.

As soon as she sighted it she picked up her baggage and made her painful way toward it, for her knees and wrist were bruised and her baggage was heavy.

A soft drip, drip greeted her as she drew nearer; something splashing down among the cinders by the track. Then she saw the tall column with its arm outstretched, and looming darker among the sage-brush the outlines of a water-tank. It was so she recognized the engine's drinking-tank, and knew that she had mistaken a pause to water the engine for a regular stop at a station.

Her soul sank within her as she came up to the dripping water and laid her hand upon the dark upright, as if in some way it could help her. She dropped her baggage and stood, trembling, gazing around upon the beautiful, lonely scene in horror; and then, like a mirage against the distance, there melted on her frightened eyes a vision of her father and mother sitting around the library lamp at home, as they sat every evening. They were probably reading and talking at this very minute, and trying not to miss her on this her first venture away from the home into the great world to teach. What would they say if they could see their beloved daughter, whom they had sheltered all these years and let go forth so reluctantly now, in all her confidence of youth, bound by almost absurd promises to be careful and not run any risks.

Yet here she was, standing alone beside a water-tank in the midst of an Arizona plain, no knowing how many miles from anywhere, at somewhere between nine and ten o'clock at night! It seemed incredible that it had really happened! Perhaps she was dreaming! A few moments before in the bright car, surrounded by drowsy fellow-travelers, almost at her journey's end, as she supposed; and now, having merely done as she thought right, she was stranded here!

She rubbed her eyes and looked again up the track, half expecting to see the train come back for her. Surely, surely the conductor, or the porter who had been so kind, would discover that she was gone, and do something about it. They couldn't leave her here alone on the prairie! It would be too dreadful!

That vision of her father and mother off against the purple-green distance, how it shook her! The lamp looked bright and cheerful, and she could see her father's head with its heavy white hair. He turned to look at her mother to tell her of something he read in the paper. They were sitting there, feeling contented and almost happy about her, and she, their little girl—all her dignity as school-teacher dropped from her like a garment now—she was standing in this empty space alone, with only an engine's water-tank to keep her from dying, and only the barren, desolate track to connect her with the world of men and women. She dropped her head upon her breast and the tears came, sobbing, choking, raining down. Then off in the distance she heard a low, rising howl of some snarling, angry beast, and she lifted her head and stood in trembling terror, clinging to the tank.

That sound was coyotes or wolves howling. She had read about them, but had not expected to experience them in such a situation. How confidently had she accepted the position which offered her the opening she had sought for the splendid career that she hoped was to follow! How fearless had she been! Coyotes, nor Indians, nor wild cowboy students—nothing had daunted her courage. Besides, she told her mother it was very different going to a town from what it would be if she were a missionary going to the wilds. It was an important school she was to teach, where her Latin and German and mathematical achievements had won her the place above several other applicants, and where her well-known tact was expected to work wonders. But what were Latin and German and mathematics now? Could they show her how to climb a water-tank? Would tact avail with a hungry wolf?

The howl in the distance seemed to come nearer. She cast frightened eyes to the unresponsive water-tank looming high and dark above her. She must get up there somehow. It was not safe to stand here a minute. Besides, from that height she might be able to see farther, and perhaps there would be a light somewhere and she might cry for help.

Investigation showed a set of rude spikes by which the trainmen were wont to climb up, and Margaret prepared to ascend them. She set her suit-case dubiously down at the foot. Would it be safe to leave it there? She had read how coyotes carried off a hatchet from a camping-party, just to get the leather thong which was bound about the handle. She could not afford to lose her things. Yet how could she climb and carry that heavy burden with her? A sudden thought came.

Her simple traveling-gown was finished with a silken girdle, soft and long, wound twice about her waist and falling in tasseled ends. Swiftly she untied it and knotted one end firmly to the handle of her suit-case, tying the other end securely to her wrist. Then slowly, cautiously, with many a look upward, she began to climb.

It seemed miles, though in reality it was but a short distance. The howling beasts in the distance sounded nearer now and continually, making her heart beat wildly. She was stiff and bruised from her falls, and weak with fright. The spikes were far apart, and each step of progress was painful and difficult. It was good at last to rise high enough to see over the water-tank and feel a certain confidence in her defense.

But she had risen already beyond the short length of her silken tether, and the suit-case was dragging painfully on her arm. She was obliged to steady herself where she stood and pull it up before she could go on. Then she managed to get it swung up to the top of the tank in a comparatively safe place. One more long spike step and she was beside it.

The tank was partly roofed over, so that she had room enough to sit on the edge without danger of falling in and drowning. For a few minutes she could only sit still and be thankful and try to get her breath back again after the climb; but presently the beauty of the night began to cast its spell over her. That wonderful blue of the sky! It hadn't ever before impressed her that skies were blue at night. She would have said they were black or gray. As a matter of fact, she didn't remember to have ever seen so much sky at once before, nor to have noticed skies in general until now.

This sky was so deeply, wonderfully blue, the stars so real, alive and sparkling, that all other stars she had ever seen paled before them into mere imitations. The spot looked like one of Taylor's pictures of the Holy Land. She half expected to see a shepherd with his crook and sheep approaching her out of the dim shadows, or a turbaned, white-robed David with his lifted hands of prayer standing off among the depths of purple darkness. It would not have been out of keeping if a walled city with housetops should be hidden behind the clumps of sage-brush farther on. 'Twas such a night and such a scene as this, perhaps, when the wise men started to follow the star!

But one cannot sit on the edge of a water-tank in the desert night alone and muse long on art and history. It was cold up there, and the howling seemed nearer than before. There was no sign of a light or a house anywhere, and not even a freight train sent its welcome clatter down the track. All was still and wide and lonely, save that terrifying sound of the beasts; such stillness as she had not ever thought could be—a fearful silence as a setting for the awful voices of the wilds.

The bruises and scratches she had acquired set up a fine stinging, and the cold seemed to sweep down and take possession of her on her high, narrow seat. She was growing stiff and cramped, yet dared not move much. Would there be no train, nor any help? Would she have to sit there all night? It looked so very near to the ground now. Could wild beasts climb, she wondered?

Then in the interval of silence that came between the calling of those wild creatures there stole a sound. She could not tell at first what it was. A slow, regular, plodding sound, and quite far away. She looked to find it, and thought she saw a shape move out of the sage-brush on the other side of the track, but she could not be sure. It might be but a figment of her brain, a foolish fancy from looking so long at the huddled bushes on the dark plain. Yet something prompted her to cry out, and when she heard her own voice she cried again and louder, wondering why she had not cried before.

"Help! Help!" she called; and again: "Help! Help!"

The dark shape paused and turned toward her. She was sure now. What if it were a beast instead of a human! Terrible fear took possession of her; then, to her infinite relief, a nasal voice sounded out: "Who's thar?"

But when she opened her lips to answer, nothing but a sob would come to them for a minute, and then she could only cry, pitifully: "Help! Help!"

"Whar be you?" twanged the voice; and now she could see a horse and rider like a shadow moving toward her down the track.

CHAPTER II

The horse came to a standstill a little way from the track, and his rider let forth a stream of strange profanity. The girl shuddered and began to think a wild beast might be preferable to some men. However, these remarks seemed to be a mere formality. He paused and addressed her: "Heow'd yeh git up thar? D'j'yeh drap er climb?"

He was a little, wiry man with a bristly, protruding chin. She could see that, even in the starlight. There was something about the point of that stubby chin that she shrank from inexpressibly. He was not a pleasant man to look upon, and even his voice was unprepossessing. She began to think that even the night with its loneliness and unknown perils was preferable to this man's company.

"I got off the train by mistake, thinking it was my station, and before I discovered it the train had gone and left me," Margaret explained, with dignity.

"Yeh didn't 'xpect it t' sit reound on th' plain while you was galli-vantin' up water-tanks, did yeh?"

Cold horror froze Margaret's veins. She was dumb for a second. "I am on my way to Ashland station. Can you tell me how far it is from here and how I can get there?" Her tone was like icicles.

"It's a little matter o' twenty miles, more 'r less," said the man protruding his offensive chin. "The walkin's good. I don't know no other way from this p'int at this time o' night. Yeh might set still till th' mornin' freight goes by an' drap atop o' one of the kyars."

"Sir!" said Margaret, remembering her dignity as a teacher.

The man wheeled his horse clear around and looked up at her impudently. She could smell bad whisky on his breath. "Say, you must be some young highbrow, ain't yeh? Is thet all yeh want o' me? 'Cause ef 'tis I got t' git on t' camp. It's a good five mile yet, an' I 'ain't hed no grub sence noon."

The tears suddenly rushed to the girl's eyes as the horror of being alone in the night again took possession of her. This dreadful man frightened her, but the thought of the loneliness filled her with dismay.

"Oh!" she cried, forgetting her insulted dignity, "you're not going to leave me up here alone, are you? Isn't there some place near here where I could stay overnight?"

"Thur ain't no palace hotel round these diggin's, ef that's what you mean," the man leered at her. "You c'n come along t' camp 'ith me ef you ain't too stuck up."

"To camp!" faltered Margaret in dismay, wondering what her mother would say. "Are there any ladies there?"

A loud guffaw greeted her question. "Wal, my woman's thar, sech es she is; but she ain't no highflier like you. We mostly don't hev ladies to camp, But I got t' git on. Ef you want to go too, you better light down pretty speedy, fer I can't wait."

In fear and trembling Margaret descended her rude ladder step by step, primitive man seated calmly on his horse, making no attempt whatever to assist her.

"This ain't no baggage-car," he grumbled, as he saw the suit-case in her hand. "Well, h'ist yerself up thar; I reckon we c'n pull through somehow. Gimme the luggage."

Margaret stood appalled beside the bony horse and his uncouth rider. Did he actually expect her to ride with him? "Couldn't I walk?" she faltered, hoping he would offer to do so.

"'T's up t' you," the man replied, indifferently. "Try 't an' see!" He spoke to the horse, and it started forward eagerly, while the girl in horror struggled on behind. Over rough, uneven ground, between greasewood, sage-brush, and cactus, back into the trail. The man, oblivious of her presence, rode contentedly on, a silent shadow on a dark horse wending a silent way between the purple-green clumps of other shadows, until, bewildered, the girl almost lost sight of them. Her breath came short, her ankle turned, and she fell with both hands in a stinging bed of cactus. She cried out then and begged him to stop.

"L'arned yer lesson, hev yeh, sweety?" he jeered at her, foolishly. "Well, get in yer box, then."

He let her struggle up to a seat behind himself with very little assistance, but when she was seated and started on her way she began to wish she had stayed behind and taken any perils of the way rather than trust herself in proximity to this creature.

From time to time he took a bottle from his pocket and swallowed a portion of its contents, becoming fluent in his language as they proceeded on their way. Margaret remained silent, growing more and more frightened every time the bottle came out. At last he offered it to her. She declined it with cold politeness, which seemed to irritate the little man, for he turned suddenly fierce.

"Oh, yer too fine to take a drap fer good comp'ny, are yeh? Wal, I'll show yeh a thing er two, my pretty lady. You'll give me a kiss with yer two cherry lips before we go another step. D'yeh hear, my sweetie?" And he turned with a silly leer to enforce his command; but with a cry of horror Margaret slid to the ground and ran back down the trail as hard as she could go, till she stumbled and fell in the shelter of a great sage-bush, and lay sobbing on the sand.

The man turned bleared eyes toward her and watched until she disappeared. Then sticking his chin out wickedly, he slung her suit-case after her and called: "All right, my pretty lady; go yer own gait an' l'arn yer own lesson." He started on again, singing a drunken song.

Under the blue, starry dome alone sat Margaret again, this time with no friendly water-tank for her defense, and took counsel with herself. The howling coyotes seemed to be silenced for the time; at least they had become a minor quantity in her equation of troubles. She felt now that man was her greatest menace, and to get away safely from him back to that friendly water-tank and the dear old railroad track she would have pledged her next year's salary. She stole softly to the place where she had heard the suit-case fall, and, picking it up, started on the weary road back to the tank. Could she ever find the way? The trail seemed so intangible a thing, her sense of direction so confused. Yet there was nothing else to do. She shuddered whenever she thought of the man who had been her companion on horseback.

When the man reached camp he set his horse loose and stumbled into the door of the log bunk-house, calling loudly for something to eat.

The men were sitting around the room on the rough benches and bunks, smoking their pipes or stolidly staring into the dying fire. Two smoky kerosene-lanterns that hung from spikes driven high in the logs cast a weird light over the company, eight men in all, rough and hardened with exposure to stormy life and weather. They were men with unkempt beards and uncombed hair, their coarse cotton shirts open at the neck, their brawny arms bare above the elbow, with crimes and sorrows and hard living written large across their faces.

There was one, a boy in looks, with smooth face and white skin healthily flushed in places like a baby's. His face, too, was hard and set in sternness like a mask, as if life had used him badly; but behind it was a fineness of feature and spirit that could not be utterly hidden. They called him the Kid, and thought it was his youth that made him different from them all, for he was only twenty-four, and not one of the rest was under forty. They were doing their best to help him get over that innate fineness that was his natural inheritance, but although he stopped at nothing, and played his part always with the ease of one old in the ways of the world, yet he kept a quiet reserve about him, a kind of charm beyond which they had not been able to go.

He was playing cards with three others at the table when the man came in, and did not look up at the entrance.

The woman, white and hopeless, appeared at the door of the shed-room when the man came, and obediently set about getting his supper; but her lifeless face never changed expression.

"Brung a gal 'long of me part way," boasted the man, as he flung himself into a seat by the table. "Thought you fellers might like t' see 'er, but she got too high an' mighty fer me, wouldn't take a pull at th' bottle 'ith me, 'n' shrieked like a catamount when I kissed 'er. Found 'er hangin' on th' water-tank. Got off 't th' wrong place. One o' yer highbrows out o' th' parlor car! Good lesson fer 'er!"

The Boy looked up from his cards sternly, his keen eyes boring through the man. "Where is she now?" he asked, quietly; and all the men in the room looked up uneasily. There was that tone and accent again that made the Boy alien from them. What was it?

The man felt it and snarled his answer angrily. "Dropped 'er on th' trail, an' threw her fine-lady b'longin's after 'er. Ain't got no use fer thet kind. Wonder what they was created fer? Ain't no good to nobody, not even 'emselves." And he laughed a harsh cackle that was not pleasant to hear.

The Boy threw down his cards and went out, shutting the door. In a few minutes the men heard two horses pass the end of the bunkhouse toward the trail, but no one looked up nor spoke. You could not have told by the flicker of an eyelash that they knew where the Boy had gone.

She was sitting in the deep shadow of a sage-bush that lay on the edge of the trail like a great blot, her suit-case beside her, her breath coming short with exertion and excitement, when she heard a cheery whistle in the distance. Just an old love-song dating back some years and discarded now as hackneyed even by the street pianos at home; but oh, how good it sounded!

From the desert I come to thee!

The ground was cold, and struck a chill through her garments as she sat there alone in the night. On came the clear, musical whistle, and she peered out of the shadow with eager eyes and frightened heart. Dared she risk it again? Should she call, or should she hold her breath and keep still, hoping he would pass her by unnoticed? Before she could decide two horses stopped almost in front of her and a rider swung himself down. He stood before her as if it were day and he could see her quite plainly.

"You needn't be afraid," he explained, calmly. "I thought I had better look you up after the old man got home and gave his report. He was pretty well tanked up and not exactly a fit escort for ladies. What's the trouble?"

Like an angel of deliverance he looked to her as he stood in the starlight, outlined in silhouette against the wide, wonderful sky: broad shoulders, well-set head, close-cropped curls, handsome contour even in the darkness. There was about him an air of quiet strength which gave her confidence.

"Oh, thank you!" she gasped, with a quick little relieved sob in her voice. "I am so glad you have come. I was—just a little—frightened, I think." She attempted to rise, but her foot caught in her skirt and she sank wearily back to the sand again.

The Boy stooped over and lifted her to her feet. "You certainly are some plucky girl!" he commented, looking down at her slender height as she stood beside him. "A 'little frightened,' were you? Well, I should say you had a right to be."

"Well, not exactly frightened, you know," said Margaret, taking a deep breath and trying to steady her voice. "I think perhaps I was more mortified than frightened, to think I made such a blunder as to get off the train before I reached my station. You see, I'd made up my mind not to be frightened, but when I heard that awful howl of some beast—And then that terrible man!" She shuddered and put her hands suddenly over her eyes as if to shut out all memory of it.

"More than one kind of beasts!" commented the Boy, briefly. "Well, you needn't worry about him; he's having his supper and he'll be sound asleep by the time we get back."

"Oh, have we got to go where he is?" gasped Margaret. "Isn't there some other place? Is Ashland very far away? That is where I am going."

"No other place where you could go to-night. Ashland's a good twenty-five miles from here. But you'll be all right. Mom Wallis'll look out for you. She isn't much of a looker, but she has a kind heart. She pulled me through once when I was just about flickering out. Come on. You'll be pretty tired. We better be getting back. Mom Wallis'll make you comfortable, and then you can get off good and early in the morning."

Without an apology, and as if it were the common courtesy of the desert, he stooped and lifted her easily to the saddle of the second horse, placed the bridle in her hands, then swung the suit-case up on his own horse and sprang into the saddle.

CHAPTER III

He turned the horses about and took charge of her just as if he were accustomed to managing stray ladies in the wilderness every day of his life and understood the situation perfectly; and Margaret settled wearily into her saddle and looked about her with content.

Suddenly, again, the wide wonder of the night possessed her. Involuntarily she breathed a soft little exclamation of awe and delight. Her companion turned to her questioningly.

"Does it always seem so big here—so—limitless?" she asked in explanation. "It is so far to everywhere it takes one's breath away, and yet the stars hang close, like a protection. It gives one the feeling of being alone in the great universe with God. Does it always seem so out here?"

He looked at her curiously, her pure profile turned up to the wide dome of luminous blue above. His voice was strangely low and wondering as he answered, after a moment's silence: "No, it is not always so," he said. "I have seen it when it was more like being alone in the great universe with the devil."

There was a tremendous earnestness in his tone that the girl felt meant more than was on the surface. She turned to look at the fine young face beside her. In the starlight she could not make out the bitter hardness of lines that were beginning to be carved about his sensitive mouth. But there was so much sadness in his voice that her heart went out to him in pity.

"Oh," she said, gently, "it would be awful that way. Yes, I can understand. I felt so, a little, while that terrible man was with me." And she shuddered again at the remembrance.

Again he gave her that curious look. "There are worse things than Pop Wallis out here," he said, gravely. "But I'll grant you there's some class to the skies. It's a case of 'Where every prospect pleases and only man is vile.'" And with the words his tone grew almost flippant. It hurt her sensitive nature, and without knowing it she half drew away a little farther from him and murmured, sadly: "Oh!" as if he had classed himself with the "man" he had been describing. Instantly he felt her withdrawal and grew grave again, as if he would atone.

"Wait till you see this sky at the dawn," he said. "It will burn red fire off there in the east like a hearth in a palace, and all this dome will glow like a great pink jewel set in gold. If you want a classy sky, there you have it! Nothing like it in the East!"

There was a strange mingling of culture and roughness in his speech. The girl could not make him out; yet there had been a palpitating earnestness in his description that showed he had felt the dawn in his very soul.

"You are—a—poet, perhaps?" she asked, half shyly. "Or an artist?" she hazarded.

He laughed roughly and seemed embarrassed. "No, I'm just a— bum! A sort of roughneck out of a job."

She was silent, watching him against the starlight, a kind of embarrassment upon her after his last remark. "You—have been here long?" she asked, at last.

"Three years." He said it almost curtly and turned his head away, as if there were something in his face he would hide.

She knew there was something unhappy in his life. Unconsciously her tone took on a sympathetic sound. "And do you get homesick and want to go back, ever?" she asked.

His tone was fairly savage now. "No!"

The silence which followed became almost oppressive before the Boy finally turned and in his kindly tone began to question her about the happenings which had stranded her in the desert alone at night.

So she came to tell him briefly and frankly about herself, as he questioned—how she came to be in Arizona all alone.

"My father is a minister in a small town in New York State. When I finished college I had to do something, and I had an offer of this

Ashland school through a friend of ours who had a brother out here. Father and mother would rather have kept me nearer home, of course, but everybody says the best opportunities are in the West, and this was a good opening, so they finally consented. They would send post-haste for me to come back if they knew what a mess I have made of things right at the start—getting out of the train in the desert."

"But you're not discouraged?" said her companion, half wonder-ingly. "Some nerve you have with you. I guess you'll manage to hit it off in Ashland. It's the limit as far as discipline is concerned, I under-stand, but I guess you'll put one over on them. I'll bank on you after to-night, sure thing!"

She turned a laughing face toward him. "Thank you!" she said. "But I don't see how you know all that. I'm sure I didn't do anything particularly nervy. There wasn't anything else to do but what I did, if I'd tried."

"Most girls would have fainted and screamed, and fainted again when they were rescued," stated the Boy, out of a vast experience. "I never fainted in my life," said Margaret Earle, with disdain. "I don't think I should care to faint out in the vast universe like this. It would be rather inopportune, I should think."

Then, because she suddenly realized that she was growing very chummy with this stranger in the dark, she asked the first question that came into her head. "What was your college?"

That he had not been to college never entered her head. There was something in his speech and manner that made it a foregone conclusion.

It was as if she had struck him forcibly in his face, so sudden and sharp a silence ensued for a second. Then he answered, gruffly, "Yale," and plunged into an elaborate account of Arizona in its early ages, including a detailed description of the cliff-dwellers and their homes, which were still to be seen high in the rocks of the cañons not many miles to the west of where they were riding.

Margaret was keen to hear it all, and asked many questions, declaring her intention of visiting those cliff-caves at her earliest opportunity. It was so wonderful to her to be actually out here where were all sorts of queer things about which she had read and wondered. It did not occur to her, until the next day, to realize that her companion had of intention led her off the topic of himself and kept her from asking any more personal questions.

He told her of the petrified forest just over some low hills off to the left; acres and acres of agatized chips and trunks of great trees all turned to eternal stone, called by the Indians "Yeitso's bones," after the great giant of that name whom an ancient Indian hero killed. He described the coloring of the brilliant days in Arizona, where you stand on the edge of some flat-topped mesa and look off through the clear air to mountains that seem quite near by, but are in reality more than two hundred miles away. He pictured the strange colors and lights of the place; ledges of rock, yellow, white and green, drab and maroon, and tumbled piles of red boulders, shadowy buttes in the distance, serrated cliffs against the horizon, not blue, but rosy pink in the heated haze of the air, and perhaps a great, lonely eagle poised above the silent, brilliant waste.

He told it not in book language, with turn of phrase and smoothly flowing sentences, but in simple, frank words, as a boy might describe a picture to one he knew would appreciate it—for her sake, and not because he loved to put it into words; but in a new, stumbling way letting out the beauty that had somehow crept into his heart in spite of all the rough attempts to keep all gentle things out of his nature.

The girl, as she listened, marveled more and more what manner of youth this might be who had come to her out of the desert night.

She forgot her weariness as she listened, in the thrill of wonder over the new mysterious country to which she had come. She forgot that she was riding through the great darkness with an utter stranger, to a place she knew not, and to experiences most dubious. Her fears had fled and she was actually enjoying herself, and responding to the wonderful story of the place with soft-murmured exclamations of delight and wonder.

From time to time in the distance there sounded forth those awful blood-curdling howls of wild beasts that she had heard when she sat alone by the water-tank, and each time she heard a shudder passed through her and instinctively she swerved a trifle toward her companion, then straightened up again and tried to seem not to notice. The Boy saw and watched her brave attempts at self-control with deep appreciation. But suddenly, as they rode and talked, a dark form appeared across their way a little ahead, lithe and stealthy and furry, and two awful eyes like green lamps glared for an instant, then disappeared silently among the mesquite bushes.

She did not cry out nor start. Her very veins seemed frozen with horror, and she could not have spoken if she tried. It was all over in a second and the creature gone, so that she almost doubted her senses and wondered if she had seen aright. Then one hand went swiftly to her throat and she shrank toward her companion.

"There is nothing to fear," he said, reassuringly, and laid a strong hand comfortingly across the neck of her horse. "The pussy-cat was as unwilling for our company as we for hers. Besides, look here!"—and he raised his hand and shot into the air. "She'll not come near us now."

"I am not afraid!" said the girl, bravely. "At least, I don't think I am—very! But it's all so new and unexpected, you know. Do people around here always shoot in that—well—unpremeditated fashion?"

They laughed together.

"Excuse me," he said. "I didn't realize the shot might startle you even more than the wildcat. It seems I'm not fit to have charge of a lady. I told you I was a roughneck."

"You're taking care of me beautifully," said Margaret Earle, loyally, "and I'm glad to get used to shots if that's the thing to be expected often."

Just then they came to the top of the low, rolling hill, and ahead in the darkness there gleamed a tiny, wizened light set in a blotch of blackness. Under the great white stars it burned a sickly red and seemed out of harmony with the night.

"There we are!" said the Boy, pointing toward it. "That's the bunk-house. You needn't be afraid. Pop Wallis'll be snoring by this time, and we'll come away before he's about in the morning. He always sleeps late after he's been off on a bout. He's been gone three days, selling some cattle, and he'll have a pretty good top on."

The girl caught her breath, gave one wistful look up at the wide, starry sky, a furtive glance at the strong face of her protector, and submitted to being lifted down to the ground.

Before her loomed the bunk-house, small and mean, built of logs, with only one window in which the flicker of the lanterns menaced, with unknown trials and possible perils for her to meet.

10

WILD BILL'S LAST TRAIL

BY NED BUNTLINE

Ned Buntline was the pen name of author and entrepreneur Edward Zane Carroll Judson, who cranked out hundreds of stories that he published in his Ned Buntline's Own magazine. Meeting a buffalo hunter named William Cody, Buntline, who claimed to have given Cody the nickname "Buffalo Bill," turned this 1976 novel about the man into a stage play in which he persuaded Cody to perform. Because of his theatrical fame, Cody creates his legendary Wild West stage show.

Here, however, are chapters from Wild Bill's Last Trail, *a 1976 saga about another actual person, Wild Bill Hickok, one that is thoroughly fictitious (Hickok refused to talk to Buntline)—but a real cliffhanger.*

As soon as the auburn-haired man who called himself Jack had left the German restaurant, he went to a livery-stable nearby, called for his own horse, which was kept there, and the instant it was saddled he mounted, and at a gallop rode westward from the town.

He did not draw rein for full an hour, and then he had covered somewhere between eight and ten miles of ground, following no course or trail, but riding in a course as straight as the flight of an arrow.

He halted then in a small ravine, nearly hidden by a growth of thick brush, and gave a peculiar whistle. Thrice had this sounded, when a man came cautiously out of the ravine, or rather out of its mouth. He was tall, slender, yet seemed to possess the bone and muscle of a giant. His eyes were jet black, fierce and flashing, and his face had a stern, almost classic beauty of feature, which would have made him a model in the ancient age of sculpture. He carried a repeating rifle, two revolvers, and a knife in his belt. His dress was buckskin, from head to foot.

"You are Persimmon Bill?" said Jack, in a tone of inquiry.

"Yes. Who are you, and how came you by the signal that called me out?"

"A woman in town gave it to me, knowing she could trust me."

"Was her first name Addie?"

"Her last name was Neidic."

"All right. I see she has trusted you. What do you want?"

"Help in a matter of revenge."

"Good! You can have it. How much help is wanted?"

"I want one man taken from a party, alive, when he gets beyond civilized help, so that I can see him tortured. I want him to die by inches."

"How large is his party, and where are they now?"

"The party numbers between twenty and thirty; they are in camp in the edge of Laramie, and will start for the Black Hills in a few days."

"If all the party are wiped out but the one you want, will it matter to you?"

"No; they are his friends, and as such I hate them!"

"All right. Get me a list of their numbers and names, how armed, what animals and stores they have, every fact, so I can be ready. They will never get more than half way to the Hills, and the one you want shall be delivered, bound into your hands. All this, and more, will I do for her who sent you here!"

"You love her?"

"She loves me! I'm not one to waste much breath on talking love. My Ogallalla Sioux warriors know me as the soldier-killer. Be cautious when you go back, and give no hint to any one but Addie Neidic that there is a living being in Dead Man's Hollow, for so this ravine is called in there."

"Do not fear. I am safe, for I counsel with no one. I knew Addie Neidic before I came here, met her by accident, revealed myself and wants, and she sent me to you."

"It is right. Go back, and be cautious to give the signal if you seek me, or you might lose your scalp before you saw me."

"My scalp?"

"Yes; my guards are vigilant and rough."

"Your guards?"

Persimmon Bill laughed at the look of wonder in the face of his visitor, and with his hand to his mouth, gave a shrill, warbling cry. In a second this mouth of the ravine was fairly blocked with armed and painted warriors—Sioux, of the Ogallalla tribe. There were not less than fifty of them.

"You see my guards—red devils, who will do my bidding at all times, and take a scalp on their own account every chance they get," said Persimmon Bill.

Then he took an eagle feather, with its tip dipped in crimson, from the coronet of the chief, and handed it, in the presence of all the Indians, to Jack. "Keep thus, and when out on the plains, wear it in your hat, where it can be seen, and the Sioux will ever pass you unharmed, and you can safely come and go among them. Now go back, get the list and all the news you can, and bring it here as soon as you can. Tell Addie to ride out with you when you come next."

Jack placed the feather in a safe place inside his vest, bowed his head, and wheeling his horse, turned toward the town. Before he had ridden a hundred yards he looked back. Persimmon Bill had vanished, not an Indian was in sight, and no one unacquainted with their vicinity could have seen a sign to show that such dangerous beings were near. No smoke rose above the trees, no horses were feeding around, nothing to break the apparent solitude of the scene.

"And that was Persimmon Bill?" muttered the auburn-haired rider, as he galloped back. "So handsome, it does not seem as if he could be the murderer they call him. And yet, if all is true, he has slain tens, where Wild Bill has killed one. No matter, he will be useful to me. That is all I care for now."

A WARNING, CHAPTER III

When Wild Bill and Sam Chichester entered the saloon alluded to in our first chapter, they were hailed by several jovial-looking men, one of whom Wild Bill warmly responded to as California Joe, while he grasped the hand of another fine-looking young man whom he called Captain Jack.

"Come, Crawford," said he, addressing the last named, "let's wet up! I'm dry as an empty powder-horn!"

"No benzine for me, Bill," replied Crawford, or "Captain Jack." "I've not touched a drop of the poison in six months."

"What? Quit drinking, Jack? Is the world coming to an end?"

"I suppose it will sometime. But that has nothing to do with my drinking. I promised old Cale Durg to quit, and I've done it. And I never took a better trail in my life. I'm fresh as a daisy, strong as a full-grown elk, and happy as an antelope on a wide range."

"All right, Jack. But I must drink. Come, boys—all that will—come up and wet down at my expense."

California Joe and most of the others joined in the invitation, and Captain Jack took a cigar rather than "lift a shingle from the roof," as he said.

"Where are you bound, Bill?" asked Captain Jack, as Bill placed his empty glass on the counter, and turned around.

"To the Black Hills with your crowd—that is if I live to get there."

"Live! You haven't any thought of dying, have you? I never saw you look better."

"Then I'll make a healthy-looking corpse, Jack. For I tell you my time is nearly up; I've felt it in my bones this six months. I've seen ghosts in my dreams, and felt as if they were around me when I was awake. It's no use, Jack, when a chap's time comes he has got to go."

"Nonsense, Bill; don't think of anything like that. A long life and a merry one—that's my motto. We'll go out to the Black Hills, dig out our fortunes, and then get out of the wilderness to enjoy life."

"Boy, I've never known the happiness outside of the wilderness that I have in it. What you kill there is what was made for killing—the food we need. What one kills among civilization is only too apt to be of his own kind." And Bill shuddered as if he thought of the many he had sent into untimely graves.

"Stuff, Bill! You're half crazed by your dramatic trip. You've acted so much, that reality comes strange. Let's go out to camp and have a talk about what is ahead of us."

"Not till I buy a horse, Jack. I want a good horse under me once more; I've ridden on cars and steamboats till my legs ache for a change."

"There's a sale's stable close by. Let's go and see what stock is there," said Sam Chichester.

"Agreed!" cried all hands, and soon Bill and his friends were at the stable, looking at some dozen or more horses which were for sale.

"There's the beauty I want," said Wild Bill, pointing to a black horse, full sixteen hands high, and evidently a thoroughbred. "Name your price, and he is my meat!"

"That horse isn't for sale now. He was spoken for an hour ago, or maybe less by a cash customer of mine—a red-haired chap from Texas."

"Red-haired chap from Texas!" muttered Bill, "Red-haired cusses from Texas are always crossin' my trail. That chap from Abilene was a Texas cattle-man, with hair as red as fire. Where is your cash customer, Mr. Liveryman?"

"Gone out riding somewhere," replied the stable-keeper.

"When he comes back, tell him Wild Bill wants that horse, and I reckon he'll let Wild Bill buy him, if he knows when he is well off! I wouldn't give two cusses and an amen for all the rest of the horses in your stable; I want *him*!"

"I'll tell Jack," said the stableman; "but I don't think it will make much odds with him. He has as good as bought the horse, for he offered me the money on my price, but I couldn't change his five hundred-dollar treasury note. It'll take more than a name to scare him. He always goes fully armed."

"You tell him what I said, and that I'm a-coming here at sunset for that horse," said Bill, and he strode away, followed by his crowd.

An hour later the auburn-haired man from Texas reined in his own horse, a fiery mustang from his own native plains, in front of the stable. Though the horse was all afoam with sweat, showing that it had been ridden far and fast; it did not pant or show a sign of weariness. It was of a stock which will run from rise of sun to its going down, and yet plunge forward in the chill of the coming night.

"You want the Black Hawk horse you spoke for this morning, don't you?" asked the stableman, as Jack dismounted.

"Of course I do. I've got the change; there is his price. Three hundred dollars you said?"

"Yes; but there's been a chap here looking at that horse who told me to tell you his name, and that he intended to take that horse. I told him a man had bought it, but he said: 'Tell him Wild Bill wants it, and that Wild Bill will come at sunset to take it.'"

"He will?"

It was hissed rather than spoken, while the young Texan's face grew white as snow, his blue eyes darkening till they seemed almost black. "He will! Let him try it! A sudden death is too good for the blood-stained wretch! But if he will force it on, why let it come. The horse is bought: let him come at sunset if he dares!" And the young man handed the stable-keeper three one-hundred-dollar greenback notes.

GIVE UP THAT HORSE, OR DIE!, CHAPTER IV

Leaving the livery-stable, the young Texan went directly to the German restaurant, and asked for Willie Pond. He was shown up to the room, recently engaged by the traveler, and found him engaged in cleaning a pair of fine, silver mounted Remington revolvers.

"Getting ready, I see," said the Texan. "I have bought you a horse— the best in this whole section; I gave three hundred dollars. There is your change."

"Keep the two hundred to buy stores with for our trip," said Pond.

"No need of it. I've laid in all the stores we need. You can buy your-self a couple of blankets and an India-rubber for wet weather. A couple of tin cans of pepper and salt is all that I lay in when I'm going to rough it on the plains. The man that can't kill all the meat he needs isn't fit to go there."

"Maybe you're right. The less we are burdened the better for our horses. Are we likely to meet Indians on the route?"

"None that will hurt *me*—or you, when you're in my company. The Sioux know me and will do me no harm."

"That is good. The Indians were my only dread."

"I've a favor to ask."

"It is granted before you ask it—what is it?"

"I want to break your horse to the saddle before you try it. You are not so used to the saddle, I reckon, as I am. I will take a ride at sunset, and bring him around here for you to look at."

"That is right. I am only thankful to have you ride him first, though you may find me a better rider than you think!"

"Perhaps. But he looks wild, and I like to tame wild uns. I'll have him here between sundown and dark."

"All right. I told you I'd see to getting arms. I had these revolvers, and cartridges for them, but I want a light repeating rifle. Get me a good one, with as much ammunition as you think I'll need!"

"All right. I'll get a new model Winchester. They rattle out lead faster than any other tool I ever carried."

The Texan now left. He had not spoken of Wild Bill's desire to possess that horse, because he had an idea that Mr. Willie Pond would weaken, and give up the horse, rather than risk bloodshed for its possession. And perhaps he had another idea—a mysterious one, which we do not care to expose at this stage of the story.

This young Texan hastened from the German restaurant to a small, neat house in the outskirts of the town. Knocking in a very peculiar manner, he was admitted at once by a tall and strikingly beautiful young woman, whom he addressed as if well acquainted with her.

"I'm here, Addie, and I've seen *him*."

"You found him all right, when you told him who sent you, did you not?" asked the lady, leading the way to a sitting-room in the rear of the cottage.

"Yes, ready to do anything for one you recommend."

"Poor Bill! A braver man and a truer friend never lived. He loves me, and I fear it will be his ruin, for he will too often come within the reach of those who would destroy him, if they only knew where and how to reach him. Persecution and cruelty placed him on the bloody path he has had to follow, and now—now he is an outlaw, beyond all chance for mercy, should he ever be taken."

"He never will be taken, guarded as he is."

"You saw his guards, then?"

"Yes, forty or fifty of them, and I would rather have them as friends than foes. He wants you to ride out with me to meet him when I go next with some information that he needs."

"When will that be?" asked the lady.

"In the early morning, or perhaps to-night, if nothing happens to me between now and sunset to make it unnecessary!"

"Between now and sunset? That is within two hours. Do you anticipate any danger?"

"Not much. I have a little task before me. I have a horse to break, and a man known as Will Bill to tame."

"Wild Bill!—the dead-shot, the desperado, who has killed at least one man for every year of his life?"

"Yes, the same. But ask me no more questions now. After I have tamed him I will report—or, if he has settled me, there will be no need of it."

"Do not run this risk."

"It must be done. He has, in a manner, defied me, and I accept his defiance!"

"Surely he does not know—"

"No, he knows nothing of what you would say if I did not interrupt you. Nor do I intend he shall at present. It is enough that you know it, and will care for both my body and my good name, should I fail."

"You know I will. But you must not fall."

"I do not intend to. I think I can crush him by a look and a word. I shall try, at least. If all goes well, I will be here by eight to-night to arrange for our visit."

"I hope you will come, and safely."

"I will, Addie. Until the cup of vengeance is full, Heaven will surely spare me. But I must go. I have no time to spare."

The young Texan glanced at the chambers of a handsome six-shooter which he carried, to see if it was ready for use, replaced it in his belt, and then, with a cheerful smile, left the room and house.

Hastening to the stable, he selected a saddle, lengthened the stirrups to suit himself, took a stout bridle from among a lot hanging in the store-room, and accompanied by the stable-keeper, approached the newly purchased Black Hawk horse.

"I may as well have him ready," he said; "for if Wild Bill is to be here at sunset, that time is close at hand. You say the horse has not been ridden?"

"No," said the stable-keeper. "My regular breaker was not here when I bought him. Black Joe tried to mount him, but the horse scared him."

"Well, I'll soon see what he is made of, if I can get saddle and bridle on him," said the Texan.

They now together approached the large box stall in which the stallion was kept. The horse, almost perfect in symmetry, black as night, with a fierce, wild look, turned to front them as they approached the barred entrance.

"Steady, boy—steady!" cried the Texan, as he sprang lightly over the bars, and at once laid his hand on the arched neck of the horse.

To the wonder of the stableman, the horse, instead of rearing back or plunging at the intruder, turned his eyes upon him, and with a kind of tremor in his frame, seemed to wait to see what his visitor meant.

"So! Steady, Black Hawk! Steady, old boy!" continued the Texan, kindly passing his hand over the horse's neck and down his face.

The horse uttered a low neigh, and seemed by his looks pleased with his attentions.

"That beats me!" cried the stable-keeper. "Old Joe had to lasso him and draw him down to a ringbolt before he could rub him off."

"Hand me the saddle and bridle," said the Texan, still continuing to "pet" the beautiful and spirited animal. In a few seconds, without difficulty, the same kind and skillful hands had the horse both saddled and bridled.

The Texan now led the horse out on the street, where quite a crowd seemed to be gathering, perhaps drawn there by some rumor of a fight in embryo.

And as he glanced up the street the Texan saw Wild Bill himself, with his six-shooters in his belt, come striding along, with California Joe and a dozen more at his heels.

In a second, the Texan vaulted upon the back of the horse, which made one wild leap that would have unseated most riders, and then reared on its hind legs as if it would fall back and crush its would-be master.

At this instant, Wild Bill rushing forward, pistol in hand, shouted: "Give up that horse, or die!"

A SQUARE BACK-DOWN, CHAPTER V

The Texan paid no heed to the words of the desperado, but bending forward on the horse with his full weight, drove his spurs deeply into its flanks. Startled and stung with pain, the noble animal, at one wild bound, leaped far beyond where Bill and his friends stood, and in a second more sped in terrific leaps along the street.

"The cowardly cuss is running away!" yelled Bill derisively.

"It is false! He is *no* coward! He will tame the horse first and then *you!*" cried a voice so close that Bill turned in amazement to see who dare thus to speak to him, the "Terror of the West."

"A woman!" he muttered, fiercely, as he saw a tall and queenly-looking girl standing there, with flashing eyes, which did not drop at his gaze.

"*Yes*—a woman, who has heard of Wild Bill, and neither fears nor admires him!" she said, undauntedly.

"Is the fellow that rode off on the horse your husband or lover that you take his part?" asked Bill, half angrily and half wondering at the temerity of the lovely girl who thus braved his anger.

"He is neither," she replied, scornfully.

"I'm glad of it. I shall not make you a widow or deprive you of a future husband when he comes under my fire, if he should be fool enough to come back."

"He comes now. See for yourself. He has tamed the horse—now comes your turn, coward and braggart!"

Bill was white with anger; but she was a woman, mind no matter what he felt, too well he knew the chivalry of the far West to raise a hand or even speak a threatening word to her. But he heard men around him murmur her name.

It was Addie Neidic.

And then he turned his eyes upon the black horse and rider. The animal, completely under control, though flecked with foam, came down the street slowly and gently, bearing his rider with an air of pride rather than submission. As he passed the German restaurant, the rider raised his hat in salutation to Willie Pond, who stood in his window, and said, in a cheerful voice: "Remain in your room. I have news for you and will be there soon."

Without checking his horse the rider kept on until he was within half a length of the horse of Wild Bill, then checking the animal, he said, in a mocking tone: "You spoke to me just as I rode away. I've come back to hear you out."

What was the matter with Wild Bill? He stood staring wildly at the Texan, his own face white as if a mortal fear had come upon him.

"Where have I seen that face before?" he gasped. "Can the dead come back to life?"

The Texan bent forward till his own face almost touched that of Wild Bill and hissed out one word in a shrill whisper: "Sister!"

It was all he said, but the instant Wild Bill heard it, he shrieked out: "'Tis him—'tis him I shot at Abilene!" and with a shuddering groan he sank senseless to the pavement.

In an instant Bill's friends, who had looked in wonder at this strange scene, sprang to his aid, and, lifting his unconscious form, carried it into the saloon where Bill had met Californian Joe, Captain Jack, and the rest of their crowd.

Left alone, the young Texan said a few words to Addie Neidic, then dismounted and told the stable-keeper to keep that horse saddled and bridled, and to get his own Texan mustang ready for use. "I must be out of town before sunrise, or Wild Bill and his friends may have questions to ask that I don't want to answer just now," he said.

And then, he walked a little way with Miss Neidic, talking earnestly. But soon he left her, and while she kept on in the direction of her own house, he turned and went to the German restaurant.

Entering the room of Willie Pond, he said, abruptly: "If you want to go to the Black Hills with me on your own horse we'll have to leave this section mighty sudden. Wild Bill has set his mind on having the horse I bought and broke for you, and he has a rough crowd to back him up."

"If I had known Bill wanted the horse so badly I could have got along with another," said Pond, rather quietly.

"What! let *him* have the horse? Why it hasn't its equal on the plains or in the mountains. It is a thoroughbred—a regular racer, which a sporting man was taking through to the Pacific coast on speculation. He played faro, lost, got broke, and put the horse up for a tenth of its value. I got him for almost nothing compared to his worth. On that horse you can keep out of the way of any red who scours the plains. If you don't want him I do, for Wild Bill shall never put a leg over his back!"

"I'll keep him. Don't get mad. I'll keep him and go whenever you are ready," said Pond, completely mastered by the excitement which this young Texan exhibited.

"Well, we'll get the horses out of town and in a safe place to-night. And for yourself, I'll take you to the house of a lady friend of mine to stay to-night and to-morrow, and by to-morrow night I'll know all I want to about the movements of the other party, and we can move so as to be just before or behind them, as you and I will decide best."

"All right, Jack. I leave it to you. Are you sure the horse will be safe for me to ride?"

"Yes. A horse like that once broken is broken for life. They never forget their first lesson. A mongrel breed, stupid, resentful, and tricky, is different. Be ready to mount when I lead him around, I will send for your traveling-bag, and you will find it at the house where we stop."

"I will be ready," said Pond.

The Texan now left, and Pond watched him as he hurried off to the stable. "The man hates Wild Bill with a deadly hatred!" he murmured. "I must learn the cause. Perhaps it is a providence that I have fallen in with him, and I have concluded to keep his company to the Black Hills. But I must call the landlord and close up my account before the other comes back with the horses."

The German was so put out by the sudden giving up of a room, which he hoped to make profitable, that he asked an extra day's rent, and to his surprise, got it.

11

HUNTING TRIPS OF A RANCHMAN

BY THEODORE ROOSEVELT

Fifteen years before being elected to the presidency, Theodore Roosevelt mourned the death in 1884 of both his wife and his mother. In an effort to assuage his grief, Roosevelt went west to the outdoors he had grown to love. While operating a cattle ranch in the Dakotas, he recorded his hunting and other adventures in Hunting Trips of a Ranchman, *an 1885 volume still prized for its accurate depiction of frontier life.*

But few bears are found in the immediate neighborhood of my ranch; and though I have once or twice seen their tracks in the Bad Lands, I have never had any experience with the animals themselves except during the elk-hunting trip on the Bighorn Mountains, described in the preceding chapter.

The grizzly bear undoubtedly comes in the category of dangerous game, and is, perhaps, the only animal in the United States that can be fairly so placed, unless we count the few jaguars found north of the Rio Grande. But the danger of hunting the grizzly has been greatly exaggerated, and the sport is certainly very much safer than it was at the beginning of this century. The first hunters who came into contact with this great bear were men belonging to that hardy and adventurous class of backwoodsmen which had filled the wild country between the Appalachian Mountains and the Mississippi. These men carried but one weapon: the long-barrelled, small-bored pea-rifle, whose bullets ran seventy to the pound, the amount of powder and lead being a little less than that contained in the cartridge of a thirty-two calibre Winchester. In the Eastern States almost all the hunting was done in the woodland; the shots were mostly obtained at short distance, and deer and black bear were the largest game; moreover, the pea-rifles were marvellously accurate for close range, and their owners were famed the world over for their skill as marksmen. Thus these rifles had so far proved plenty good enough for the work they had to do, and indeed had done excellent service as military weapons in the ferocious wars that the men of the border carried on with their Indian neighbors, and even in conflict with more civilized foes, as at the battles of King's Mountain and New Orleans. But when the restless frontiersmen pressed out over the Western plains, they encountered in the grizzly a beast of far greater bulk and more savage temper than any of those found in the Eastern woods, and their small-bore rifles were utterly inadequate weapons with which to cope with him. It is small wonder that he was considered by them to be almost invulnerable, and extraordinarily tenacious of life. He would be a most unpleasant antagonist now to a man armed only with a thirty-two calibre rifle, that carried but a single shot and was loaded at the muzzle. A rifle, to be of use in this sport, should carry a ball weighing from half an ounce to an ounce. With the old pea-rifles the shot had to be in the eye or heart; and accidents to the hunter were very common. But the introduction of heavy breech-loading repeaters has greatly lessened the danger, even in the very few and far-off places where the grizzlies are as ferocious as formerly. For nowadays these great bears are undoubtedly much better aware of the death-dealing power of men, and, as a consequence, much less fierce, than was the case with their forefathers, who so unhesitatingly attacked the early Western travelers and explorers. Constant contact with rifle-carrying hunters, for a period extending over many generations of bear-life, has taught the grizzly by bitter experience that man is his undoubted overlord, as far as fighting goes; and this knowledge has become an hereditary characteristic. No grizzly will assail a man now unprovoked, and one will almost always rather run than fight; though if he is wounded or thinks himself cornered he will attack his foes with a headlong, reckless fury that renders him one of the most dangerous of wild beasts. The ferocity of all wild animals depends largely upon the amount of resistance they are accustomed to meet with, and the quantity of molestation to which they are subjected.

The change in the grizzly's character during the last half century has been precisely paralleled by the change in the characters of his northern cousin, the polar bear, and of the South African lion. When the Dutch and Scandinavian sailors first penetrated the Arctic seas, they were kept in constant dread of the white bear, who regarded a man as simply an erect variety of seal, quite as good eating as the common kind. The records of these early explorers are filled with examples of the ferocious and man-eating propensities of the polar bears; but in the accounts of most of the later Arctic expeditions they are portrayed as having learned wisdom, and being now most anxious to keep out of the way of the hunters. A number of my sporting friends have killed white bears, and none of them were ever even charged. And in South Africa the English sportsmen and Dutch boers have taught the lion to be a very different creature from what it was when the first white man reached that continent. If the Indian tiger had been a native of the United States, it would now be one of the most shy of beasts.

Of late years our estimate of the grizzly's ferocity has been lowered; and we no longer accept the tales of uneducated hunters as being proper authority by which to judge it. But we should make a parallel reduction in the cases of many foreign animals and their describers. Take, for example, that purely melodramatic beast, the North African lion, as portrayed by Jules Gérard, who bombastically describes himself as "le tueur des lions." Gérard's accounts are self-evidently in large part fictitious, while if true they would prove less for the bravery of the lion than for the phenomenal cowardice, incapacity, and bad marksmanship of the Algerian Arabs. Doubtless Gérard was a great hunter; but so is many a Western plainsman, whose account of the grizzlies he has killed would be wholly untrustworthy. Take for instance the following from page 223 of "La Chasse au Lion": "The inhabitants had assembled one day to the number of two or three hundred with the object of killing (the lion) or driving it out of the country. The attack took place at sunrise; at mid-day five hundred cartridges had been expended; the Arabs carried off one of their number dead and six wounded, and the lion remained master of the field of battle." Now if three hundred men could fire five hundred shots at a lion without hurting him, it merely shows that they were wholly incapable of hurting anything, or else that M. Gérard was more expert with the long-bow than with the rifle. Gérard's whole book is filled with equally preposterous nonsense; yet a great many people seriously accept this same book as trustworthy authority for the manners and ferocity of the North African lion. It would be quite as sensible to accept M. Jules Verne's stories as being valuable contributions to science. A good deal of the lion's reputation is built upon just such stuff.

How the prowess of the grizzly compares with that of the lion or tiger would be hard to say; I have never shot either of the latter myself, and my brother, who has killed tigers in India, has never had a chance at a grizzly. Any one of the big bears we killed on the mountains would, I should think, have been able to make short work of either a lion or a tiger; for the grizzly is greatly superior in bulk and muscular power to either of the great cats, and its teeth are as large as theirs, while its claws, though blunter, are much longer; nevertheless, I believe that a lion or a tiger would be fully as dangerous to a hunter or other human being, on account of the superior speed of its charge, the lightning-like rapidity of its movements, and its apparently sharper senses. Still, after all is said, the man should have a thoroughly trustworthy weapon and a fairly cool head, who would follow into his own haunts and slay grim Old Ephraim.

A grizzly will only fight if wounded or cornered, or, at least, if he thinks himself cornered. If a man by accident stumbles on to one close up, he is almost certain to be attacked really more from fear than from any other motive; exactly the same reason that makes a rattlesnake strike at a passer-by. I have personally known of but one instance of a grizzly turning on a hunter before being wounded. This happened to a friend of mine, a Californian ranchman, who, with two or three of his men, was following a bear that had carried off one of his sheep. They got the bear into a cleft in the mountain from which there was no escape, and he suddenly charged back through the line of his pursuers, struck down one of the horsemen, seized the arm of the man in his jaws and broke it as if it had been a pipe stem, and was only killed after a most lively fight, in which, by repeated charges, he at one time drove every one of his assailants off the field.

But two instances have come to my personal knowledge where a man has been killed by a grizzly. One was that of a hunter at the foot of the Bighorn Mountains who had chased a large bear and finally wounded him. The animal turned at once and came straight at the man, whose second shot missed. The bear then closed and passed on, after striking only a single blow; yet that one blow, given with all the power of its thick, immensely muscular forearm, armed with nails as strong as so many hooked steel spikes, tore out the man's collar-bone and snapped through three or four ribs. He never recovered from the shock, and died that night.

The other instance occurred to a neighbor of mine—who has a small ranch on the Little Missouri—two or three years ago. He was out on a mining trip, and was prospecting with two other men near the head-water of the Little Missouri, in the Black Hills country. They were walking down along the river, and came to a point of land, thrust out into it, which was densely covered with brush and fallen timber. Two of the party walked round by the edge of the stream, but the third, a German, and a very powerful fellow, followed a well-beaten game trail, leading through the bushy point. When they were some forty yards apart the two men heard an agonized shout from the German, and at the same time the loud coughing growl, or roar, of a bear. They turned just in time to see their companion struck a terrible blow on the head by a grizzly, which must have been roused from its lair by his almost stepping on it; so close was it that he had no time to fire his rifle, but merely held it up over his head as a guard. Of course it was struck down, the claws of the great brute at the same time shattering his skull like an egg-shell. Yet the man staggered on some ten feet before he fell; but when he did he never spoke or moved again. The two others killed the bear after a short, brisk struggle, as he was in the midst of a most determined charge.

In 1872, near Fort Wingate, New Mexico, two soldiers of a cavalry regiment came to their death at the claws of a grizzly bear. The army surgeon who attended them told me the particulars, as far as they were known. The men were mail carriers, and one day did not come in at the appointed time. Next day, a relief party was sent out to look for them, and after some search found the bodies of both, as well as that of one of the horses. One of the men still showed signs of life; he came to his senses before dying, and told the story. They had seen a grizzly and pursued it on horseback, with their Spencer rifles. On coming close, one had fired into its side, when it turned with marvellous quickness for so large and unwieldy an animal, and struck down the horse, at the same time inflicting a ghastly wound on the rider. The other man dismounted and came up to the rescue of his companion. The bear then left the latter and attacked the other. Although hit by the bullet, it charged home and threw the man down, and then lay on him and deliberately bit him to death, while his groans and cries were frightful to hear. Afterward it walked off into the bushes without again offering to molest the already mortally wounded victim of its first assault.

At certain times the grizzly works a good deal of havoc among the herds of the stockmen. A friend of mine, a ranchman in Montana, told me that one fall bears became very plenty around his ranches, and caused him severe loss, killing with ease even full-grown beef-steers. But one of them once found his intended quarry too much for him. My friend had a stocky, rather vicious range stallion, which had been grazing one day near a small thicket of bushes, and, towards evening, came galloping in with three or four gashes in his haunch, that looked as if they had been cut with a dull axe. The cowboys knew at once that he had been assailed by a bear, and rode off to the thicket near which he had been feeding. Sure enough a bear, evidently in a very bad temper, sallied out as soon as the thicket was surrounded, and, after a spirited fight and a succession of charges, was killed. On examination, it was found that his under jaw was broken, and part of his face smashed in, evidently by the stallion's hoofs. The horse had been feeding when the bear leaped out at him but failed to kill at the first stroke; then the horse lashed out behind, and not only freed himself, but also severely damaged his opponent.

Doubtless, the grizzly could be hunted to advantage with dogs, which would not, of course, be expected to seize him, but simply to find and bay him, and distract his attention by barking and nipping. Occasionally a bear can be caught in the open and killed with the aid of horses. But nine times out of ten the only way to get one is to put on moccasins and still-hunt it in its own haunts, shooting it at close quarters. Either its tracks should be followed until the bed wherein it lies during the day is found, or a given locality in which it is known to exist should be carefully beaten through, or else a bait should be left out and a watch kept on it to catch the bear when he has come to visit it.

For some days after our arrival on the Bighorn range we did not come across any grizzly.

Although it was still early in September, the weather was cool and pleasant, the nights being frosty; and every two or three days there was a flurry of light snow, which rendered the labor of tracking much more easy. Indeed, throughout our stay on the mountains, the peaks were snow-capped almost all the time. Our fare was excellent, consisting of elk venison, mountain grouse, and small trout; the last caught in one of the beautiful little lakes that lay almost up by timber line. To us, who had for weeks been accustomed to make small fires from dried brush, or from sage-brush roots, which we dug out of the ground, it was a treat to sit at night before the roaring and crackling pine logs; as the old teamster quaintly put it, we had at last come to a land "where the wood grew on trees." There were plenty of black-tail deer in the woods, and we came across a number of bands of cow and calf elk, or of young bulls; but after several days' hunting, we were still without any head worth taking home, and had seen no sign of grizzly, which was the game we were especially anxious to kill; for neither Merrifield nor I had ever seen a wild bear alive.

Sometimes we hunted in company; sometimes each of us went out alone; the teamster, of course, remaining in to guard camp and cook. One day we had separated; I reached camp early in the afternoon, and waited a couple of hours before Merrifield put in an appearance.

At last I heard a shout—the familiar long-drawn Ei-koh-h-h of the cattle-men,—and he came in sight galloping at speed down an open glade, and waving his hat, evidently having had good luck; and when he reined in his small, wiry, cow-pony, we saw that he had packed behind his saddle the fine, glossy pelt of a black bear. Better still, he announced that he had been off about ten miles to a perfect tangle of ravines and valleys where bear sign was very thick; and not of black bear either but of grizzly. The black bear (the only one we got on the mountains) he had run across by accident, while riding up a valley in which there was a patch of dead timber grown up with berry bushes. He noticed a black object which he first took to be a stump; for during the past few days we had each of us made one or two clever stalks up to charred logs which our imagination converted into bears. On coming near, however, the object suddenly took to its heels; he followed over frightful ground at the pony's best pace, until it stumbled and fell down. By this time he was close on the bear, which had just reached the edge of the wood.

Picking himself up, he rushed after it, hearing it growling ahead of him; after running some fifty yards the sounds stopped, and he stood still listening. He saw and heard nothing, until he happened to cast his eyes upwards, and there was the bear, almost overhead, and about twenty-five feet up a tree; and in as many seconds afterwards it came down to the ground with a bounce, stone dead. It was a young bear, in its second year, and had probably never before seen a man, which accounted for the ease with which it was treed and taken. One minor result of the encounter was to convince Merrifield—the list of whose faults did not include lack of self-confidence—that he could run down any bear; in consequence of which idea we on more than one subsequent occasion went through a good deal of violent exertion.

Merrifield's tale made me decide to shift camp at once, and go over to the spot where the bear-tracks were so plenty. Next morning we were off, and by noon pitched camp by a clear brook, in a valley with steep, wooded sides, but with good feed for the horses in the open bottom. We rigged the canvas wagon sheet into a small tent, sheltered by the trees from the wind, and piled great pine logs near by where we wished to place the fire; for a night camp in the sharp fall weather is cold and dreary unless there is a roaring blaze of flame in front of the tent.

That afternoon we again went out, and I shot a fine bull elk. I came home alone toward nightfall, walking through a reach of burnt forest, where there was nothing but charred tree-trunks and black mould. When nearly through it I came across the huge, half-human footprints of a great grizzly, which must have passed by within a few minutes. It gave me rather an eerie feeling in the silent, lonely woods, to see for the first time the unmistakable proofs that I was in the home of the mighty lord of the wilderness. I followed the tracks in the fading twilight until it became too dark to see them any longer, and then shouldered my rifle and walked back to camp.

That evening we almost had a visit from one of the animals we were after. Several times we had heard at night the musical calling of the bull elk—a sound to which no writer has as yet done justice. This particular night, when we were in bed and the fire was smouldering, we were roused by a ruder noise—a kind of grunting or roaring whine, answered by the frightened snorts of the ponies. It was a bear which had evidently not seen the fire, as it came from behind the bank, and had probably been attracted by the smell of the horses. After it made out what we were it stayed round a short while, again uttered its peculiar roaring grunt, and went off; we had seized our rifles and had run out into the woods, but in the darkness could see nothing; indeed it was rather lucky we did not stumble across the bear, as he could have made short work of us when we were at such a disadvantage.

Next day we went off on a long tramp through the woods and along the sides of the canyons. There were plenty of berry bushes growing in clusters; and all around these there were fresh tracks of bear. But the grizzly is also a flesh-eater, and has a great liking for carrion. On visiting the place where Merrifield had killed the black bear, we found that the grizzlies had been there before us, and had utterly devoured the carcass, with cannibal relish. Hardly a scrap was left, and we turned our steps toward where lay the bull elk I had killed. It was quite late in the afternoon when we reached the place. A grizzly had evidently been at the carcass during the preceding night, for his great footprints were in the ground all around it, and the carcass itself was gnawed and torn, and partially covered with earth and leaves—for the grizzly has a curious habit of burying all of his prey that he does not at the moment need. A great many ravens had been feeding on the body, and they wheeled about over the tree tops above us, uttering their barking croaks.

The forest was composed mainly of what are called ridge-pole pines, which grow close together, and do not branch out until the stems are thirty or forty feet from the ground. Beneath these trees we walked over a carpet of pine needles, upon which our moccasined feet made no sound. The woods seemed vast and lonely, and their silence was broken now and then by the strange noises always to be heard in the great forests, and which seem to mark the sad and ever-lasting unrest of the wilderness. We climbed up along the trunk of a dead tree which had toppled over until its upper branches struck in the limb crotch of another, that thus supported it at an angle half-way in its fall. When above the ground far enough to prevent the bear's smelling us, we sat still to wait for his approach; until, in the gathering gloom, we could no longer see the sights of our rifles, and could but dimly make out the carcass of the great elk. It was useless to wait lon-ger; and we clambered down and stole out to the edge of the woods. The forest here covered one side of a steep, almost canyon-like ravine, whose other side was bare except of rock and sage-brush. Once out from under the trees there was still plenty of light, although the sun had set, and we crossed over some fifty yards to the opposite hill-side, and crouched down under a bush to see if perchance some animal might not also leave the cover. To our right the ravine sloped down-ward toward the valley of the Bighorn River, and far on its other side we could catch a glimpse of the great main chain of the Rockies, their snow peaks glinting crimson in the light of the set sun. Again we waited quietly in the growing dusk until the pine trees in our front blended into one dark, frowning mass. We saw nothing; but the wild creatures of the forest had begun to stir abroad. The owls hooted dis-mally from the tops of the tall trees, and two or three times a harsh wailing cry, probably the voice of some lynx or wolverine, arose from the depths of the woods. At last, as we were rising to leave, we heard the sound of the breaking of a dead stick, from the spot where we knew the carcass lay. It was a sharp, sudden noise, perfectly distinct from the natural creaking and snapping of the branches; just such a sound as would be made by the tread of some heavy creature. "Old Ephraim" had come back to the carcass. A minute afterward, listening with strained ears, we heard him brush by some dry twigs. It was entirely too dark to go in after him; but we made up our minds that on the morrow he should be ours.

Early next morning we were over at the elk carcass, and, as we expected, found that the bear had eaten his fill at it during the night. His tracks showed him to be an immense fellow, and were so fresh that we doubted if he had left long before we arrived; and we made up our minds to follow him up and try to find his lair. The bears that lived on these mountains had evidently been little disturbed; indeed, the Indians and most of the white hunters are rather chary of meddling with "Old Ephraim," as the mountain men style the grizzly, unless they get him at a disadvantage; for the sport is fraught with some danger and but small profit. The bears thus seemed to have very little fear of harm, and we thought it likely that the bed of the one who had fed on the elk would not be far away.

My companion was a skillful tracker, and we took up the trail at once. For some distance it led over the soft, yielding carpet of moss and pine needles, and the footprints were quite easily made out, although we could follow them but slowly; for we had, of course, to keep a sharp look-out ahead and around us as we walked noiselessly on in the sombre half-light always prevailing under the great pine trees, through whose thickly interlacing branches stray but few beams of light, no matter how bright the sun may be outside. We made no sound ourselves, and every little sudden noise sent a thrill through me as I peered about with each sense on the alert. Two or three of the ravens that we had scared from the carcass flew overhead, croaking hoarsely; and the pine tops moaned and sighed in the slight breeze—for pine trees seem to be ever in motion, no matter how light the wind.

After going a few hundred yards the tracks turned off on a well-beaten path made by the elk; the woods were in many places cut up by these game trails, which had often become as distinct as ordinary foot-paths. The beast's footprints were perfectly plain in the dust, and he had lumbered along up the path until near the middle of the hillside, where the ground broke away and there were hollows and boulders. Here there had been a windfall, and the dead trees lay among the living, piled across one another in all directions; while between and around them sprouted up a thick growth of young spruces and other evergreens. The trail turned off into the tangled thicket, within which it was almost certain we would find our quarry. We could still follow the tracks, by the slight scrapes of the claws on the bark, or by the bent and broken twigs; and we advanced with noiseless caution, slowly climbing over the dead tree trunks and upturned stumps, and not letting a branch rustle or catch on our clothes. When in the middle of the thicket we crossed what was almost a breastwork of fallen logs, and Merrifield, who was leading, passed by the upright stem of a great pine. As soon as he was by it he sank suddenly on one knee, turning half round, his face fairly aflame with excitement; and as I strode past him, with my rifle at the ready, there, not ten steps off, was the great bear, slowly rising from his bed among the young spruces. He had heard us, but apparently hardly knew exactly where or what we were, for he reared up on his haunches sideways to us. Then he saw us and dropped down again on all fours, the shaggy hair on his neck and shoulders seeming to bristle as he turned toward us. As he sank down on his forefeet I had raised the rifle; his head was bent slightly down, and when I saw the top of the white bead fairly between his small, glittering, evil eyes, I pulled trigger. Half-rising up, the huge beast fell over on his side in the death throes, the ball having gone into his brain, striking as fairly between the eyes as if the distance had been measured by a carpenter's rule.

The whole thing was over in twenty seconds from the time I caught sight of the game; indeed, it was over so quickly that the grizzly did not have time to show fight at all or come a step toward us. It was the first I had ever seen, and I felt not a little proud, as I stood over the great brindled bulk, which lay stretched out at length in the cool shade of the evergreens. He was a monstrous fellow, much larger than any I have seen since, whether alive or brought in dead by the hunters. As near as we could estimate (for of course we had nothing with which to weigh more than very small portions) he must have weighed about twelve hundred pounds, and though this is not as large as some of his kind are said to grow in California, it is yet a very unusual size for a bear. He was a good deal heavier than any of our horses; and it was with the greatest difficulty that we were able to skin him. He must have been very old, his teeth and claws being all worn down and blunted; but nevertheless he had been living in plenty, for he was as fat as a prize hog, the layers on his back being a finger's length in thickness. He was still in the summer coat, his hair being short, and in color a curious brindled brown, somewhat like that of certain bull-dogs; while all the bears we shot afterward had the long thick winter fur, cinnamon or yellowish brown. By the way, the name of this bear has reference to its character and not to its color, and should, I suppose, be properly spelt grisly—in the sense of horrible, exactly as we speak of a "grisly spectre"—and not grizzly; but perhaps the latter way of spelling it is too well established to be now changed.

In killing dangerous game steadiness is more needed than good shooting. No game is dangerous unless a man is close up, for nowadays hardly any wild beast will charge from a distance of a hundred yards, but will rather try to run off; and if a man is close it is easy enough for him to shoot straight if he does not lose his head. A bear's brain is about the size of a pint bottle; and any one can hit a pint bottle off-hand at thirty or forty feet. I have had two shots at bears at close quarters, and each time I fired into the brain, the bullet in one case striking fairly between the eyes, as told above, and in the other going in between the eye and ear. A novice at this kind of sport will find it best and safest to keep in mind the old Norse viking's advice in reference to a long sword: "If you go in close enough your sword will be long enough." If a poor shot goes in close enough he will find that he shoots straight enough.

I was very proud over my first bear; but Merrifield's chief feeling seemed to be disappointment that the animal had not had time to show fight. He was rather a reckless fellow, and very confident in his own skill with the rifle; and he really did not seem to have any more fear of the grizzlies than if they had been so many jack-rabbits. I did not at all share his feelings, having a hearty respect for my foes' prowess, and in following and attacking them always took all possible care to get the chances on my side. Merrifield was sincerely sorry that we never had to stand a regular charge; while on this trip we killed five grizzlies with seven bullets, and except in the case of the she and cub, spoken of further on, each was shot about as quickly as it got sight of us. The last one we got was an old male, which was feeding on an elk carcass. We crept up to within about sixty feet, and as Merrifield had not yet killed a grizzly purely to his own gun, and I had killed three, I told him to take the shot. He at once whispered gleefully: "I'll break his leg, and we'll see what he'll do!" Having no ambition to be a participator in the antics of a three-legged bear, I hastily interposed a most emphatic veto; and with a rather injured air he fired, the bullet going through the neck just back of the head. The bear fell to the shot, and could not get up from the ground, dying in a few minutes; but first he seized his left wrist in his teeth and bit clean through it, completely separating the bones of the paw and arm. Although a smaller bear than the big one I first shot, he would probably have proved a much more ugly foe, for he was less unwieldy, and had much longer and sharper teeth and claws. I think that if my companion had merely broken the beast's leg he would have had his curiosity as to its probable conduct more than gratified.

We tried eating the grizzly's flesh but it was not good, being coarse and not well flavored; and besides, we could not get over the feeling that it had belonged to a carrion feeder. The flesh of the little black bear, on the other hand, was excellent; it tasted like that of a young pig. Doubtless, if a young grizzly, which had fed merely upon fruits, berries, and acorns, was killed, its flesh would prove good eating; but even then, it would probably not be equal to a black bear.

A day or two after the death of the big bear, we went out one afternoon on horseback, intending merely to ride down to see a great canyon lying some six miles west of our camp; indeed, we went more to look at the scenery than for any other reason, though, of course, neither of us ever stirred out of camp without his rifle. We rode down the valley in which we had camped, through alternate pine groves and open glades, until we reached the canyon, and then skirted its brink for a mile or so. It was a great chasm, many miles in length, as if the table-land had been rent asunder by some terrible and unknown force; its sides were sheer walls of rock, rising three or four hundred feet straight up in the air, and worn by the weather till they looked like the towers and battlements of some vast fortress. Between them at the bottom was a space, in some places nearly a quarter of a mile wide, in others very narrow, through whose middle foamed a deep, rapid torrent of which the sources lay far back among the snow-topped mountains around Cloud Peak. In this valley, dark-green, sombre pines stood in groups, stiff and erect; and here and there among them were groves of poplar and cotton-wood, with slender branches and trembling leaves, their bright green already changing to yellow in the sharp fall weather. We went down to where the mouth of the canyon opened out, and rode our horses to the end of a great jutting promontory of rock, thrust out into the plain; and in the cold, clear air we looked far over the broad valley of the Bighorn as it lay at our very feet, walled in on the other side by the distant chain of the Rocky Mountains.

Turning our horses, we rode back along the edge of another canyon-like valley, with a brook flowing down its centre, and its rocky sides covered with an uninterrupted pine forest—the place of all others in whose inaccessible wildness and ruggedness a bear would find a safe retreat. After some time we came to where other valleys, with steep, grass-grown sides, covered with sage-brush, branched out from it, and we followed one of these out. There was plenty of elk sign about, and we saw several black-tail deer. These last were very common on the mountains, but we had not hunted them at all, as we were in no need of meat. But this afternoon we came across a buck with remarkably fine antlers, and accordingly I shot it, and we stopped to cut off and skin out the horns, throwing the reins over the heads of the horses and leaving them to graze by themselves. The body lay near the crest of one side of a deep valley, or ravine, which headed up on the plateau a mile to our left. Except for scattered trees and bushes the valley was bare; but there was heavy timber along the crests of the hills on its opposite side. It took some time to fix the head properly, and we were just ending when Merrifield sprang to his feet and exclaimed: "Look at the bears!" pointing down into the valley below us. Sure enough there were two bears (which afterwards proved to be an old she and a nearly full-grown cub) travelling up the bottom of the valley, much too far off for us to shoot. Grasping our rifles and throwing off our hats we started off as hard as we could run, diagonally down the hill-side, so as to cut them off. It was some little time before they saw us, when they made off at a lumbering gallop up the valley. It would seem impossible to run into two grizzlies in the open, but they were going uphill and we down, and moreover the old one kept stopping. The cub would forge ahead and could probably have escaped us, but the mother now and then stopped to sit up on her haunches and look round at us, when the cub would run back to her. The upshot was that we got ahead of them, when they turned and went straight up one hill-side as we ran straight down the other behind them. By this time I was pretty nearly done out, for running along the steep ground through the sage-brush was most exhausting work; and Merrifield kept gaining on me and was well in front. Just as he disappeared over a bank, almost at the bottom of the valley, I tripped over a bush and fell full-length. When I got up I knew I could never make up the ground I had lost, and besides, could hardly run any longer; Merrifield was out of sight below, and the bears were laboring up the steep hill-side directly opposite and about three hundred yards off, so I sat down and began to shoot over Merrifield's head, aiming at the big bear. She was going very steadily and in a straight line, and each bullet sent up a puff of dust where it struck the dry soil, so that I could keep correcting my aim; and the fourth ball crashed into the old bear's flank. She lurched heavily forward, but recovered herself and reached the timber, while Merrifield, who had put on a spurt, was not far behind.

I toiled up the hill at a sort of trot, fairly gasping and sobbing for breath; but before I got to the top I heard a couple of shots and a shout.

The old bear had turned as soon as she was in the timber, and came towards Merrifield, but he gave her the death wound by firing into her chest, and then shot at the young one, knocking it over. When I came up he was just walking towards the latter to finish it with the revolver, but it suddenly jumped up as lively as ever and made off at a great pace—for it was nearly full-grown. It was impossible to fire where the tree trunks were so thick, but there was a small opening across which it would have to pass, and collecting all my energies I made a last run, got into position, and covered the opening with my rifle. The instant the bear appeared I fired, and it turned a dozen somersaults down-hill, rolling over and over; the ball had struck it near the tail and had ranged forward through the hollow of the body. Each of us had thus given the fatal wound to the bear into which the other had fired the first bullet. The run, though short, had been very sharp, and over such awful country that we were completely fagged out, and could hardly speak for lack of breath. The sun had already set, and it was too late to skin the animals; so we merely dressed them, caught the ponies—with some trouble, for they were frightened at the smell of the bear's blood on our hands,—and rode home through the darkening woods. Next day we brought the teamster and two of the steadiest pack-horses to the carcasses, and took the skins into camp.

The feed for the horses was excellent in the valley in which we were camped, and the rest after their long journey across the plains did them good. They had picked up wonderfully in condition during our stay on the mountains; but they were apt to wander very far during the night, for there were so many bears and other wild beasts around that they kept getting frightened and running off. We were very loath to leave our hunting grounds, but time was pressing, and we had already many more trophies than we could carry; so one cool morning, when the branches of the evergreens were laden with the feathery snow that had fallen overnight, we struck camp and started out of the mountains, each of us taking his own bedding behind his saddle, while the pack-ponies were loaded down with bearskins, elk and deer antlers, and the hides and furs of other game. In single file we moved through the woods, and across the canyons to the edge of the great table-land, and then slowly down the steep slope to its foot, where we found our canvas-topped wagon; and next day saw us setting out on our long journey homewards, across the three hundred weary miles of treeless and barren-looking plains country.

Last spring, since the above was written, a bear killed a man not very far from my ranch. It was at the time of the floods. Two hunters came down the river, by our ranch, on a raft, stopping to take dinner. A score or so of miles below, as we afterwards heard from the survivor, they landed, and found a bear in a small patch of brushwood. After waiting in vain for it to come out, one of the men rashly attempted to enter the thicket, and was instantly struck down by the beast, before he could so much as fire his rifle. It broke in his skull with a blow of its great paw, and then seized his arm in its jaws, biting it through and through in three places, but leaving the body and retreating into the bushes as soon as the unfortunate man's companion approached. We did not hear of the accident until too late to go after the bear, as we were just about starting to join the spring round-up.

12

ROUGHING IT, CHAPTER VI

BY MARK TWAIN

Few American authors conveyed the spirit of adventure, regional humor, and the absurdities of life better than Samuel Langhorn Clemens, better known as Mark Twain. Working in Nevada after the Civil War and trawling through the West resulted in his 1872 account entitled Roughing It.

Our new conductor (just shipped) had been without sleep for twenty hours.

Such a thing was very frequent. From St. Joseph, Missouri, to Sacramento, California, by stage-coach, was nearly nineteen hundred miles, and the trip was often made in fifteen days (the cars do it in four and a half, now), but the time specified in the mail contracts, and required by the schedule, was eighteen or nineteen days, if I remember rightly.

This was to make fair allowance for winter storms and snows, and other unavoidable causes of detention. The stage company had everything under strict discipline and good system. Over each two hundred and fifty miles of road they placed an agent or superintendent, and invested him with great authority. His beat or jurisdiction of two hundred and fifty miles was called a "division." He purchased horses, mules harness, and food for men and beasts, and distributed these things among his stage stations, from time to time, according to his judgment of what each station needed. He erected station buildings and dug wells. He attended to the paying of the station-keepers, hostlers, drivers and blacksmiths, and discharged them whenever he chose. He was a very, very great man in his "division"—a kind of Grand Mogul, a Sultan of the Indies, in whose presence common men were modest of speech and manner, and in the glare of whose greatness even the dazzling stage-driver dwindled to a penny dip. There were about eight of these kings, all told, on the overland route.

Next in rank and importance to the division-agent came the "conductor." His beat was the same length as the agent's—two hundred and fifty miles. He sat with the driver, and (when necessary) rode that fearful distance, night and day, without other rest or sleep than what he could get perched thus on top of the flying vehicle. Think of it! He had absolute charge of the mails, express matter, passengers and stage-coach, until he delivered them to the next conductor, and got his receipt for them.

Consequently he had to be a man of intelligence, decision and considerable executive ability. He was usually a quiet, pleasant man, who attended closely to his duties, and was a good deal of a gentleman. It was not absolutely necessary that the division-agent should be a gentleman, and occasionally he wasn't. But he was always a general in administrative ability, and a bull-dog in courage and determination—

otherwise the chieftainship over the lawless underlings of the overland service would never in any instance have been to him anything but an equivalent for a month of insolence and distress and a bullet and a coffin at the end of it. There were about sixteen or eighteen conductors on the overland, for there was a daily stage each way, and a conductor on every stage.

Next in real and official rank and importance, after the conductor, came my delight, the driver—next in real but not in apparent importance—for we have seen that in the eyes of the common herd the driver was to the conductor as an admiral is to the captain of the flag-ship. The driver's beat was pretty long, and his sleeping-time at the stations pretty short, sometimes; and so, but for the grandeur of his position his would have been a sorry life, as well as a hard and a wearing one. We took a new driver every day or every night (for they drove backward and forward over the same piece of road all the time), and therefore we never got as well acquainted with them as we did with the conductors; and besides, they would have been above being familiar with such rubbish as passengers, anyhow, as a general thing. Still, we were always eager to get a sight of each and every new driver as soon as the watch changed, for each and every day we were either anxious to get rid of an unpleasant one, or loath to part with a driver we had learned to like and had come to be sociable and friendly with. And so the first question we asked the conductor whenever we got to where we were to exchange drivers, was always, "Which is him?" The grammar was faulty, maybe, but we could not know, then, that it would go into a book some day. As long as everything went smoothly, the overland driver was well enough situated, but if a fellow driver got sick suddenly it made trouble, for the coach must go on, and so the potentate who was about to climb down and take a luxurious rest after his long night's siege in the midst of wind and rain and darkness, had to stay where he was and do the sick man's work. Once, in the Rocky Mountains, when I found a driver sound asleep on the box, and the mules going at the usual break-neck pace, the conductor said never mind him, there was no danger, and he was doing double duty—had driven seventy-five miles on one coach, and was now going back over it on this without rest or sleep. A hundred and fifty miles of holding back of six vindictive mules and keeping them from climbing the trees! It sounds incredible, but I remember the statement well enough.

The station-keepers, hostlers, etc., were low, rough characters, as already described; and from western Nebraska to Nevada a considerable sprinkling of them might be fairly set down as outlaws—fugitives from justice, criminals whose best security was a section of country which was without law and without even the pretense of it. When the "division-agent" issued an order to one of these parties he did it with the full understanding that he might have to enforce it with a navy six-shooter, and so he always went "fixed" to make things go along smoothly.

Now and then a division-agent was really obliged to shoot a hostler through the head to teach him some simple matter that he could have taught him with a club if his circumstances and surroundings had been different. But they were snappy, able men, those division-agents, and when they tried to teach a subordinate anything, that subordinate generally "got it through his head."

A great portion of this vast machinery—these hundreds of men and coaches, and thousands of mules and horses—was in the hands of Mr. Ben Holliday. All the western half of the business was in his hands. This reminds me of an incident of Palestine travel which is pertinent here, so I will transfer it just in the language in which I find it set down in my Holy Land note-book:

No doubt everybody has heard of Ben Holliday—a man of prodigious energy, who used to send mails and passengers flying across the continent in his overland stage-coaches like a very whirlwind—two thousand long miles in fifteen days and a half, by the watch! But this fragment of history is not about Ben Holliday, but about a young New York boy by the name of Jack, who traveled with our small party of pilgrims in the Holy Land (and who had traveled to California in Mr. Holliday's overland coaches three years before, and had by no means forgotten it or lost his gushing admiration of Mr. H.) Aged nineteen, Jack was a good boy—a good-hearted and always well-meaning boy, who had been reared in the city of New York, and although he was bright and knew a great many useful things, his Scriptural education had been a good deal neglected—to such a degree, indeed, that all Holy Land history was fresh and new to him, and all Bible names mysteries that had never disturbed his virgin ear.

Also in our party was an elderly pilgrim who was the reverse of Jack, in that he was learned in the Scriptures and an enthusiast concerning them. He was our encyclopedia, and we were never tired of listening to his speeches, nor he of making them. He never passed a celebrated locality, from Bashan to Bethlehem, without illuminating it with an oration. One day, when camped near the ruins of Jericho, he burst forth with something like this:

"Jack, do you see that range of mountains over yonder that bounds the Jordan valley? The mountains of Moab, Jack! Think of it, my boy—the actual mountains of Moab—renowned in Scripture history! We are actually standing face to face with those illustrious crags and peaks—and for all we know" [dropping his voice impressively], "our eyes may be resting at this very moment upon the spot WHERE LIES THE MYSTERIOUS GRAVE OF MOSES! Think of it, Jack!"

"Moses who?" (falling inflection).

"Moses who! Jack, you ought to be ashamed of yourself—you ought to be ashamed of such criminal ignorance. Why, Moses, the great guide, soldier, poet, lawgiver of ancient Israel! Jack, from this spot where we stand, to Egypt, stretches a fearful desert three hundred miles in extent—and across that desert that wonderful man brought the children of Israel!—guiding them with unfailing sagacity for forty years over the sandy desolation and among the obstructing rocks and hills, and landed them at last, safe and sound, within sight of this very spot; and where we now stand they entered the Promised Land with anthems of rejoicing! It was a wonderful, wonderful thing to do, Jack! Think of it!"

"Forty years? Only three hundred miles? Humph! Ben Holliday would have fetched them through in thirty-six hours!"

The boy meant no harm. He did not know that he had said anything that was wrong or irreverent. And so no one scolded him or felt offended with him—and nobody could but some ungenerous spirit incapable of excusing the heedless blunders of a boy.

At noon on the fifth day out, we arrived at the "Crossing of the South Platte," alias "Julesburg," alias "Overland City," four hundred and seventy miles from St. Joseph—the strangest, quaintest, funniest frontier town that our untraveled eyes had ever stared at and been astonished with.

CHAPTER VII

It did seem strange enough to see a town again after what appeared to us such a long acquaintance with deep, still, almost lifeless and houseless solitude! We tumbled out into the busy street feeling like meteoric people crumbled off the corner of some other world, and wakened up suddenly in this. For an hour we took as much interest in Overland

City as if we had never seen a town before. The reason we had an hour to spare was because we had to change our stage (for a less sumptuous affair, called a "mud-wagon") and transfer our freight of mails. Presently we got under way again. We came to the shallow, yellow, muddy South Platte, with its low banks and its scattering flat sandbars and pigmy islands—a melancholy stream straggling through the centre of the enormous flat plain, and only saved from being impossible to find with the naked eye by its sentinel rank of scattering trees standing on either bank. The Platte was "up," they said—which made me wish I could see it when it was down, if it could look any sicker and sorrier. They said it was a dangerous stream to cross, now, because its quicksands were liable to swallow up horses, coach and passengers if an attempt was made to ford it. But the mails had to go, and we made the attempt. Once or twice in midstream the wheels sunk into the yielding sands so threateningly that we half believed we had dreaded and avoided the sea all our lives to be shipwrecked in a "mud-wagon" in the middle of a desert at last. But we dragged through and sped away toward the setting sun.

Next morning, just before dawn, when about five hundred and fifty miles from St. Joseph, our mud-wagon broke down. We were to be delayed five or six hours, and therefore we took horses, by invitation, and joined a party who were just starting on a buffalo hunt. It was noble sport galloping over the plain in the dewy freshness of the morning, but our part of the hunt ended in disaster and disgrace, for a wounded buffalo bull chased the passenger Bemis nearly two miles, and then he forsook his horse and took to a lone tree. He was very sullen about the matter for some twenty-four hours, but at last he began to soften little by little, and finally he said:

"Well, it was not funny, and there was no sense in those gawks making themselves so facetious over it. I tell you I was angry in earnest for awhile. I should have shot that long gangly lubber they called Hank, if I could have done it without crippling six or seven other people—but of course I couldn't, the old 'Allen's' so confounded comprehensive. I wish those loafers had been up in the tree; they wouldn't have wanted to laugh so. If I had had a horse worth a cent—but no, the minute he saw that buffalo bull wheel on him and give a bellow, he raised straight up in the air and stood on his heels. The saddle began to slip, and I took him round the neck and laid close to him, and began to pray. Then he came down and stood up on the other end awhile, and the bull actually stopped pawing sand and bellowing to contemplate the inhuman spectacle.

"'Then the bull made a pass at him and uttered a bellow that sounded perfectly frightful, it was so close to me, and that seemed to literally prostrate my horse's reason, and make a raving distracted maniac of him, and I wish I may die if he didn't stand on his head for a quarter of a minute and shed tears. He was absolutely out of his mind—he was, as sure as truth itself, and he really didn't know what he was doing. Then the bull came charging at us, and my horse dropped down on all fours and took a fresh start—and then for the next ten minutes he would actually throw one hand-spring after another so fast that the bull began to get unsettled, too, and didn't know where to start in—and so he stood there sneezing, and shovelling dust over his back, and bellowing every now and then, and thinking he had got a fifteen-hundred dollar circus horse for breakfast, certain. Well, I was first out on his neck—the horse's, not the bull's—and then underneath, and next on his rump, and sometimes head up, and sometimes heels—but I tell you it seemed solemn and awful to be ripping and tearing and carrying on so in the presence of death, as you might say. Pretty soon the bull made a snatch for us and brought away some of my horse's tail (I suppose, but do not know, being pretty busy at the time), but something made him hungry for solitude and suggested to him to get up and hunt for it.

"And then you ought to have seen that spider legged old skeleton go! And you ought to have seen the bull cut out after him, too—head down, tongue out, tail up, bellowing like everything, and actually mowing down the weeds, and tearing up the earth, and boosting up the sand like a whirlwind! By George, it was a hot race! I and the saddle were back on the rump, and I had the bridle in my teeth and holding on to the pommel with both hands. First we left the dogs behind; then we passed a jackass rabbit; then we overtook a cayote, and were gaining on an antelope when the rotten girth let go and threw me about thirty yards off to the left, and as the saddle went down over the horse's rump he gave it a lift with his heels that sent it more than four hundred yards up in the air, I wish I may die in a minute if he didn't. I fell at the foot of the only solitary tree there was in nine counties adjacent (as any creature could see with the naked eye), and the next second I had hold of the bark with four sets of nails and my teeth, and the next second after that I was astraddle of the main limb and blaspheming my luck in a way that made my breath smell of brimstone. I had the bull, now, if he did not think of one thing. But that one thing I dreaded. I dreaded it very seriously. There was a possibility that the bull might not think of it, but there were greater chances that he would. I made up my mind what I would do in case he did. It was a little over forty feet to the ground from where I sat. I cautiously unwound the lariat from the pommel of my saddle—"

"Your saddle? Did you take your saddle up in the tree with you?"

"Take it up in the tree with me? Why, how you talk. Of course I didn't. No man could do that. It fell in the tree when it came down."

"Oh—exactly."

"Certainly. I unwound the lariat, and fastened one end of it to the limb. It was the very best green raw-hide, and capable of sustaining tons. I made a slip-noose in the other end, and then hung it down to see the length. It reached down twenty-two feet—half way to the ground. I then loaded every barrel of the Allen with a double charge. I felt satisfied. I said to myself, if he never thinks of that one thing that I dread, all right—but if he does, all right anyhow—I am fixed for him. But don't you know that the very thing a man dreads is the thing that always happens? Indeed it is so. I watched the bull, now, with anxiety—anxiety which no one can conceive of who has not been in such a situation and felt that at any moment death might come. Presently a thought came into the bull's eye. I knew it! said I—if my nerve fails now, I am lost. Sure enough, it was just as I had dreaded, he started in to climb the tree—"

"What, the bull?"

"Of course—who else?"

"But a bull can't climb a tree."

"He can't, can't he? Since you know so much about it, did you ever see a bull try?"

"No! I never dreamt of such a thing."

"Well, then, what is the use of your talking that way, then? Because you never saw a thing done, is that any reason why it can't be done?"

"Well, all right—go on. What did you do?"

"The bull started up, and got along well for about ten feet, then slipped and slid back. I breathed easier. He tried it again—got up a little higher—slipped again. But he came at it once more, and this time he was careful. He got gradually higher and higher, and my spirits went down more and more. Up he came—an inch at a time—with his eyes hot, and his tongue hanging out. Higher and higher—hitched his foot over the stump of a limb, and looked up, as much as to say, 'You are my meat, friend.' Up again—higher and higher, and getting more excited the closer he got. He was within ten feet of me! I took a long breath,— and then said I, 'It is now or never.' I had the coil of the lariat all ready; I paid it out slowly, till it hung right over his head; all of a sudden I let go of the slack, and the slipnoose fell fairly round his neck! Quicker than lightning I out with the Allen and let him have it in the face. It was an awful roar, and must have scared the bull out of his senses. When the smoke cleared away, there he was, dangling in the air, twenty foot from the ground, and going out of one convulsion into another faster than you could count! I didn't stop to count, anyhow—I shinned down the tree and shot for home."

"Bemis, is all that true, just as you have stated it?"

"I wish I may rot in my tracks and die the death of a dog if it isn't."

"Well, we can't refuse to believe it, and we don't. But if there were some proofs—"

"Proofs! Did I bring back my lariat?"

"No."

"Did I bring back my horse?"

"No."

"Did you ever see the bull again?"

"No."

"Well, then, what more do you want? I never saw anybody as particular as you are about a little thing like that."

I made up my mind that if this man was not a liar he only missed it by the skin of his teeth. This episode reminds me of an incident of my brief sojourn in Siam, years afterward. The European citizens of a town in the neighborhood of Bangkok had a prodigy among them by the name of Eckert, an Englishman—a person famous for the number, ingenuity and imposing magnitude of his lies. They were always repeating his most celebrated falsehoods, and always trying to "draw him out" before strangers; but they seldom succeeded. Twice he was invited to the house where I was visiting, but nothing could seduce him into a specimen lie. One day a planter named Bascom, an influential man, and a proud and sometimes irascible one, invited me to ride over with him and call on Eckert. As we jogged along, said he:

"Now, do you know where the fault lies? It lies in putting Eckert on his guard. The minute the boys go to pumping at Eckert he knows perfectly well what they are after, and of course he shuts up his shell. Anybody might know he would. But when we get there, we must play him finer than that. Let him shape the conversation to suit himself— let him drop it or change it whenever he wants to. Let him see that nobody is trying to draw him out. Just let him have his own way. He will soon forget himself and begin to grind out lies like a mill. Don't get impatient—just keep quiet, and let me play him. I will make him lie. It does seem to me that the boys must be blind to overlook such an obvious and simple trick as that."

Eckert received us heartily—a pleasant-spoken, gentle-mannered creature. We sat in the veranda an hour, sipping English ale, and talking about the king, and the sacred white elephant, the Sleeping Idol, and all manner of things; and I noticed that my comrade never led the conversation himself or shaped it, but simply followed Eckert's lead, and betrayed no solicitude and no anxiety about anything. The effect was shortly perceptible. Eckert began to grow communicative; he grew more and more at his ease, and more and more talkative and sociable. Another hour passed in the same way, and then all of a sudden Eckert said:

"Oh, by the way! I came near forgetting. I have got a thing here to astonish you. Such a thing as neither you nor any other man ever heard of—I've got a cat that will eat cocoanut! Common green cocoanut— and not only eat the meat, but drink the milk. It is so—I'll swear to it."

A quick glance from Bascom—a glance that I understood—then: "Why, bless my soul, I never heard of such a thing. Man, it is impossible."

"I knew you would say it. I'll fetch the cat."

He went in the house. Bascom said: "There—what did I tell you? Now, that is the way to handle Eckert. You see, I have petted him along patiently, and put his suspicions to sleep. I am glad we came. You tell the boys about it when you go back. Cat eat a cocoanut—oh, my! Now, that is just his way, exactly—he will tell the absurdest lie, and trust to luck to get out of it again.

"Cat eat a cocoanut—the innocent fool!"

Eckert approached with his cat, sure enough.

Bascom smiled. Said he: "I'll hold the cat—you bring a cocoanut."

Eckert split one open, and chopped up some pieces. Bascom smuggled a wink to me, and proffered a slice of the fruit to puss. She snatched it, swallowed it ravenously, and asked for more!

We rode our two miles in silence, and wide apart. At least I was silent, though Bascom cuffed his horse and cursed him a good deal, notwithstanding the horse was behaving well enough. When I branched off homeward, Bascom said:

"Keep the horse till morning. And—you need not speak of this—foolishness to the boys."

13

PART I—NOTES BY FLOOD AND FIELD

BY BRET HARTE

Bret Harte rose to national prominence as editor of the Overland Monthly, *a San Francisco-based magazine of western lore. His best-known short stories include "The Luck of Roaring Camp," "The Outcasts of Poker Flat," and this 1869 "Notes by Flood and Field," in which he romanticized the hardscrabble lives and conflicts of the early California settlers.*

It was near the close of an October day that I began to be disagreeably conscious of the Sacramento Valley. I had been riding since sunrise, and my course through the depressing monotony of the long level landscape affected me more like a dull dyspeptic dream than a business journey, performed under that sincerest of natural phenomena—a California sky.

The recurring stretches of brown and baked fields, the gaping fissures in the dusty trail, the hard outline of the distant hills, and the herds of slowly moving cattle, seemed like features of some glittering stereoscopic picture that never changed. Active exercise might have removed this feeling, but my horse by some subtle instinct had long since given up all ambitious effort, and had lapsed into a dogged trot.

It was autumn, but not the season suggested to the Atlantic reader under that title. The sharply defined boundaries of the wet and dry seasons were prefigured in the clear outlines of the distant hills. In the dry atmosphere the decay of vegetation was too rapid for the slow hectic which overtakes an Eastern landscape, or else Nature was too practical for such thin disguises. She merely turned the Hippocratic face to the spectator, with the old diagnosis of Death in her sharp, contracted features.

In the contemplation of such a prospect there was little to excite any but a morbid fancy. There were no clouds in the flinty blue heavens, and the setting of the sun was accompanied with as little ostentation as was consistent with the dryly practical atmosphere. Darkness soon followed, with a rising wind, which increased as the shadows deepened on the plain. The fringe of alder by the watercourse began to loom up as I urged my horse forward. A half-hour's active spurring brought me to a corral, and a little beyond a house, so low and broad it seemed at first sight to be half-buried in the earth.

My second impression was that it had grown out of the soil, like some monstrous vegetable, its dreary proportions were so in keeping with the vast prospect. There were no recesses along its roughly boarded walls for vagrant and unprofitable shadows to lurk in the daily sunshine. No projection for the wind by night to grow musical over, to wail, whistle, or whisper to; only a long wooden shelf containing a chilly-looking tin basin and a bar of soap. Its uncurtained windows were red with the sinking sun, as though bloodshot and inflamed from a too-long unlidded existence. The tracks of cattle led to its front door, firmly closed against the rattling wind.

To avoid being confounded with this familiar element, I walked to the rear of the house, which was connected with a smaller building by a slight platform. A grizzled, hard-faced old man was standing there, and met my salutation with a look of inquiry, and, without speaking, led the way to the principal room. As I entered, four young men who were reclining by the fire slightly altered their attitudes of perfect repose, but beyond that betrayed neither curiosity nor interest. A hound started from a dark corner with a growl, but was immediately kicked by the old man into obscurity, and silenced again. I can't tell why, but I instantly received the impression that for a long time the group by the fire had not uttered a word or moved a muscle. Taking a seat, I briefly stated my business.

Was a United States surveyor. Had come on account of the Espiritu Santo Rancho. Wanted to correct the exterior boundaries of township lines, so as to connect with the near exteriors of private grants. There had been some intervention to the old survey by a Mr. Tryan who had preempted adjacent—"settled land warrants," interrupted the old man. "Ah, yes! Land warrants—and then this was Mr. Tryan?"

I had spoken mechanically, for I was preoccupied in connecting other public lines with private surveys as I looked in his face. It was certainly a hard face, and reminded me of the singular effect of that mining operation known as "ground sluicing"; the harder lines of underlying character were exposed, and what were once plastic curves and soft outlines were obliterated by some powerful agency.

There was a dryness in his voice not unlike the prevailing atmosphere of the valley, as he launched into an EX PARTE statement of the contest, with a fluency, which, like the wind without, showed frequent and unrestrained expression. He told me—what I had already learned—that the boundary line of the old Spanish grant was a creek, described in the loose phraseology of the DESENO as beginning in the VALDA or skirt of the hill, its precise location long the subject of litigation. I listened and answered with little interest, for my mind was still distracted by the wind which swept violently by the house, as well as by his odd face, which was again reflected in the resemblance that the silent group by the fire bore toward him. He was still talking, and the wind was yet blowing, when my confused attention was aroused by a remark addressed to the recumbent figures.

"Now, then, which on ye'll see the stranger up the creek to Altascar's, tomorrow?"

There was a general movement of opposition in the group, but no decided answer.

"Kin you go, Kerg?"

"Who's to look up stock in Strarberry perar-ie?"

This seemed to imply a negative, and the old man turned to another hopeful, who was pulling the fur from a mangy bearskin on which he was lying, with an expression as though it were somebody's hair.

"Well, Tom, wot's to hinder you from goin'?"

"Mam's goin' to Brown's store at sunup, and I s'pose I've got to pack her and the baby agin."

I think the expression of scorn this unfortunate youth exhibited for the filial duty into which he had been evidently beguiled was one of the finest things I had ever seen.

"Wise?"

Wise deigned no verbal reply, but figuratively thrust a worn and patched boot into the discourse. The old man flushed quickly.

"I told ye to get Brown to give you a pair the last time you war down the river."

"Said he wouldn't without 'en order. Said it was like pulling gum teeth to get the money from you even then."

There was a grim smile at this local hit at the old man's parsimony, and Wise, who was clearly the privileged wit of the family, sank back in honorable retirement.

"Well, Joe, ef your boots are new, and you aren't pestered with wimmin and children, p'r'aps you'll go," said Tryan, with a nervous twitching, intended for a smile, about a mouth not remarkably mirthful.

Tom lifted a pair of bushy eyebrows, and said shortly: "Got no saddle."

"Wot's gone of your saddle?"

"Kerg, there"—indicating his brother with a look such as Cain might have worn at the sacrifice.

"You lie!" returned Kerg, cheerfully.

Tryan sprang to his feet, seizing the chair, flourishing it around his head and gazing furiously in the hard young faces which fearlessly met his own. But it was only for a moment; his arm soon dropped by his side, and a look of hopeless fatality crossed his face. He allowed me to take the chair from his hand, and I was trying to pacify him by the assurance that I required no guide when the irrepressible Wise again lifted his voice:

"Theer's George comin'! why don't ye ask him? He'll go and introduce you to Don Fernandy's darter, too, ef you ain't pertickler."

The laugh which followed this joke, which evidently had some domestic allusion (the general tendency of rural pleasantry), was followed by a light step on the platform, and the young man entered. Seeing a stranger present, he stopped and colored, made a shy salute and colored again, and then, drawing a box from the corner, sat down, his hands clasped lightly together and his very handsome bright blue eyes turned frankly on mine. Perhaps I was in a condition to receive the romantic impression he made upon me, and I took it upon myself to ask his company as guide, and he cheerfully assented. But some domestic duty called him presently away.

The fire gleamed brightly on the hearth, and, no longer resisting the prevailing influence, I silently watched the spurting flame, listening to the wind which continually shook the tenement. Besides the one chair which had acquired a new importance in my eyes, I presently discovered a crazy table in one corner, with an ink bottle and pen; the latter in that greasy state of decomposition peculiar to country taverns and farmhouses. A goodly array of rifles and double-barreled guns stocked the corner; half a dozen saddles and blankets lay near, with a mild flavor of the horse about them. Some deer and bear skins completed the inventory. As I sat there, with the silent group around me, the shadowy gloom within and the dominant wind without, I found it difficult to believe I had ever known a different existence. My profession had often led me to wilder scenes, but rarely among those whose unrestrained habits and easy unconsciousness made me feel so lonely and uncomfortable. I shrank closer to myself, not without grave doubts—which I think occur naturally to people in like situations—that this was the general rule of humanity and I was a solitary and somewhat gratuitous exception.

It was a relief when a laconic announcement of supper by a weak-eyed girl caused a general movement in the family. We walked across the dark platform, which led to another low-ceiled room. Its entire length was occupied by a table, at the farther end of which a weak-eyed woman was already taking her repast as she at the same time gave nourishment to a weak-eyed baby. As the formalities of introduction had been dispensed with, and as she took no notice of me, I was enabled to slip into a seat without discomposing or interrupting her. Tryan extemporized a grace, and the attention of the family became absorbed in bacon, potatoes, and dried apples.

The meal was a sincere one. Gentle gurglings at the upper end of the table often betrayed the presence of the "wellspring of pleasure." The conversation generally referred to the labors of the day, and comparing notes as to the whereabouts of missing stock. Yet the supper was such a vast improvement upon the previous intellectual feast that when a chance allusion of mine to the business of my visit brought out the elder Tryan, the interest grew quite exciting. I remember he inveighed bitterly against the system of ranch-holding by the "greasers," as he was pleased to term the native Californians. As the same ideas have been sometimes advanced under more pretentious circumstances they may be worthy of record.

"Look at 'em holdin' the finest grazin' land that ever lay outer doors. Whar's the papers for it? Was it grants? Mighty fine grants—most of 'em made arter the 'Merrikans got possession. More fools the 'Merrikans for lettin' 'em hold 'em. Wat paid for 'em? 'Merrikan and blood money.

"Didn't they oughter have suthin' out of their native country? Wot for? Did they ever improve? Got a lot of yaller-skinned diggers, not so sensible as n*****s to look arter stock, and they a sittin' home and smokin'. With their gold and silver candlesticks, and missions, and crucifixens, priests and graven idols, and sich? Them sort things wurent allowed in Mizzoori."

At the mention of improvements, I involuntarily lifted my eyes, and met the half laughing, half embarrassed look of George. The act did not escape detection, and I had at once the satisfaction of seeing that the rest of the family had formed an offensive alliance against us.

"It was agin Nater, and agin God," added Tryan. "God never intended gold in the rocks to be made into heathen candlesticks and crucifixens. That's why he sent 'Merrikans here. Nater never intended such a climate for lazy lopers. She never gin six months' sunshine to be slept and smoked away."

How long he continued and with what further illustration I could not say, for I took an early opportunity to escape to the sitting-room. I was soon followed by George, who called me to an open door leading to a smaller room, and pointed to a bed. "You'd better sleep there tonight," he said, "you'll be more comfortable, and I'll call you early."

I thanked him, and would have asked him several questions which were then troubling me, but he shyly slipped to the door and vanished.

A shadow seemed to fall on the room when he had gone. The "boys" returned, one by one, and shuffled to their old places. A larger log was thrown on the fire, and the huge chimney glowed like a furnace, but it did not seem to melt or subdue a single line of the hard faces that it lit. In half an hour later, the furs which had served as chairs by day undertook the nightly office of mattresses, and each received its owner's full-length figure. Mr. Tryan had not returned, and I missed George. I sat there until, wakeful and nervous, I saw the fire fall and shadows mount the wall. There was no sound but the rushing of the wind and the snoring of the sleepers. At last, feeling the place insupportable, I seized my hat and opening the door, ran out briskly into the night.

The acceleration of my torpid pulse in the keen fight with the wind, whose violence was almost equal to that of a tornado, and the familiar faces of the bright stars above me, I felt as a blessed relief. I ran not knowing whither, and when I halted, the square outline of the house was lost in the alder bushes. An uninterrupted plain stretched before me, like a vast sea beaten flat by the force of the gale. As I kept on I noticed a slight elevation toward the horizon, and presently my progress was impeded by the ascent of an Indian mound. It struck me forcibly as resembling an island in the sea. Its height gave me a better view of the expanding plain. But even here I found no rest. The ridiculous interpretation Tryan had given the climate was somehow sung in my ears, and echoed in my throbbing pulse as, guided by the star, I sought the house again.

But I felt fresher and more natural as I stepped upon the platform. The door of the lower building was open, and the old man was sitting beside the table, thumbing the leaves of a Bible with a look in his face as though he were hunting up prophecies against the "Greaser." I turned to enter, but my attention was attracted by a blanketed figure lying beside the house, on the platform. The broad chest heaving with healthy slumber, and the open, honest face were familiar. It was George, who had given up his bed to the stranger among his people. I was about to wake him, but he lay so peaceful and quiet, I felt awed and hushed. And I went to bed with a pleasant impression of his handsome face and tranquil figure soothing me to sleep.

I was awakened the next morning from a sense of lulled repose and grateful silence by the cheery voice of George, who stood beside my bed, ostentatiously twirling a riata, as if to recall the duties of the day to my sleep-bewildered eyes. I looked around me. The wind had been magically laid, and the sun shone warmly through the windows. A dash of cold water, with an extra chill on from the tin basin, helped to brighten me. It was still early, but the family had already breakfasted and dispersed, and a wagon winding far in the distance showed that the unfortunate Tom had already "packed" his relatives away. I felt more cheerful—there are few troubles Youth cannot distance with the start of a good night's rest. After a substantial breakfast, prepared by George, in a few moments we were mounted and dashing down the plain.

We followed the line of alder that defined the creek, now dry and baked with summer's heat, but which in winter, George told me, overflowed its banks. I still retain a vivid impression of that morning's ride, the far-off mountains, like silhouettes, against the steel-blue sky, the crisp dry air, and the expanding track before me, animated often by the well-knit figure of George Tryan, musical with jingling spurs and picturesque with flying riata. He rode powerful native roan, wild-eyed, untiring in stride and unbroken in nature. Alas! the curves of beauty were concealed by the cumbrous MACHILLAS of the Spanish saddle, which levels all equine distinctions. The single rein lay loosely on the cruel bit that can gripe, and if need be, crush the jaw it controls.

Again the illimitable freedom of the valley rises before me, as we again bear down into sunlit space. Can this be "Chu Chu," staid and respectable filly of American pedigree—Chu Chu, forgetful of plank roads and cobblestones, wild with excitement, twinkling her small white feet beneath me? George laughs out of a cloud of dust. "Give her her head; don't you see she likes it?" and Chu Chu seems to like it, and whether bitten by native tarantula into native barbarism or emulous of the roan, "blood" asserts itself, and in a moment the peaceful servitude of years is beaten out in the music of her clattering hoofs. The creek widens to a deep gully. We dive into it and up on the opposite side, carrying a moving cloud of impalpable powder with us. Cattle are scattered over the plain, grazing quietly or banded together in vast restless herds. George makes a wide, indefinite sweep with the riata, as if to include them all in his vaquero's loop, and says, "Ours!"

"About how many, George?"

"Don't know."

"How many?"

"Well, p'r'aps three thousand head," says George, reflecting. "We don't know, takes five men to look 'em up and keep run."

"What are they worth?"

"About thirty dollars a head."

I make a rapid calculation, and look my astonishment at the laughing George. Perhaps a recollection of the domestic economy of the Tryan household is expressed in that look, for George averts his eye and says, apologetically: "I've tried to get the old man to sell and build, but you know he says it ain't no use to settle down, just yet. We must keep movin'. In fact, he built the shanty for that purpose, lest titles should fall through, and we'd have to get up and move stakes further down."

Suddenly his quick eye detects some unusual sight in a herd we are passing, and with an exclamation he puts his roan into the center of the mass. I follow, or rather Chu Chu darts after the roan, and in a few moments we are in the midst of apparently inextricable horns and hoofs.

"TORO!" shouts George, with vaquero enthusiasm, and the band opens a way for the swinging riata. I can feel their steaming breaths, and their spume is cast on Chu Chu's quivering flank.

Wild, devilish-looking beasts are they; not such shapes as Jove might have chosen to woo a goddess, nor such as peacefully range the downs of Devon, but lean and hungry Cassius-like bovines, economically got up to meet the exigencies of a six months' rainless climate, and accustomed to wrestle with the distracting wind and the blinding dust.

"That's not our brand," says George; "they're strange stock," and he points to what my scientific eye recognizes as the astrological sign of Venus deeply seared in the brown flanks of the bull he is chasing. But the herd are closing round us with low mutterings, and George has again recourse to the authoritative "TORO," and with swinging riata divides the "bossy bucklers" on either side. When we are free, and breathing somewhat more easily, I venture to ask George if they ever attack anyone.

"Never horsemen—sometimes footmen. Not through rage, you know, but curiosity. They think a man and his horse are one, and if they meet a chap afoot, they run him down and trample him under hoof, in the pursuit of knowledge. But," adds George, "here's the lower bench of the foothills, and here's Altascar's corral, and that white building you see yonder is the casa."

A whitewashed wall enclosed a court containing another adobe building, baked with the solar beams of many summers. Leaving our horses in the charge of a few peons in the courtyard, who were basking lazily in the sun, we entered a low doorway, where a deep shadow and an agreeable coolness fell upon us, as sudden and grateful as a plunge in cool water, from its contrast with the external glare and heat. In the center of a low-ceiled apartment sat an old man with a black-silk handkerchief tied about his head, the few gray hairs that escaped from its folds relieving his gamboge-colored face. The odor of CIGARRITOS was as incense added to the cathedral gloom of the building.

As Senor Altascar rose with well-bred gravity to receive us, George advanced with such a heightened color, and such a blending of tenderness and respect in his manner, that I was touched to the heart by so much devotion in the careless youth. In fact, my eyes were still dazzled by the effect of the outer sunshine, and at first I did not see the white teeth and black eyes of Pepita, who slipped into the corridor as we entered.

It was no pleasant matter to disclose particulars of business which would deprive the old señor of the greater part of that land we had just ridden over, and I did it with great embarrassment. But he listened calmly—not a muscle of his dark face stirring—and the smoke curling placidly from his lips showed his regular respiration. When I had finished, he offered quietly to accompany us to the line of demarcation.

George had meanwhile disappeared, but a suspicious conversation in broken Spanish and English, in the corridor, betrayed his vicinity. When he returned again, a little absent-minded, the old man, by far the coolest and most self-possessed of the party, extinguished his black-silk cap beneath that stiff, uncomely sombrero which all native Californians affect. A serape thrown over his shoulders hinted that he was waiting. Horses are always ready saddled in Spanish ranchos, and in half an hour from the time of our arrival we were again "loping" in the staring sunlight.

But not as cheerfully as before. George and myself were weighed down by restraint, and Altascar was gravely quiet. To break the silence, and by way of a consolatory essay, I hinted to him that there might be further intervention or appeal, but the proffered oil and wine were returned with a careless shrug of the shoulders and a sententious "QUE BUENO?—Your courts are always just."

The Indian mound of the previous night's discovery was a bearing monument of the new line, and there we halted. We were surprised to find the old man Tryan waiting us. For the first time during our interview the old Spaniard seemed moved, and the blood rose in his yellow cheek. I was anxious to close the scene, and pointed out the corner boundaries as clearly as my recollection served.

"The deputies will be here tomorrow to run the lines from this initial point, and there will be no further trouble, I believe, gentlemen." Senor Altascar had dismounted and was gathering a few tufts of dried grass in his hands. George and I exchanged glances. He presently arose from his stooping posture, and advancing to within a few paces of Joseph Tryan, said, in a voice broken with passion: "And I, Fernando Jesus Maria Altascar, put you in possession of my land in the fashion of my country."

He threw a sod to each of the cardinal points. "I don't know your courts, your judges, or your CORREGIDORES. Take the LLANO!—

and take this with it. May the drought seize your cattle till their tongues hang down as long as those of your lying lawyers! May it be the curse and torment of your old age, as you and yours have made it of mine!"

We stepped between the principal actors in this scene, which only the passion of Altascar made tragical, but Tryan, with a humility but ill concealing his triumph, interrupted: "Let him curse on. He'll find 'em coming home to him sooner than the cattle he has lost through his sloth and pride. The Lord is on the side of the just, as well as agin all slanderers and revilers."

Altascar but half guessed the meaning of the Missourian, yet sufficiently to drive from his mind all but the extravagant power of his native invective. "Stealer of the Sacrament! Open not!—open not, I say, your lying, Judas lips to me! Ah! half-breed, with the soul of a coyote!—car-r-r-ramba!"

With his passion reverberating among the consonants like distant thunder, he laid his hand upon the mane of his horse as though it had been the gray locks of his adversary, swung himself into the saddle and galloped away.

George turned to me: "Will you go back with us tonight?"

I thought of the cheerless walls, the silent figures by the fire, and the roaring wind, and hesitated. "Well then, goodby."

"Goodby, George."

Another wring of the hands, and we parted. I had not ridden far when I turned and looked back. The wind had risen early that afternoon, and was already sweeping across the plain. A cloud of dust traveled before it, and a picturesque figure occasionally emerging therefrom was my last indistinct impression of George Tryan.

14

A NARRATIVE OF THE OLD TRAIL DAYS

BY ANDY ADAMS

Unlike many if not most other Western writers, Andy Adams was indeed a cowboy. His The Log of a Cowboy: A Narrative of the Old Trail Days *chronicles a five-month cattle drive from Texas to Montana. Although a work of fiction, the 1903 account was based on the author's ranching experiences and is as realistic an account of a cattle drive as can be found in print.*

On the morning of April 1, 1882, our Circle Dot herd started on its long tramp to the Blackfoot Agency in Montana. With six men on each side, and the herd strung out for three quarters of a mile, it could only be compared to some mythical serpent or Chinese dragon, as it moved forward on its sinuous, snail-like course. Two riders, known as point men, rode out and well back from the lead cattle, and by riding forward and closing in as occasion required, directed the course of the herd. The main body of the herd trailed along behind the leaders like an army in loose marching order, guarded by outriders, known as swing men, who rode well out from the advancing column, warding off range cattle and seeing that none of the herd wandered away or dropped out. There was no driving to do; the cattle moved of their own free will as in ordinary travel. Flood seldom gave orders; but, as a number of us had never worked on the trail before, at breakfast on the morning of our start he gave in substance these general directions:

"Boys, the secret of trailing cattle is never to let your herd know that they are under restraint. Let everything that is done be done voluntarily by the cattle. From the moment you let them off the bed ground in the morning until they are bedded at night, never let a cow take a step, except in the direction of its destination. In this manner you can loaf away the day, and cover from fifteen to twenty miles, and the herd in the mean time will enjoy all the freedom of an open range. Of course, it's long, tiresome hours to the men; but the condition of the herd and saddle stock demands sacrifices on our part, if any have to be made. And I want to caution you younger boys about your horses; there is such a thing as having ten horses in your string, and at the same time being afoot. You are all well mounted, and on the condition of the *remuda* depends the success and safety of the herd. Accidents will happen to horses, but don't let it be your fault; keep your saddle blankets dry and clean, for no better word can be spoken of a man than that he is careful of his horses. Ordinarily a man might get along with six or eight horses, but in such emergencies as we are liable to meet, we have not a horse to spare, and a man afoot is useless."

And as all of us younger boys learned afterward, there was plenty of good, solid, horse-sense in Flood's advice; for before the trip ended there were men in our outfit who were as good as afoot, while others had their original mounts, every one fit for the saddle. Flood had insisted on a good mount of horses, and Lovell was cowman enough to know that what the mule is to the army the cow-horse is to the herd.

The first and second day out there was no incident worth mentioning. We traveled slowly, hardly making an average day's drive. The third morning Flood left us, to look out a crossing on the Arroyo Colorado. On coming down to receive the herd, we had crossed this sluggish bayou about thirty-six miles north of Brownsville. It was a deceptive-looking stream, being over fifty feet deep and between bluff banks. We ferried our wagon and saddle horses over, swimming the loose ones. But the herd was keeping near the coast line for the sake of open country, and it was a question if there was a ford for the wagon as near the coast as our course was carrying us. The murmurings of the Gulf had often reached our ears the day before, and herds had been known, in former years, to cross from the mainland over to Padre Island, the intervening Laguna Madre being fordable.

We were nooning when Flood returned with the news that it would be impossible to cross our wagon at any point on the bayou, and that we would have to ford around the mouth of the stream. Where the fresh and salt water met in the laguna, there had formed a delta, or shallow bar; and by following its contour we would not have over twelve to fourteen inches of water, though the half circle was nearly two miles in length. As we would barely have time to cross that day, the herd was at once started, veering for the mouth of the Arroyo Colorado. On reaching it, about the middle of the afternoon, the foreman led the way, having crossed in the morning and learned the ford. The wagon followed, the saddle horses came next, while the herd brought up the rear. It proved good footing on the sandbar, but the water in the laguna was too salty for the cattle, though the loose horses lay down and wallowed in it. We were about an hour in crossing, and on reaching the mainland met a vaquero, who directed us to a large fresh-water lake a few miles inland, where we camped for the night.

It proved an ideal camp, with wood, water, and grass in abundance, and very little range stock to annoy us. We had watered the herd just before noon, and before throwing them upon the bed ground for the night, watered them a second time. We had a splendid camp-fire that night, of dry live oak logs, and after supper was over and the first guard had taken the herd, smoking and story telling were the order of the evening. The camp-fire is to all outdoor life what the evening fireside is to domestic life. After the labors of the day are over, the men gather around the fire, and the social hour of the day is spent in yarning. The stories told may run from the sublime to the ridiculous, from a true incident to a base fabrication, or from a touching bit of pathos to the most vulgar vulgarity.

"Have I ever told this outfit my experience with the vigilantes when I was a kid?" inquired Bull Durham. There was a general negative response, and he proceeded. "Well, our folks were living on the Frio at the time, and there was a man in our neighborhood who had an outfit of four men out beyond Nueces Cañon hunting wild cattle for their hides. It was necessary to take them out supplies about every so often, and on one trip he begged my folks to let me go along for company. I was a slim slip of a colt about fourteen at the time, and as this man was a friend of ours, my folks consented to let me go along. We each had a good saddle horse, and two pack mules with provisions and ammunition for the hunting camp. The first night we made camp, a boy overtook us with the news that the brother of my companion had been accidentally killed by a horse, and of course he would have to return. Well, we were twenty miles on our way, and as it would take some little time to go back and return with the loaded mules, I volunteered, like a fool kid, to go on and take the packs through.

"The only question was, could I pack and unpack. I had helped him at this work, double-handed, but now that I was to try it alone, he showed me what he called a squaw hitch, with which you can lash a pack single-handed. After putting me through it once or twice, and satisfying himself that I could do the packing, he consented to let me go on, he and the messenger returning home during the night. The next morning I packed without any trouble and started on my way. It would take me two days yet, poking along with heavy packs, to reach the hunters. Well, I hadn't made over eight or ten miles the first morning, when, as I rounded a turn in the trail, a man stepped out from behind a rock, threw a gun in my face, and ordered me to hold up my hands. Then another appeared from the opposite side with his gun leveled on me. Inside of half a minute a dozen men galloped up from every quarter, all armed to the teeth. The man on leaving had given me his gun for company, one of these old smoke-pole, cap-and-ball six-shooters, but I must have forgotten what guns were for, for I elevated my little hands nicely. The leader of the party questioned me as to who I was, and what I was doing there, and what I had in those packs. That once, at least, I told the truth. Every mother's son of them was cursing and cross-questioning me in the same breath. They ordered me off my horse, took my gun, and proceeded to verify my tale by unpacking the mules. So much ammunition aroused their suspicions, but my story was as good as it was true, and they never shook me from the truth of it. I soon learned that robbery was not their motive, and the leader explained the situation.

"A vigilance committee had been in force in that county for some time, trying to rid the country of lawless characters. But lawlessness got into the saddle, and had bench warrants issued and served on every member of this vigilance committee. As the vigilantes numbered several hundred, there was no jail large enough to hold such a number, so they were released on parole for appearance at court. When court met, every man served with a capias—"

"Hold on! hold your horses just a minute," interrupted Quince Forrest, "I want to get that word. I want to make a memorandum of it, for I may want to use it myself sometime. Capias? Now I have it; go ahead."

"When court met, every man served with a bench warrant from the judge presiding was present, and as soon as court was called to order, a squad of men arose in the court room, and the next moment the judge fell riddled with lead. Then the factions scattered to fight it out, and I was passing through the county while matters were active.

"They confiscated my gun and all the ammunition in the packs, but helped me to repack and started me on my way. A happy thought struck one of the men to give me a letter, which would carry me through without further trouble, but the leader stopped him, saying, 'Let the boy alone. Your letter would hang him as sure as hell's hot, before he went ten miles farther.' I declined the letter. Even then I didn't have sense enough to turn back, and inside of two hours I was rounded up by the other faction. I had learned my story perfectly by this time, but those packs had to come off again for everything to be examined. There was nothing in them now but flour and salt and such things—nothing that they might consider suspicious. One fellow in this second party took a fancy to my horse, and offered to help hang me on general principles, but kinder counsels prevailed. They also helped me to repack, and I started on once more. Before I reached my destination the following evening, I was held up seven different times. I got so used to it that I was happily disappointed every shelter I passed, if some man did not step out and throw a gun in my face.

"I had trouble to convince the cattle hunters of my experiences, but the absence of any ammunition, which they needed worst, at last led them to give credit to my tale. I was expected home within a week, as I was to go down on the Nueces on a cow hunt which was making up, and I only rested one day at the hunters' camp. On their advice, I took a different route on my way home, leaving the mules behind me. I never saw a man the next day returning, and was feeling quite gala on my good fortune. When evening came on, I sighted a little ranch house some distance off the trail, and concluded to ride to it and stay overnight. As I approached, I saw that some one lived there, as there were chickens and dogs about, but not a person in sight. I dismounted and knocked on the door, when, without a word, the door was thrown wide open and a half dozen guns were poked into my face. I was ordered into the house and given a chance to tell my story again. Whether my story was true or not, they took no chances on me, but kept me all night. One of the men took my horse to the stable and cared for him, and I was well fed and given a place to sleep, but not a man offered a word of explanation, from which I took it they did not belong to the vigilance faction. When it came time to go to bed, one man said to me, 'Now, sonny, don't make any attempt to get away, and don't move out of your bed without warning us, for you'll be shot as sure as you do. We won't harm a hair on your head if you're telling us the truth; only do as you're told, for we'll watch you.'

"By this time I had learned to obey orders while in that county, and got a fair night's sleep, though there were men going and coming all night. The next morning I was given my breakfast; my horse, well cuffed and saddled, was brought to the door, and with this parting advice I was given permission to go: 'Son, if you've told us the truth, don't look back when you ride away. You'll be watched for the first ten miles after leaving here, and if you've lied to us it will go hard with you. Now, remember, don't look back, for these are times when no one cares to be identified.' I never questioned that man's advice; it was 'die dog or eat the hatchet' with me. I mounted my horse, waved the usual parting courtesies, and rode away. As I turned into the trail about a quarter mile from the house, I noticed two men ride out from behind the stable and follow me. I remembered the story about Lot's wife looking back, though it was lead and not miracles that I was afraid of that morning.

"For the first hour I could hear the men talking and the hoofbeats of their horses, as they rode along always the same distance behind me. After about two hours of this one-sided joke, as I rode over a little hill, I looked out of the corner of my eye back at my escort, still about a quarter of a mile behind me. One of them noticed me and raised his gun, but I instantly changed my view, and the moment the hill hid me, put spurs to my horse, so that when they reached the brow of the hill, I was half a mile in the lead, burning the earth like a canned dog. They threw lead close around me, but my horse lengthened the distance between us for the next five miles, when they dropped entirely out of sight. By noon I came into the old stage road, and by the middle of the afternoon reached home after over sixty miles in the saddle without a halt."

Just at the conclusion of Bull's story, Flood rode in from the herd, and after picketing his horse, joined the circle. In reply to an inquiry from one of the boys as to how the cattle were resting, he replied,—

"This herd is breaking into trail life nicely. If we'll just be careful with them now for the first month, and no bad storms strike us in the night, we may never have a run the entire trip. That last drink of water they had this evening gave them a night-cap that'll last them until morning. No, there's no danger of any trouble to-night."

For fully an hour after the return of our foreman, we lounged around the fire, during which there was a full and free discussion of stampedes. But finally, Flood, suiting the action to the word by arising, suggested that all hands hunt their blankets and turn in for the night. A quiet wink from Bull to several of the boys held us for the time being, and innocently turning to Forrest, Durham inquired,—

"Where was—when was—was it you that was telling some one about a run you were in last summer? I never heard you tell it. Where was it?"

"You mean on the Cimarron last year when we mixed two herds," said Quince, who had taken the bait like a bass and was now fully embarked on a yarn. "We were in rather close quarters, herds ahead and behind us, when one night here came a cow herd like a cyclone and swept right through our camp. We tumbled out of our blankets and ran for our horses, but before we could bridle—"

Bull had given us the wink, and every man in the outfit fell back, and the snoring that checked the storyteller was like a chorus of rip saws running through pine knots. Forrest took in the situation at a glance, and as he arose to leave, looked back and remarked, "you must all think that's smart."

Before he was out of hearing, Durham said to the rest of us, "a few doses like that will cure him of sucking eggs and acting smart, interrupting folks."

15

ARIZONA NIGHTS

BY STEWART EDWARD WHITE

Stewart Edward White was a consummate outdoorsman (Theodore Roosevelt acknowledged his facility with firearms) as well as a writer on many subjects, especially the American West. This chapter from his 1907 novel Arizona Nights *displays how Western justice could be sure and swift . . . and well suited to the situation.*

After the rain that had held us holed up at the Double R over one day, we discussed what we should do next.

"The flats will be too boggy for riding, and anyway the cattle will be in the high country," the Cattleman summed up the situation. "We'd bog down the chuck-wagon if we tried to get back to the J. H. But now after the rain the weather ought to be beautiful. What shall we do?"

"Was you ever in the Jackson country?" asked Uncle Jim. "It's the wildest part of Arizona. It's a big country and rough, and no one lives there, and there's lots of deer and mountain lions and bear. Here's my dogs. We might have a hunt."

"Good!" said we.

We skirmished around and found a condemned army pack saddle with aparejos, and a sawbuck saddle with kyacks. On these, we managed to condense our grub and utensils. There were plenty of horses, so our bedding we bound flat about their naked barrels by means of the squaw-hitch. Then we started.

That day furnished us with a demonstration of what Arizona horses can do. Our way led first through a canon-bed filled with rounded boulders and rocks, slippery and unstable. Big cottonwoods and oaks grew so thick as partially to conceal the cliffs on either side of us. The rim-rock was mysterious with caves; beautiful with hanging gardens of tree ferns and grasses growing thick in long transverse crevices; wonderful in colour and shape. We passed the little canons fenced off by the rustlers as corrals into which to shunt from the herds their choice of beeves.

The Cattleman shook his head at them. "Many a man has come from Texas and established a herd with no other asset than a couple of horses and a branding-iron," said he.

Then we worked up gradually to a divide, whence we could see a range of wild and rugged mountains on our right. They rose by slopes and ledges, steep and rough, and at last ended in the thousand-foot cliffs of the buttes, running sheer and unbroken for many miles. During all the rest of our trip they were to be our companions, the only constant factors in the tumult of lesser peaks, precipitous canons, and twisted systems in which we were constantly involved.

The sky was sun-and-shadow after the rain. Each and every Arizonan predicted clearing.

"Why, it almost never rains in Arizona," said Jed Parker. "And when it does it quits before it begins."

Nevertheless, about noon a thick cloud gathered about the tops of the Galiuros above us. Almost immediately it was dissipated by the wind, but when the peaks again showed, we stared with astonishment to see that they were white with snow. It was as though a magician had passed a sheet before them the brief instant necessary to work his great transformation. Shortly the sky thickened again, and it began to rain.

Travel had been precarious before; but now its difficulties were infinitely increased. The clay sub-soil to the rubble turned slippery and adhesive. On the sides of the mountains it was almost impossible to keep a footing. We speedily became wet, our hands puffed and purple, our boots sodden with the water that had trickled from our clothing into them.

"Over the next ridge," Uncle Jim promised us, "is an old shack that I fixed up seven years ago. We can all make out to get in it."

Over the next ridge, therefore, we slipped and slid, thanking the god of luck for each ten feet gained. It was growing cold. The cliffs and palisades near at hand showed dimly behind the falling rain; beyond them waved and eddied the storm mists through which the mountains revealed and concealed proportions exaggerated into unearthly grandeur. Deep in the clefts of the box canons the streams were filling. The roar of their rapids echoed from innumerable precipices. A soft swish of water usurped the world of sound.

Nothing more uncomfortable or more magnificent could be imagined. We rode shivering. Each said to himself, "I can stand this—right now—at the present moment. Very well; I will do so, and I will refuse to look forward even five minutes to what I may have to stand," which is the true philosophy of tough times and the only effective way to endure discomfort.

By luck we reached the bottom of that cañon without a fall. It was wide, well grown with oak trees, and belly deep in rich horse feed— an ideal place to camp were it not for the fact that a thin sheet of water a quarter of an inch deep was flowing over the entire surface of the ground. We spurred on desperately, thinking of a warm fire and a chance to steam.

The roof of the shack had fallen in, and the floor was six inches deep in adobe mud.

We did not dismount—that would have wet our saddles—but sat on our horses taking in the details. Finally Uncle Jim came to the front with a suggestion.

"I know of a cave," said he, "close under a butte. It's a big cave, but it has such a steep floor that I'm not sure as we could stay in it; and it's back the other side of that ridge."

"I don't know how the ridge is to get back over—it was slippery enough coming this way—and the cave may shoot us out into space, but I'd like to LOOK at a dry place anyway," replied the Cattleman.

We all felt the same about it, so back over the ridge we went. About half way down the other side Uncle Jim turned sharp to the right, and as the "hog back" dropped behind us, we found ourselves out on the steep side of a mountain, the perpendicular cliff over us to the right, the river roaring savagely far down below our left, and sheets of water glazing the footing we could find among the boulders and debris. Hardly could the ponies keep from slipping sideways on the slope, as we proceeded farther and farther from the solidity of the ridge behind us, we experienced the illusion of venturing out on a tight rope over abysses of space. Even the feeling of danger was only an illusion, however, composite of the falling rain, the deepening twilight, and the night that had already enveloped the plunge of the canon below. Finally Uncle Jim stopped just within the drip from the cliffs.

"Here she is," said he.

We descended eagerly. A deer bounded away from the base of the buttes. The cave ran steep, in the manner of an inclined tunnel, far up into the dimness. We had to dig our toes in and scramble to make way up it at all, but we found it dry, and after a little search discovered a foot-ledge of earth sufficiently broad for a seat.

"That's all right," quoth Jed Parker. "Now, for sleeping places."

We scattered. Uncle Jim and Charley promptly annexed the slight overhang of the cliff whence the deer had jumped. It was dry at the moment, but we uttered pessimistic predictions if the wind should change. Tom Rich and Jim Lester had a little tent, and insisted on descending to the canon-bed.

"Got to cook there, anyways," said they, and departed with the two pack mules and their bed horse.

That left the Cattleman, Windy Bill, Jed Parker, and me. In a moment Windy Bill came up to us whispering and mysterious.

"Get your cavallos and follow me," said he.

We did so. He led us two hundred yards to another cave, twenty feet high, fifteen feet in diameter, level as a floor.

"How's that?" he cried in triumph. "Found her just now while I was rustling nigger-heads for a fire."

We unpacked our beds with chuckles of joy, and spread them carefully within the shelter of the cave. Except for the very edges, which did not much matter, our blankets and "so-guns," protected by the canvas "tarp," were reasonably dry. Every once in a while a spasm of conscience would seize one or the other of us.

"It seems sort of mean on the other fellows," ruminated Jed Parker.

"They had their first choice," cried we all.

"Uncle Jim's an old man," the Cattleman pointed out.

But Windy Bill had thought of that. "I told him of this yere cave first. But he allowed he was plumb satisfied."

We finished laying out our blankets. The result looked good to us. We all burst out laughing.

"Well, I'm sorry for those fellows," cried the Cattleman. We hobbled our horses and descended to the gleam of the fire, like guilty conspirators. There we ate hastily of meat, bread and coffee, merely for the sake of sustenance. It certainly amounted to little in the way of pleasure. The water from the direct rain, the shivering trees, and our hat brims accumulated in our plates faster than we could bail it out. The dishes were thrust under a canvas. Rich and Lester decided to remain with their tent, and so we saw them no more until morning.

We broke off back-loads of mesquite and toiled up the hill, tasting thickly the high altitude in the severe labour. At the big cave we dumped down our burdens, transported our fuel piecemeal to the vicinity of the narrow ledge, built a good fire, sat in a row, and lit our pipes. In a few moments, the blaze was burning high, and our bodies had ceased shivering. Fantastically the firelight revealed the knobs and crevices, the ledges and the arching walls. Their shadows leaped, following the flames, receding and advancing like playful beasts. Far above us was a single tiny opening through which the smoke was sucked as through a chimney. The glow ruddied the men's features. Outside was thick darkness, and the swish and rush and roar of rising waters. Listening, Windy Bill was reminded of a story. We leaned back comfortably against the sloping walls of the cave, thrust our feet toward the blaze, smoked, and hearkened to the tale of Windy Bill.

"There's a tur'ble lot of water running loose here, but I've seen the time and place where even what is in that drip would be worth a gold mine. That was in the emigrant days. They used to come over south of here, through what they called Emigrant Pass, on their way to Cali-forny. I was a kid then, about eighteen year old, and what I didn't know about Injins and Agency cattle wasn't a patch of alkali. I had a kid out-fit of h'ar bridle, lots of silver and such, and I used to ride over and be the handsome boy before such outfits as happened along.

"They were queer people, most of 'em from Missoury and such-like southern seaports, and they were tur'ble sick of travel by the time they come in sight of Emigrant Pass. Up to Santa Fe they mostly hiked along any old way, but once there they herded up together in bunches of twenty wagons or so, 'count of our old friends, Geronimo and Loco. A good many of 'em had horned cattle to their wagons, and they crawled along about two miles an hour, hotter'n hell with the blower on, nothin' to look at but a mountain a week way, chuck full of alkali, plenty of sage-brush and rattlesnakes—but mighty little water.

"Why, you boys know that country down there. Between the Chir-icahua Mountains and Emigrant Pass it's maybe a three or four days' journey for these yere bull-slingers. Mostly they filled up their bellies and their kegs, hoping to last through, but they sure found it drier than cork legs, and generally long before they hit the Springs their tongues was hangin' out a foot. You see, for all their plumb nerve in comin' so far, the most of them didn't know sic'em. They were plumb innocent in regard to savin' their water, and Injins, and such; and the long-haired buckskin fakes they picked up at Santa Fe for guides wasn't much better.

"That was where Texas Pete made his killing.

"Texas Pete was a tough citizen from the Lone Star. He was about as broad as he was long, and wore all sorts of big whiskers and black eyebrows. His heart was very bad. You never COULD tell where Texas Pete was goin' to jump next. He was a side-winder and a diamond-back and a little black rattlesnake all rolled into one. I believe that Texas

Pete person cared about as little for killin' a man as for takin' a drink—and he shorely drank without an effort. Peaceable citizens just spoke soft and minded their own business; unpeaceable citizens Texas Pete used to plant out in the sagebrush.

"Now this Texas Pete happened to discover a water hole right out in the plumb middle of the desert. He promptly annexed said water hole, digs her out, timbers her up, and lays for emigrants.

"He charged two bits a head—man or beast—and nobody got a mouthful till he paid up in hard coin.

"Think of the wads he raked in! I used to figure it up, just for the joy of envyin' him, I reckon. An average twenty-wagon outfit, first and last, would bring him in somewheres about fifty dollars—and besides he had forty-rod at four bits a glass. And outfits at that time were thicker'n spatter.

"We used all to go down sometimes to watch them come in. When they see that little canvas shack and that well, they begun to cheer up and move fast. And when they see that sign, 'Water, two bits a head,' their eyes stuck out like two raw oysters.

"Then come the kicks. What a howl they did raise, shorely. But it didn't do no manner of good. Texas Pete didn't do nothin' but sit there and smoke, with a kind of sulky gleam in one corner of his eye. He didn't even take the trouble to answer, but his Winchester lay across his lap. There wasn't no humour in the situation for him.

"'How much is your water for humans?' asks one emigrant.

"'Can't you read that sign?' Texas Pete asks him.

"'But you don't mean two bits a head for HUMANS!' yells the man. 'Why, you can get whisky for that!'

"'You can read the sign, can't you?' insists Texas Pete.

"'I can read it all right,' says the man, tryin' a new deal, 'but they tell me not to believe more'n half I read.'

"But that don't go; and Mr. Emigrant shells out with the rest.

"I didn't blame them for raisin' their howl. Why, at that time the regular water holes was chargin' five cents a head from the government freighters, and the motto was always 'Hold up Uncle Sam,' at that. Once in a while some outfit would get mad and go chargin' off dry; but it was a long, long way to the Springs, and mighty hot and dusty. Texas Pete and his one lonesome water hole shorely did a big business.

"Late one afternoon me and Gentleman Tim was joggin' along above Texas Pete's place. It was a tur'ble hot day—you had to prime yourself to spit—and we was just gettin' back from drivin' some beef up to the troops at Fort Huachuca. We was due to cross the Emigrant Trail—she's wore in tur'ble deep—you can see the ruts to-day. When we topped the rise we see a little old outfit just makin' out to drag along.

"It was one little schooner all by herself, drug along by two poor old cavallos that couldn't have pulled my hat off. Their tongues was out, and every once in a while they'd stick in a chuck-hole. Then a man would get down and put his shoulder to the wheel, and everybody'd take a heave, and up they'd come, all a-trembling and weak.

"Tim and I rode down just to take a look at the curiosity.

"A thin-lookin' man was drivin', all humped up.

"'Hullo, stranger,' says I, 'ain't you 'fraid of Injins?'

"'Yes,' says he.

"'Then why are you travellin' through an Injin country all alone?'

"'Couldn't keep up,' says he. 'Can I get water here?'

"'I reckon,' I answers.

"He drove up to the water trough there at Texas Pete's, me and Gentleman Tim followin' along because our trail led that way. But he hadn't more'n stopped before Texas Pete was out.

"'Cost you four bits to water them hosses,' says he.

"The man looked up kind of bewildered. 'I'm sorry,' says he, 'I ain't got no four bits. I got my roll lifted off'n me.'

"'No water, then,' growls Texas Pete back at him.

"The man looked about him helpless.

"'How far is it to the next water?' he asks me. 'Twenty mile,' I tells him.

"'My God!' he says, to himself-like.

"Then he shrugged his shoulders very tired. 'All right. It's gettin' the cool of the evenin'; we'll make it.' He turns into the inside of that old schooner. 'Gi' me the cup, Sue.'

"A white-faced woman who looked mighty good to us alkalis opened the flaps and gave out a tin cup, which the man pointed out to fill.

"'How many of you is they?' asks Texas Pete.

"'Three,' replies the man, wondering.

"'Well, six bits, then,' says Texas Pete, 'cash down.'

"At that the man straightens up a little. 'I ain't askin' for no water for my stock,' says he, 'but my wife and baby has been out in this sun all day without a drop of water. Our cask slipped a hoop and bust just this side of Dos Cabesas. The poor kid is plumb dry.'

"'Two bits a head,' says Texas Pete.

"At that the woman comes out, a little bit of a baby in her arms. The kid had fuzzy yellow hair, and its face was flushed red and shiny. 'Shorely you won't refuse a sick child a drink of water, sir,' says she.

"But Texas Pete had some sort of a special grouch; I guess he was just beginning to get his snowshoes off after a fight with his own forty-rod.

"'What the hell are you-all doin' on the trail without no money at all?' he growls, 'and how do you expect to get along? Such plumb tenderfeet drive me weary.'

"'Well,' says the man, still reasonable, 'I ain't got no money, but I'll give you six bits' worth of flour or trade or an'thin' I got.'

"'I don't run no truck-store,' snaps Texas Pete, and turns square on his heel and goes back to his chair.

"'Got six bits about you?' whispers Gentleman Tim to me.

"'Not a red,' I answers.

"Gentleman Tim turns to Texas Pete. 'Let 'em have a drink, Pete. I'll pay you next time I come down.'

"'Cash down,' growls Pete.

"'You're the meanest man I ever see,' observes Tim. 'I wouldn't speak to you if I met you in hell carryin' a lump of ice in your hand.'

"'You're the softest I ever see,' sneers Pete. 'Don't they have any genooine Texans down your way?'

"'Not enough to make it disagreeable,' says Tim.

"'That lets you out,' growls Pete, gettin' hostile and handlin' of his rifle.

"Which the man had been standin' there bewildered, the cup hangin' from his finger. At last, lookin' pretty desperate, he stooped down to dig up a little of the wet from an overflow puddle lyin' at his feet. At the same time the hosses, left sort of to themselves and bein' drier than a covered bridge, drug forward and stuck their noses in the trough.

"Gentleman Tim and me was sittin' there on our hosses, a little to one side. We saw Texas Pete jump up from his chair, take a quick aim, and cut loose with his rifle. It was plumb unexpected to us. We hadn't thought of any shootin', and our six-shooters was tied in, 'count of the jumpy country we'd been drivin' the steers over. But Gentleman Tim, who had unslung his rope, aimin' to help the hosses out of the chuckhole, snatched her off the horn, and with one of the prettiest twenty-foot flip throws I ever see done he snaked old Texas Pete right out of his wicky-up, gun and all. The old renegade did his best to twist around for a shot at us; but it was no go; and I never enjoyed hog-tying a critter more in my life than I enjoyed hog-tying Texas Pete. Then we turned to see what damage had been done.

"We were some relieved to find the family all right, but Texas Pete had bored one of them poor old crow-bait hosses plumb through the head.

"'It's lucky for you, you don't get the old man,' says Gentleman Tim very quiet and polite.

"Which Gentleman Tim was an Irishman, and I'd been on the range long enough with him to know that when he got quiet and polite it was time to dodge behind something.

"'I hope, sir,' says he to the stranger, 'that you will give your wife and baby a satisfying drink. As for your hoss, pray do not be under any apprehension. Our friend, Mr. Texas Pete, here, has kindly consented to make good any deficiencies from his own corral.'

"Tim could talk high, wide, and handsome when he set out to.

"The man started to say something; but I managed to herd him to one side.

"'Let him alone,' I whispers. 'When he talks that way, he's mad; and when he's mad, it's better to leave nature to supply the lightnin' rods.'

"He seemed to sabe all right, so we built us a little fire and started some grub, while Gentleman Tim walked up and down very grand and fierce.

"By and by he seemed to make up his mind. He went over and untied Texas Pete.

"'Stand up, you hound,' says he. 'Now listen to me. If you make a break to get away, or if you refuse to do just as I tell you, I won't shoot you, but I'll march you up country and see that Geronimo gets you.'

"He sorted out a shovel and pick, made Texas Pete carry them right along the trail a quarter, and started him to diggin' a hole. Texas Pete started in hard enough, Tim sittin' over him on his hoss, his six-shooter loose, and his rope free. The man and I stood by, not darin' to say a word. After a minute or so Texas Pete began to work slower and slower. By and by he stopped. 'Look here,' says he, 'is this here thing my grave?'

"'I am goin' to see that you give the gentleman's hoss decent interment,' says Gentleman Tim very polite.

"'Bury a hoss!' growls Texas Pete. But he didn't say any more. Tim cocked his six-shooter.

"'Perhaps you'd better quit panting and sweat a little,' says he.

"'Texas Pete worked hard for a while, for Tim's quietness was beginning to scare him up the worst way. By and by he had got down maybe four or five feet, and Tim got off his hoss.

"'I think that will do,' says he.

"'You may come out. Billy, my son, cover him. Now, Mr. Texas Pete,' he says, cold as steel, 'there is the grave. We will place the hoss in it. Then I intend to shoot you and put you in with the hoss, and write you an epitaph that will be a comfort to such travellers of the Trail as are honest, and a warnin' to such as are not. I'd as soon kill you now as an hour from now, so you may make a break for it if you feel like it.'

"He stooped over to look into the hole. I thought he looked an extra long time, but when he raised his head his face had changed complete. 'March!' says he very brisk.

"We all went back to the shack. From the corral Tim took Texas Pete's best team and hitched her to the old schooner.

"'There,' says he to the man. 'Now you'd better hit the trail. Take that whisky keg there for water. Good-bye.'

"We sat there without sayin' a word for some time after the schooner had pulled out. Then Tim says, very abrupt: 'I've changed my mind.' He got up. 'Come on, Billy,' says he to me. 'We'll just leave our friend tied up. I'll be back to-morrow to turn you loose. In the meantime it won't hurt you a bit to be a little uncomfortable, and hungry—and thirsty.'

"We rode off just about sundown, leavin' Texas Pete lashed tight.

"Now all this knocked me hell-west and crooked, and I said so, but I couldn't get a word out of Gentleman Tim. All the answer I could get was just little laughs.

"We drawed into the ranch near midnight, but next mornin' Tim had a long talk with the boss, and the result was that the whole outfit was instructed to arm up with a pick or a shovel apiece, and to get set for Texas Pete's. We got there a little after noon, turned the old boy out—without firearms—and then began to dig at a place Tim told us to, near that grave of Texas Pete's. In three hours we had the finest water-hole developed you ever want to see. Then the boss stuck up a sign that said: PUBLIC WATER-HOLE. WATER, FREE.

"'Now you old skin,' says he to Texas Pete, 'charge all you want to on your own property. But if I ever hear of your layin' claim to this other hole, I'll shore make you hard to catch.'

"Then we rode off home. You see, when Gentleman Tim inspected that grave, he noted indications of water; and it struck him that runnin' the old renegade out of business was a neater way of gettin' even than merely killin' him.

Somebody threw a fresh mesquite on the fire. The flames leaped up again, showing a thin trickle of water running down the other side of the cave. The steady downpour again made itself prominent through the re-established silence.

"What did Texas Pete do after that?" asked the Cattleman.

"Texas Pete?" chuckled Windy Bill. "Well, he put in a heap of his spare time lettin' Tim alone."

16

THE TWO-GUN MAN

BY CHARLES ALDEN SELTZER

~~~~~~

Charles Alden Seltzer was one of the stalwarts of Western fiction, with many novels and magazine short stories to his credit. Sixteen of his stories were made into movies. His ability to capture the spirit of the Old West is delightfully evident in these opening chapters of this 1911 shoot-'em-up saga, The Two-Gun Man.

~~~~~~

From the crest of Three Mile Slope the man on the pony could see the town of Dry Bottom straggling across the gray floor of the flat, its low, squat buildings looking like so many old boxes blown there by an idle wind, or unceremoniously dumped there by a careless fate and left, regardless, to carry out the scheme of desolation.

Apparently the rider was in no hurry, for, as the pony topped the rise and the town burst suddenly into view, the little animal pricked up its ears and quickened its pace, only to feel the reins suddenly tighten and to hear the rider's voice gruffly discouraging haste. Therefore, the pony pranced gingerly, alert, champing the bit impatiently, picking its way over the lumpy hills of stone and cactus, but holding closely to the trail.

The man lounged in the saddle, his strong, well-knit body swaying gracefully, his eyes, shaded by the brim of his hat, narrowed with slight mockery and interest as he gazed steadily at the town that lay before him.

"I reckon that must be Dry Bottom," he said finally, mentally taking in its dimensions. "If that's so, I've only got twenty miles to go."

Halfway down the slope, and still a mile and a half from the town, the rider drew the pony to a halt. He dropped the reins over the high pommel of the saddle, drew out his two guns, one after the other, rolled the cylinders, and returned the guns to their holsters. He had heard something of Dry Bottom's reputation and in examining his pistols he was merely preparing himself for an emergency. For a moment after he had replaced the weapons he sat quietly in the saddle. Then he shook out the reins, spoke to the pony, and the little animal set forward at a slow lope.

An ironic traveler, passing through Dry Bottom in its younger days, before civic spirit had definitely centered its efforts upon things nomenclatural, had hinted that the town should be known as "dry" because of the fact that while it boasted seven buildings, four were saloons; and that "bottom" might well be used as a suffix, because, in the nature of things, a town of seven buildings, four of which were saloons, might reasonably expect to descend to the very depths of moral iniquity.

The ironic traveler had spoken with prophetic wisdom. Dry Bottom was trying as best it knew how to wallow in the depths of sin. Unlovely, soiled, desolate of verdure, dumped down upon a flat of sand in a treeless waste, amid cactus, crabbed yucca, scorpions, horned toads, and rattlesnakes, Dry Bottom had forgotten its morals, subverted its principles, and neglected its God.

As the rider approached to within a few hundred yards of the edge of town he became aware of a sudden commotion. He reined in his pony, allowing it to advance at a walk, while with alert eyes he endeavored to search out the cause of the excitement. He did not have long to watch for the explanation.

A man had stepped out of the door of one of the saloons, slowly walking twenty feet away from it toward the center of the street. Immediately other men had followed. But these came only to a point just outside the door. For some reason which was not apparent to the rider, they were giving the first man plenty of room.

The rider was now able to distinguish the faces of the men in the group, and he gazed with interested eyes at the man who had first issued from the door of the saloon.

The man was tall—nearly as tall as the rider—and in his every movement seemed sure of himself. He was young, seemingly about thirty-five, with shifty, insolent eyes and a hard mouth whose lips were just now curved into a self-conscious smile.

The rider had now approached to within fifty feet of the man, halting his pony at the extreme end of the hitching rail that skirted the front of the saloon. He sat carelessly in the saddle, his gaze fixed on the man.

The men who had followed the first man out, to the number of a dozen, were apparently deeply interested, though plainly skeptical. A short, fat man, who was standing near the saloon door, looked on with a half-sneer. Several others were smiling blandly. A tall man on the extreme edge of the crowd, near the rider, was watching the man in the street gravely. Other men had allowed various expressions to creep into their faces. But all were silent.

Not so the man in the street. Plainly, here was conceit personified, and yet a conceit mingled with a maddening insolence. His expression told all that this thing which he was about to do was worthy of the closest attention. He was the axis upon which the interest of the universe revolved.

Certainly he knew of the attention he was attracting. Men were approaching from the other end of the street, joining the group in front of the saloon—which the rider now noticed was called the "Silver Dollar." The newcomers were inquisitive; they spoke in low tones to the men who had arrived before them, gravely inquiring the cause.

But the man in the street seemed not disturbed by his rapidly swelling audience. He stood in the place he had selected, his insolent eyes roving over the assembled company, his thin, expressive lips opening a very little to allow words to filter through them.

"Gents," he said, "you're goin' to see some shootin'! I told you in the Silver Dollar that I could keep a can in the air while I put five holes in it. There's some of you gassed about bein' showed, not believin'. An' now I'm goin' to show you!"

He reached down and took up a can that had lain at his feet, removing the red lithographed label, which had a picture of a large tomato in the center of it. The can was revealed, naked and shining in the white sunlight. The man placed the can in his left hand and drew his pistol with the right.

Then he tossed the can into the air. While it still rose, his weapon exploded, the can shook spasmodically and turned clear over. Then in rapid succession followed four other explosions, the last occurring just before the can reached the ground. The man smiled, still holding the smoking weapon in his hand.

The tall man on the extreme edge of the group now stepped forward and examined the can, while several other men crowded about to look. There were exclamations of surprise. It was curious to see how quickly enthusiasm and awe succeeded skepticism.

"He's done it, boys!" cried the tall man, holding the can aloft. "Bored it in five places!" He stood erect, facing the crowd. "I reckon that's some shootin'!" He now threw a glance of challenge and defiance about him. "I've got a hundred dollars to say that there ain't another man in this here town can do it!"

Several men tried, but none equaled the first man's performance. Many of the men could not hit the can at all. The first man watched their efforts, sneers twitching his lips as man after man failed.

Presently all had tried. Watching closely, the rider caught an expression of slight disappointment on the tall man's face. The rider was the only man who had not yet tried his skill with the pistol, and the man in the street now looked up at him, his eyes glittering with an insolent challenge. As it happened, the rider glanced at the shooter at the instant the latter had turned to look up at him. Their eyes met fairly, the shooter's conveying a silent taunt. The rider smiled, slight mockery glinting his eyes.

Apparently the stranger did not care to try his skill. He still sat lazily in the saddle, his gaze wandering languidly over the crowd. The latter plainly expected him to take part in the shooting match and was impatient over his inaction.

"Two-gun," sneered a man who stood near the saloon door. "I wonder what he totes them two guns for?"

The shooter heard and turned toward the man who had spoken, his lips wreathed satirically.

"I reckon he wouldn't shoot nothin' with them," he said, addressing the man who had spoken.

Several men laughed! The tall man who had revealed interest before now raised a hand, checking further comment.

"That offer of a hundred to the man who can beat that shootin' still goes," he declared. "An' I'm taking off the condition. The man that tries don't have to belong to Dry Bottom. No stranger is barred!"

The stranger's glance again met the shooter's. The latter grinned felinely. Then the rider spoke. The crowd gave him its polite attention.

"I reckon you-all think you've seen some shootin'," he said in a steady, even voice, singularly free from boast. "But I reckon you ain't seen any real shootin'." He turned to the tall, grave-faced man. "I ain't got no hundred," he said, "but I'm goin' to show you."

He still sat in the saddle. But now with an easy motion he swung down and hitched his pony to the rail.

THE STRANGER SHOOTS

The stranger seemed taller on the ground than in the saddle and an admirable breadth of shoulder and slenderness of waist told eloquently of strength. He could not have been over twenty-five or six. Yet certain hard lines about his mouth, the glint of mockery in his eyes, the pronounced forward thrust of the chin, the indefinable force that seemed to radiate from him, told the casual observer that here was a man who must be approached with care.

But apparently the shooter saw no such signs. In the first glance that had been exchanged between the two men there had been a lack of ordinary cordiality. And now, as the rider slid down from his pony and advanced toward the center of the street, the shooter's lips curled. Writhing through them came slow-spoken words.

"You runnin' sheep, stranger?"

The rider's lips smiled, but his eyes were steady and cold. In them shone a flash of cold humor. He stood, quietly contemplating his insulter.

Smiles appeared on the faces of several of the onlookers. The tall man with the grave face watched with a critical eye. The insult had been deliberate, and many men crouched, plainly expecting a serious outcome. But the stranger made no move toward his guns, and when he answered he might have been talking about the weather, so casual was his tone.

"I reckon you think you're a plum man," he said quietly. "But if you are, you ain't showed it much—buttin' in with that there wise observation. An' there's some men who think that shootin' at a man is more excitin' than shootin' at a can."

There was a grim quality in his voice now. He leaned forward slightly, his eyes cold and alert. The shooter sneered experimentally. Again the audience smiled.

But the tall man now stepped forward. "You've made your play, stranger," he said quietly. "I reckon it's up to you to make good."

"Correct," agreed the stranger. "I'm goin' to show you some real shootin'. You got another can?"

Some one dived into the Silver Dollar and returned in a flash with another tomato can. This the stranger took, removing the label, as the shooter had done. Then, smiling, he took a position in the center of the street, the can in his right hand.

He did not draw his weapon as the shooter had done, but stood loosely in his place, his right hand still grasping the can, the left swinging idly by his side. Apparently he did not mean to shoot. Sneers reached the faces of several men in the crowd. The shooter growled, "Fourflush."

There was a flash as the can rose twenty feet in the air, propelled by the right hand of the stranger. As the can reached the apex of its climb the stranger's right hand descended and grasped the butt of the weapon at his right hip. There was a flash as the gun came out; a gasp of astonishment from the watchers. The can was arrested in the first foot of its descent by the shock of the first bullet striking it. It jumped up and out and again began its interrupted fall, only to stop dead still in the air as another bullet struck it. There was an infinitesimal pause, and then twice more the can shivered and jumped. No man in the crowd but could tell that the bullets were striking true.

The can was still ten feet in the air and well out from the stranger. The latter whipped his weapon to a level, the bullet striking the can and driving it twenty feet from him. Then it dropped. But when it was within five feet of the ground the stranger's gun spoke again. The can leaped, careened sideways, and fell, shattered, to the street, thirty feet distant from the stranger.

Several men sprang forward to examine it.

"Six times!" ejaculated the tall man in an awed tone. "An' he didn't pull his gun till he'd throwed the can!"

He approached the stranger, drawing him confidentially aside. The crowd slowly dispersed, loudly proclaiming the stranger's ability with the six-shooter. The latter took his honors lightly, the mocking smile again on his face.

"I'm lookin' for a man who can shoot," said the tall man, when the last man of the crowd had disappeared into the saloon.

The stranger smiled. "I reckon you've just seen some shootin'," he returned.

The tall man smiled mirthlessly. "You particular about what you shoot at?" he inquired.

The stranger's lips straightened coldly. "I used to have that habit," he returned evenly.

"Hard luck?" queried the tall man.

"I'm rollin' in wealth," stated the stranger, with an ironic sneer.

The tall man's eyes glittered. "Where you from?" he questioned.

"You c'n have three guesses," returned the stranger, his eyes narrowing with the mockery that the tall man had seen in them before.

The tall man adopted a placative tone. "I ain't wantin' to butt into your business," he said. "I was wantin' to find out if any one around here knowed you."

"This town didn't send any reception committee to meet me, did they?" smiled the stranger.

"Correct," said the tall man. He leaned closer. "You willin' to work your guns for me for a hundred a month?"

The stranger looked steadily into the tall man's eyes.

"You've been right handy askin' questions," he said. "Mebbe you'll answer some. What's your name?"

"Stafford," returned the tall man. "I'm managin' the Two Diamond, over on the Ute."

The stranger's eyelashes flickered slightly. His eyes narrowed quizzically. "What you wantin' of a gun-man?" he asked.

"Rustler," returned the other shortly.

The stranger smiled. "Figger on shootin' him?" he questioned.

Stafford hesitated. "Well, no," he returned. "That is, not until I'm sure I've got the right one." He seized the stranger's arm in a confidential grip. "You see," he explained, "I don't know just where I'm at. There's been a rustler workin' on the herd, an' I ain't been able to get close enough to find out who it is. But rustlin' has got to be stopped. I've sent over to Raton to get a man named Ned Ferguson, who's been workin' for Sid Tucker, of the Lazy J. Tucker wrote me quite a while back, tellin' me that this man was plum slick at nosin' out rustlers. He was to come to the Two Diamond two weeks ago. But he ain't showed up, an' I've about concluded that he ain't comin'. An' so I come over to Dry Bottom to find a man."

"You've found one," smiled the stranger.

Stafford drew out a handful of double eagles and pressed them into the other's hand. "I'm goin' over to the Two Diamond now," he said. "You'd better wait a day or two, so's no one will get wise. Come right to me, like you was wantin' a job."

He started toward the hitching rail for his pony, hesitated and then walked back.

"I didn't get your name," he smiled.

The stranger's eyes glittered humorously. "It's Ferguson," he said quietly.

Stafford's eyes widened with astonishment. Then his right hand went out and grasped the other's.

"Well, now," he said warmly, "that's what I call luck."

Ferguson smiled. "Mebbe it's luck," he returned. "But before I go over to work for you there's got to be an understandin'. I c'n shoot some," he continued, looking steadily at Stafford, "but I ain't runnin' around the country shootin' men without cause. I'm willin' to try an' find your rustler for you, but I ain't shootin' him—unless he goes to crowdin' me mighty close."

"I'm agreein' to that," returned Stafford.

He turned again, looking back over his shoulder. "You'll sure be over?" he questioned.

"I'll be there the day after tomorrow," stated Ferguson.

He turned and went into the Silver Dollar. Stafford mounted his pony and loped rapidly out of town.

17

THE LITTLE GOLD MINERS OF THE SIERRAS

BY JOAQUIN MILLER

Joaquin Miller was the pen name of Cincinnatus Hiner Miller, a poet, journalist and author whose particular area of interest and expression was the California Gold Rush. Although he achieved great success abroad, his critical reputation in America focused on his excessive romanticism and sentimentality, as this 1886 short story shows.

Their mother had died crossing the plains, and their father had had a leg broken by a wagon wheel passing over it as they descended the Sierras, and he was for a long time after reaching the mines miserable, lame and poor.

The eldest boy, Jim Keene, as I remember him, was a bright little fellow, but wild as an Indian and full of mischief. The next eldest child, Madge, was a girl of ten, her father's favorite, and she was wild enough too. The youngest was Stumps. Poor, timid, starved Little Stumps! I never knew his real name. But he was the baby, and hardly yet out of petticoats. And he was very short in the legs, very short in the body, very short in the arms and neck; and so he was called Stumps because he looked it. In fact he seemed to have stopped growing entirely. Oh, you don't know how hard the old Plains were on everybody, when we crossed them in ox-wagons, and it took more than half a year to make the journey. The little children, those that did not die, turned brown like the Indians, in that long, dreadful journey of seven months, and stopped growing for a time.

For the first month or two after reaching the Sierras, old Mr. Keene limped about among the mines trying to learn the mystery of finding gold, and the art of digging. But at last, having grown strong enough, he went to work for wages, to get bread for his half-wild little ones, for they were destitute indeed.

Things seemed to move on well, then. Madge cooked the simple meals, and Little Stumps clung to her dress with his little pinched brown hand wherever she went, while Jim whooped it over the hills and chased jack-rabbits as if he were a greyhound. He would climb trees, too, like a squirrel. And, oh!—it was deplorable—but how he could swear!

At length some of the miners, seeing the boy must come to some bad end if not taken care of, put their heads and their pockets together and sent the children to school. This school was a mile away over the beautiful brown hills, a long, pleasant walk under the green California oaks.

Well, Jim would take the little tin dinner bucket, and his slate, and all their books under his arm and go booming ahead about half a mile in advance, while Madge with brown Little Stumps clinging to her side like a burr, would come stepping along the trail under the oak-trees as fast as she could after him.

But if a jack-rabbit, or a deer, or a fox crossed Jim's path, no matter how late it was, or how the teacher had threatened him, he would drop books, lunch, slate and all, and spitting on his hands and rolling up his sleeves, would bound away after it, yelling like a wild Indian. And some days, so fascinating was the chase, Jim did not appear at the schoolhouse at all; and of course Madge and Stumps played truant too. Sometimes a week together would pass and the Keene children would not be seen at the schoolhouse. Visits from the schoolmaster produced no lasting effect. The children would come for a day or two, then be seen no more. The schoolmaster and their father at last had a serious talk about the matter.

"What can I do with him?" said Mr. Keene.

"You'll have to put him to work," said the schoolmaster. "Set him to hunting nuggets instead of bird's-nests. I guess what the boy wants is some honest means of using his strength. He's a good boy, Mr. Keene; don't despair of him. Jim would be proud to be an 'honest miner.' Jim's a good boy, Mr. Keene."

"Well, then, thank you, Schoolmaster," said Mr. Keene. "Jim's a good boy; and Madge is good, Mr. Schoolmaster; and poor starved and stunted motherless Little Stumps, he is good as gold, Mr. Schoolmaster. And I want to be a mother to 'em—I want to be father and mother to 'em all, Mr. Schoolmaster. And I'll follow your advice. I'll put 'em all to work a-huntin' for gold."

The next day away up on the hillside under a pleasant oak, where the air was sweet and cool, and the ground soft and dotted over with flowers, the tender-hearted old man that wanted to be "father and mother both," "located" a claim. The flowers were kept fresh by a little stream of waste water from the ditch that girded the brow of the hill above. Here he set a sluice-box and put his three little miners at work with pick, pan and shovel. There he left them and limped back to his own place in the mine below.

And how they did work! And how pleasant it was here under the broad boughs of the oak, with the water rippling through the sluice on the soft, loose soil which they shoveled into the long sluice-box. They could see the mule-trains going and coming, and the clouds of dust far below which told them the stage was whirling up the valley. But Jim kept steadily on at his work day after day. Even though jack-rabbits and squirrels appeared on the very scene, he would not leave till, like the rest of the honest miners, he could shoulder his pick and pan and go down home with the setting sun.

Sometimes the men who had tried to keep the children at school, would come that way, and with a shy smile, talk very wisely about whether or not the new miners would "strike it" under the cool oak among the flowers on the hill. But Jim never stopped to talk much. He dug and wrestled away, day after day, now up to his waist in the pit.

One Saturday evening the old man limped up the hillside to help the young miners "clean up." He sat down at the head of the sluice-box and gave directions how they should turn off the most of the water, wash down the "toilings" very low, lift up the "riffle," brush down the "apron," and finally set the pan in the lower end of the "sluice-toil" and pour in the quicksilver to gather up and hold the gold.

"What for you put your hand in de water for, papa?" queried Little Stumps, who had left off his work, which consisted mainly of pulling flowers and putting them in the sluice-box to see them float away. He was sitting by his father's side, and he looked up in his face as he spoke.

"Hush, child," said the old man softly, as he again dipped his thumb and finger in his vest pocket as if about to take snuff. But he did not take snuff. Again his hand was reached down to the rippling water at the head of the sluice-box. And this time curious but obedient Little Stumps was silent.

Suddenly there was a shout, such a shout from Jim as the hills had not heard since he was a schoolboy.

He had found the "color." "Two colors! three, four, five—a dozen!" The boy shouted like a Modoc, threw down the brush and scraper, and kissed his little sister over and over, and cried as he did so; then he whispered softly to her as he again took up his brush and scraper, that it was "for papa; all for poor papa; that he did not care for himself, but he did want to help poor, tired, and crippled papa." But papa did not seem to be excited so very much.

The little miners were now continually wild with excitement. They were up and at work Monday morning at dawn. The men who were in the father's tender secret, congratulated the children heartily and made them presents of several small nuggets to add to their little horde.

In this way they kept steadily at work for half the summer. All the gold was given to papa to keep. Papa weighed it each week, and I suppose secretly congratulated himself that he was getting back about as much as he put in.

Before quite the end of the third month, Jim struck a thin bed of blue gravel. The miners who had been happily chuckling and laughing among themselves to think how they had managed to keep Jim out of mischief, began to look at each other and wonder how in the world blue gravel ever got up there on the hill. And in a few days more there was a well-defined bed of blue gravel, too; and not one of the miners could make it out.

One Saturday evening shortly after, as the old man weighed their gold he caught his breath, started, and stood up straight; straighter than he had stood since he crossed the Plains. Then he hastily left the cabin. He went up the hill to the children's claim almost without limping. Then he took a pencil and an old piece of a letter, and wrote out a notice and tacked it up on the big oak-tree, claiming those mining claims according to miners' law, for the three children. A couple of miners laughed as they went by in the twilight, to see what he was doing; and he laughed with them. But as he limped on down the hill he smiled.

That night as they sat at supper, he told the children that as they had been such faithful and industrious miners, he was going to give them each a present, besides a little gold to spend as they pleased.

So he went up to the store and bought Jim a red shirt, long black and bright gum boots, a broad-brimmed hat, and a belt. He also bought each of the other children some pretty trappings, and gave each a dollar's worth of gold dust. Madge and Stumps handed their gold back to "poor papa." But Jim was crazy with excitement. He put on his new clothes and went forth to spend his dollar. And what do you suppose he bought? I hesitate to tell you. But what he bought was a pipe and a paper of tobacco!

That red shirt, that belt and broad-brimmed hat, together with the shiny top boots, had been too much for Jim's balance. How could a man—he spoke of himself as a man now—how could a man be an "honest miner" and not smoke a pipe?

And now with his manly clothes and his manly pipe he was to be so happy! He had all that went to make up "the honest miner." True, he did not let his father know about the pipe. He hid it under his pillow at night. He meant to have his first smoke at the sluice-box, as a miner should.

Monday morning he was up with the sun and ready for his work. His father, who worked down the Gulch, had already gone before the children had finished their breakfast. So now Jim filled his brand-new pipe very leisurely; and with as much calm unconcern as if he had been smoking for forty years, he stopped to scratch a match on the door as he went out.

From under his broad hat he saw his little sister watching him, and he fairly swelled with importance as Stumps looked up at him with childish wonder. Leaving Madge to wash the few tin dishes and follow as she could with Little Stumps, he started on up the hill, pipe in mouth.

He met several miners, but he puffed away like a tug-boat against the tide, and went on. His bright new boots whetted and creaked together, the warm wind lifted the broad brim of his sombrero and his bright new red shirt was really beautiful, with the green grass and oaks for a background—and so this brave young man climbed the hill to his mine.

Ah, he was so happy!

Suddenly, as he approached the claim, his knees began to smite together, and he felt so weak he could hardly drag one foot after the other. He threw down his pick; he began to tremble and spin around. The world seemed to be turning over and over, and he trying in vain to hold on to it. He jerked the pipe from his teeth, and throwing it down on the bank, he tumbled down too, and clutching at the grass with both hands tried hard, oh! so hard, to hold the world from slipping from under him.

"O, Jim, you are white as snow," cried Madge as she came up.

"White as 'er sunshine, an' blue, an' green too, sisser. Look at brurrer 'all colors,'" piped Little Stumps pitifully.

"O, Jim, Jim—brother Jim, what is the matter?" sobbed Madge.

"Sunstroke," murmured the young man, smiling grimly, like a true Californian. "No; it is not sunstroke, it's—it's cholera," he added in dismay over his falsehood.

Poor boy! He was sorry for this second lie too. He fairly groaned in agony of body and soul.

Oh, how he did hate that pipe! How he did want to get up and jump on it and smash it into a thousand pieces! But he could not get up or turn around or move at all without betraying his unmanly secret.

A couple of miners came up, but Jim feebly begged them to go.

"Sunstroke," whispered the sister.

"No; tolera," piped poor Little Stumps.

"Get out! Leave me!" groaned the young red-shirted miner of the Sierras.

The biggest of the two miners bent over him a moment.

"Yas; it's both," he muttered. "Cholera-nicotine-fantum!" Then he looked at his partner and winked wickedly. Without a word, he took the limp young miner up in his arms and bore him down the hill to his father's cabin, while Stumps and Madge ran along at either side, and tenderly and all the time kept asking what was good for "cholera."

The other old "honest miner" lingered behind to pick up the baleful pipe which he knew was somewhere there; and when the little party was far enough down the hill, he took it up and buried it in his own capacious pocket with a half-sorrowful laugh. "Poor little miner," he sighed.

"Don't ever swear any more, Windy," pleaded the boy to the miner who had carried him down the hill, as he leaned over him, "and don't never lie. I am going to die, Windy, and I should like to be good. Windy, it ain't sunstroke, it's—"

"Hush yer mouth," growled Windy. "I know what 'tis! We've left it on the hill."

The boy turned his face to the wall. The conviction was strong upon him that he was going to die. The world spun round now very,

very fast indeed. Finally, half-rising in bed, he called Little Stumps to his side:

"Stumps, dear, good Little Stumps, if I die don't you never, never try for to smoke; for that's what's the matter with me. No, Stumps— dear little brother Stumps—don't you never try for to go the whole of the 'honest miner,' for it can't be did by a boy! We're nothing but boys, you and I, Stumps—Little Stumps."

He sank back in bed and Little Stumps and his sister cried and cried, and kissed him and kissed him.

The miners who had gathered around loved him now, every one, for daring to tell the truth and take the shame of his folly so bravely.

"I'm going to die, Windy," groaned the boy.

Windy could stand no more of it. He took Jim's hand with a cheery laugh. "Git well in half an hour," said he, "now that you've out with the truth."

And so he did. By the time his father came home he was sitting up; and he ate breakfast the next morning as if nothing had happened. But he never tried to smoke any more as long as he lived. And he never lied, and he never swore any more.

Oh, no! This Jim that I have been telling you of is "Moral Jim," of the Sierras. The mine? Oh! I almost forgot. Well, that blue dirt was the old bed of the stream, and it was ten times richer than where the miners were all at work below. Struck it! I should say so! Ask any of the old Sierras miners about "The Children's Claim," if you want to hear just how rich they struck it.

18

THE MYSTERIOUS RIDER

BY ZANE GREY

Zane Grey played such an important role in the development and popularization of the Western novel that he more than deserves to have more than one entry in this book. Unlike the gun duels and cattle stampedes with which he and, indeed, the genre are associated, here's more than a touch of old-fashioned—or perhaps eternal—romance set amid the backdrop of the Old West in this 1921 tale.

A September sun, losing some of its heat if not its brilliance, was dropping low in the west over the black Colorado range. Purple haze began to thicken in the timbered notches. Gray foothills, round and billowy, rolled down from the higher country. They were smooth, sweeping, with long velvety slopes and isolated patches of aspens that blazed in autumn gold. Splotches of red vine colored the soft gray of sage. Old White Slides, a mountain scarred by avalanche, towered with bleak rocky peak above the valley, sheltering it from the north.

A girl rode along the slope, with gaze on the sweep and range and color of the mountain fastness that was her home. She followed an old trail which led to a bluff overlooking an arm of the valley. Once it had been a familiar lookout for her, but she had not visited the place of late. It was associated with serious hours of her life. Here seven years before, when she was twelve, she had made a hard choice to please her guardian the old rancher whom she loved and called father, who had indeed been a father to her. That choice had been to go to school in Denver. Four years she had lived away from her beloved gray hills and black mountains. Only once since her return had she climbed to this height, and that occasion, too, was memorable as an unhappy hour. It had been three years ago. Today girlish ordeals and griefs seemed back in the past: she was a woman at nineteen and face to face with the first great problem in her life.

The trail came up back of the bluff, through a clump of aspens with white trunks and yellow fluttering leaves, and led across a level bench of luxuriant grass and wild flowers to the rocky edge.

She dismounted and threw the bridle. Her mustang; used to being petted, rubbed his sleek, dark head against her and evidently expected like demonstration in return, but as none was forthcoming he bent his nose to the grass and began grazing. The girl's eyes were intent upon some waving, slender, white-and-blue flowers. They smiled up wanly, like pale stars, out of the long grass that had a tinge of gold.

"Columbines," she mused, wistfully, as she plucked several of the flowers and held them up to gaze wonderingly at them, as if to see in them some revelation of the mystery that shrouded her birth and her name. Then she stood with dreamy gaze upon the distant ranges.

"Columbine! . . . So they named me those miners who found me a baby lost in the woods asleep among the columbines." She spoke aloud, as if the sound of her voice might convince her.

So much of the mystery of her had been revealed that day by the man she had always called father. Vaguely she had always been conscious of some mystery, something strange about her childhood, some relation never explained.

"No name but Columbine," she whispered, sadly, and now she understood a strange longing of her heart.

Scarcely an hour back, as she ran down the wide porch of White Slides ranch-house, she had encountered the man who had taken care of her all her life. He had looked upon her as kindly and fatherly as of old, yet with a difference. She seemed to see him as old Bill Belllounds, pioneer and rancher, of huge frame and broad face, hard and scarred and grizzled, with big eyes of blue fire.

"Collie," the old man had said, "I reckon hyar's news. A letter from Jack. . . . He's comin' home."

Belllounds had waved the letter. His huge hand trembled as he reached to put it on her shoulder. The hardness of him seemed strangely softened. Jack was his son. Buster Jack, the range had always called him, with other terms, less kind, that never got to the ears of his father. Jack had been sent away three years ago, just before Columbine's return from school. Therefore she had not seen him for over seven years. But she remembered him well—a big, rangy boy, handsome and wild, who had made her childhood almost unendurable.

"Yes my son Jack he's comin' home," said Belllounds, with a break in his voice. "An', Collie, now I must tell you somethin'."

"Yes, dad," she had replied, with strong clasp of the heavy hand on her shoulder.

"Thet's just it, lass. I ain't your dad. I've tried to be a dad to you an' I've loved you as my own. But you're not flesh an' blood of mine. An' now I must tell you."

The brief story followed. Seventeen years ago miners working a claim of Belllounds's in the mountains above Middle Park had found a child asleep in the columbines along the trail. Near that point Indians, probably Arapahoes coming across the mountains to attack the Utes, had captured or killed the occupants of a prairie-schooner. There was no other clue. The miners took the child to their camp, fed and cared for it, and, after the manner of their kind, named it Columbine. Then they brought it to Belllounds.

"Collie," said the old rancher, "it needn't never have been told, an wouldn't but fer one reason. I'm getting' old. I reckon I'd never split my property between you an' Jack. So I mean you an' him to marry. You always steadied Jack. With a wife like you'll be wal, mebbe Jack . . ."

"Dad!" burst out Columbine. "Marry Jack! . . . Why I don't even remember him!"

"Haw! Haw!" laughed Belllounds. "Wal, you dog-gone soon will. Jack's in Kremmlin, an' he'll be hyar tonight or to-morrow."

"But I . . . I don't l-love him," faltered Columbine.

The old man lost his mirth; the strong-lined face resumed its hard cast; the big eyes smoldered. Her appealing objection had wounded him. She was reminded of how sensitive the old man had always been to any reflection cast upon his son.

"Wal, thet's unlucky;" he replied, gruffly. "Mebbe you'll change. I reckon no girl could help a boy much, onless she cared for him. Anyway, you an' Jack will marry."

He had stalked away and Columbine had ridden her mustang far up the valley slope where she could be alone. Standing on the verge of the bluff, she suddenly became aware that the quiet and solitude of her lonely resting-place had been disrupted. Cattle were bawling below her and along the slope of old White Slides and on the grassy uplands above. She had forgotten that the cattle were being driven down into the lowlands for the fall round up. A great red-and-white-spotted herd was milling in the park just beneath her. Calves and yearlings were making the dust fly along the mountain slope; wild old steers were crashing in the sage, holding level, unwilling to be driven down; cows were running and lowing for their lost ones. Melodious and clear rose the clarion calls of the cowboys. The cattle knew those calls and only the wild steers kept up-grade.

Columbine also knew each call and to which cowboy it belonged. They sang and yelled and swore, but it was all music to her. Here and there along the slope, where the aspen groves clustered, a horse would flash across an open space; the dust would fly, and a cowboy would peal out a lusty yell that rang along the slope and echoed under the bluff and lingered long after the daring rider had vanished in the steep thickets.

"I wonder which is Wils," murmured Columbine, as she watched and listened, vaguely conscious of a little difference, a strange check in her remembrance of this particular cowboy. She felt the change, yet did not understand. One after one she recognized the riders on the slopes below, but Wilson Moore was not among them. He must be above her, then, and she turned to gaze across the grassy bluff, up the long, yellow slope, to where the gleaming aspens half hid a red bluff of mountain, towering aloft. Then from far to her left, high up a scrubby ridge of the slope, rang down a voice that thrilled her: "Go aloong you ooooo." Red cattle dashed pell-mell down the slope, raising the dust, tearing the brush, rolling rocks, and letting out hoarse bawls.

"Hoop-ee!" High-pitched and pealing came a clearer yell.

Columbine saw a white mustang flash out on top of the ridge, silhouetted against the blue, with mane and tail flying. His gait on that edge of steep slope proved his rider to be a reckless cowboy for whom no heights or depths had terrors. She would have recognized him from the way he rode, if she had not known the slim, erect figure. The cowboy saw her instantly. He pulled the mustang, about to plunge down the slope, and lifted him, rearing and wheeling. Then Columbine waved her hand. The cowboy spurred his horse along the crest of the ridge, disappeared behind the grove of aspens, and came in sight again around to the right, where on the grassy bench he slowed to a walk in descent to the bluff.

The girl watched him come, conscious of an unfamiliar sense of uncertainty in this meeting, and of the fact that she was seeing him differently from any other time in the years he had been a playmate, a friend, almost like a brother. He had ridden for Belllounds for years, and was a cowboy because he loved cattle well and horses better, and above all a life in the open. Unlike most cowboys, he had been to school; he had a family in Denver that objected to his wild range life, and often importuned him to come home; he seemed aloof sometimes and not readily understood.

While many thoughts whirled through Columbine's mind she watched the cowboy ride slowly down to her, and she became more concerned with a sudden restraint. How was Wilson going to take the news of this forced change about to come in her life? That thought leaped up. It gave her a strange pang. But she and he were only good friends. As to that, she reflected, of late they had not been the friends and comrades they formerly were. In the thrilling uncertainty of this meeting she had forgotten his distant manner and the absence of little attentions she had missed.

By this time the cowboy had reached the level, and with the lazy grace of his kind slipped out of the saddle. He was tall, slim, round-limbed, with the small hips of a rider, and square, though not broad shoulders. He stood straight like an Indian. His eyes were hazel, his features regular, his face bronzed. All men of the open had still lean, strong faces, but added to this in him was a steadiness of expression, a restraint that seemed to hide sadness.

"Howdy, Columbine!" he said. "What are you doing up here? You might get run over."

"Hello, Wils!" she replied, slowly. "Oh, I guess I can keep out of the way."

"Some bad steers in that bunch. If any of them run over here Pronto will leave you to walk home. That mustang hates cattle. And he only half broke, you know."

"I forgot you were driving to-day," she replied, and looked away from him. There was a moment's pause long, it seemed to her.

"What'd you come for?" he asked, curiously.

"I wanted to gather columbines. See." She held out the nodding flowers toward him. "Take one. . . . Do you like them?"

"Yes. I like columbine," he replied, taking one of them. His keen hazel eyes, softened, darkened. "Colorado's flower."

"Columbine! . . . It is my name."

"Well, could you have a better? It sure suits you."

"Why?" she asked, and she looked at him again.

"You're slender, graceful. You sort of hold your head high and proud. Your skin is white. Your eyes are blue. Not bluebell blue, but columbine blue and they turn purple when you're angry."

"Compliments! Wilson, this is new kind of talk for you," she said.

"You're different to-day."

"Yes, I am." She looked across the valley toward the westering sun, and the slight flush faded from her cheeks. "I have no right to hold my head proud. No one knows who I am, where I came from."

"As if that made any difference!" he exclaimed.

"Belllounds is not my dad. I have no dad. I was a waif. They found me in the woods a baby lost among the flowers. Columbine Belllounds I've always been. But that is not my name. No one can tell what my name really is."

"I knew your story years ago, Columbine," he replied, earnestly. "Everybody knows. Old Bill ought to have told you long before this. But he loves you. So does everybody. You must not let this knowledge sadden you. . . . I'm sorry you've never known a mother or a sister. Why, I could tell you of many orphans whose stories were different."

"You don't understand. I've been happy. I've not longed for anyone except a mother. It's only . . ."

"What don't I understand?"

"I've not told you all."

"No? Well, go on," he said slowly.

The meaning of the hesitation and the restraint that had obstructed her thought now flashed over Columbine. It lay in what Wilson Moore might think of her prospective marriage to Jack Belllounds. Still she could not guess why that should make her feel strangely uncertain of the ground she stood on or how it could cause a constraint she had to fight herself to hide. Moreover, to her annoyance, she found that she was evading his direct request for the news she had withheld.

"Jack Belllounds is coming home to-night or to-morrow," she said. Then, waiting for her companion to reply, she kept an unseeing gaze upon the scanty pines fringing Old White Slides. But no reply appeared to be forthcoming from Moore. His silence compelled her to turn to him. The cowboy's face had subtly altered; it was darker with a tinge of red under the bronze; and his lower lip was released from his teeth, even as she looked. He had his eyes intent upon the lasso he was coiling. Suddenly he faced her and the dark fire of his eyes gave her a shock.

"I've been expecting that shorthorn back for months." he said, bluntly.

"You never liked Jack?" queried Columbine, slowly. That was not what she wanted to say, but the thought spoke itself.

"I never did."

"Ever since you and he fought long ago all over . . . ?"

His sharp gesture made the coiled lasso loosen. "Ever since I licked him good, don't forget that," interrupted Wilson. The red had faded from the bronze.

"Yes, you licked him," mused Columbine. "I remember that. And Jack's hated you ever since."

"There's been no love lost."

"But, Wils, you never before talked this way against Jack," she protested.

"Well, I'm not the kind to talk behind a fellow's back. But I'm not mealy-mouthed, either, and . . ."

He did not complete the sentence, and his meaning was enigmatic. Altogether Moore seemed not like himself. The fact disturbed Columbine. Always she had confided in him. Here was a most complex situation she burned to tell him, yet somehow feared to. She felt an incomprehensible satisfaction in his bitter reference to Jack. She seemed to realize that she valued Wilson's friendship more than she had known, and now for some strange reason it was slipping from her.

"We were such good friends . . . pards," said Columbine, hurriedly and irrelevantly.

"Who?" He stared at her.

"Why, you and me."

"Oh!" His tone softened, but there was still disapproval in his glance. "What of that?"

"Something has happened to make me think I've missed you lately, that's all."

"Ahuh!" His tone held finality and bitterness, but he would not commit himself. Columbine sensed a pride in him that seemed the cause of his aloofness.

"Wilson, why have you been different lately?" she asked, plaintively.

"What's the good to tell you now?" he queried in reply.

That gave her a blank sense of actual loss. She had lived in dreams and he in realities. Right now she could not dispel her dream and understand all that he seemed to. She felt like a child, then, growing old swiftly. The strange past longing or a mother surged up in her like a strong tide. Some one to lean on, some one who loved her, some one to help her in this hour when fatality knocked at the door of her youth. How she needed that!

"It might be bad for me to tell me, but tell me, anyhow," she said, finally, answering as some one older than she had been an hour ago to something feminine that leaped up. She did not understand this impulse, but it was in her.

"No!" declared Moore, with dark red staining his face. He slapped the lasso against his saddle, and tied it with clumsy hands. He did not look at her. His tone expressed anger and amazement.

"Dad says I must marry Jack," she said, with a sudden return to her natural simplicity.

"I heard him tell that months ago," snapped Moore.

"You did! Was that why?" she whispered.

"It was," he answered, ringingly.

"But that was no reason for you to stay away from me," she declared, with rising spirit.

He laughed shortly.

"Wils, didn't you like me any more after dad said that?" she queried.

"Columbine, a girl nineteen years and about to get married ought not be a fool," he replied, with sarcasm.

"I'm not a fool," she rejoined, hotly.

"You ask fool questions."

"Well, you didn't like me afterward or you'd never have mistreated me."

"If you say I mistreated you, you say what's untrue," he replied, just as hotly.

They had never been so near a quarrel before. Columbine experienced a sensation new to her, a commingling of fear, heat, and pang, it seemed, all in one throb. Wilson was hurting her. A quiver ran all over her, along her veins, swelling and tingling.

"You mean I lie?" she flashed.

"Yes, I do, if . . ."

But before he could conclude she slapped his face. It grew pale then, while she began to tremble. "Oh I didn't intend that. Forgive me," she faltered,

He rubbed his cheek. The hurt had not been great, so far as the blow was concerned. But his eyes were dark with pain and anger.

"Oh, don't distress yourself," he burst out. "You slapped me before once, years ago for kissing you. I apologize for saying you lied. You're only out of your head. So am I."

That poured oil upon the troubled waters. The cowboy appeared to be hesitating between sudden flight and the risk of staying longer.

"Maybe that's it," replied Columbine, with a half-laugh. She was not far from tears and fury with herself. "Let us make up and be friends again."

Moore squared around aggressively. He seemed to fortify himself against something in her. She felt that. But his face grew harder and older than she had ever seen it.

"Columbine, do you know where Jack Belllounds has been for these three years?" he asked, deliberately, entirely ignoring her overtures of friendship.

"No. Somebody said Denver. Some one else said Kansas City. I never asked dad, because I knew Jack had been sent away. I supposed he was working, making a man of himself."

"Well, I hope to Heaven for your sake what you suppose comes true," returned Moore, with exceeding bitterness.

"Do you know where he has been?" asked Columbine. Some strange feeling prompted that. There was a mystery here. Wilson's agitation seemed strange and deep.

"Yes, I do." The cowboy bit that out through closing teeth, as if locking them against an almost overmastering temptation.

Columbine lost her curiosity. She was woman enough to realize that there might well be facts which would only make her situation harder.

"Wilson," she began, hurriedly, "I owe all I am to dad. He has cared for me, sent me to school. He has been so good to me. I've loved him always. It would be a shabby return for all his protection and love if I refused."

"Old Bill is the best man ever," interrupted Moore, as if to repudiate any hint of disloyalty to his employer. "Everybody in Middle Park and all over owes Bill something. He's sure good. There never was anything wrong with him except his crazy blindness about his son. Buster Jack the . . . the . . ."

Columbine put a hand over Moore's lips. "The man I must marry," she said solemnly.

"You must, you will?" he demanded.

"Of course. What else could I do? I never thought of refusing."

"Columbine!" Wilson's cry was so poignant, his gesture so violent, his dark eyes so piercing that Columbine sustained a shock that held her trembling and mute. "How can you love Jack Belllounds? You were twelve years old when you saw him last. How can you love him?"

"I don't," replied Columbine.

"Then how could you marry him?"

"I owe dad obedience. It's his hope that I can steady Jack."

"Steady Jack!" exclaimed Moore, passionately. "Why, you girl, you white-faced flower! You with your innocence and sweetness steady that damned pup! My Heavens! He was a gambler and a drunkard. He . . ."

"Hush!" implored Columbine.

"He cheated at cards," declared the cowboy, with a scorn that placed that vice as utterly base.

"But Jack was only a wild boy," replied Columbine, trying with brave words to champion the son of the man she loved as her father. "He has been sent away to work. He'll have outgrown that wildness. He'll come home a man."

"Bah!" cried Moore, harshly.

Columbine felt a sinking within her. Where was her strength? She, who could walk and ride so many miles, to become sick with an inward quaking! It was childish. She struggled to hide her weakness from him.

"It's not like you to be this way," she said. "You used to be generous. Am I to blame? Did I choose my life?"

Moore looked quickly away from her, and, standing with a hand on his horse, he was silent for a moment. The squaring of his shoulders bore testimony to his thought.

Presently he swung up into the saddle. The mustang snorted and champed the bit and tossed his head, ready to bolt.

"Forget my temper," begged the cowboy, looking down upon Columbine. "I take it all back. I'm sorry. Don't let a word of mine worry you. I was only jealous."

"Jealous!" exclaimed Columbine, wonderingly.

"Yes. That makes a fellow see red and green. Bad medicine! You never felt it."

"What were you jealous of?" asked Columbine.

The cowboy had himself in hand now and he regarded her with a grim amusement. "Well, Columbine, it's like a story," he replied. "I'm the fellow disowned by his family, a wanderer of the wilds, no good and no prospects. . . . Now our friend Jack, he's handsome and rich. He has a doting old dad. Cattle, horses, ranches! He wins the girl. See!"

Spurring his mustang, the cowboy rode away. At the edge of the slope he turned in the saddle. "I've got to drive in this bunch of cattle. It's late. You hurry home." Then he was gone. The stones cracked and rolled down under the side of the bluff.

Columbine stood where he had left her: dubious, yet with the blood still hot in her cheeks.

"Jealous? . . . He wins the girl?" she murmured in repetition to herself. "What ever could he have meant?"

The simple, logical interpretation of Wilson's words opened Columbine's mind to a disturbing possibility of which she had never dreamed. That he might love her. If he did, why had he not said so? Jealous, maybe, but he did not love her!

The next throb of thought was like a knock at a door of her heart, a door never yet opened, inside which seemed a mystery of feeling, of hope, despair, unknown longing, and clamorous voices. The woman just born in her, instinctive and self-preservative, shut that door before she had more than a glimpse inside. But then she felt her heart swell with its nameless burdens.

Pronto was grazing near at hand. She caught him and mounted. It struck her then that her hands were numb with cold. The wind had ceased fluttering the aspens, but the yellow leaves were falling, rustling. Out on the brow of the slope she faced home and the west.

A glorious Colorado sunset had just reached the wonder full height of its color and transformation. The sage slopes below her seemed rosy velvet; the golden aspens on the farther reaches were on fire at the tips; the foot hills rolled clear and mellow and rich in the light; the gulf of distance on to the great black range was veiled in mountain purple; and the dim peaks beyond the range stood up, sunset-flushed and grand. The narrow belt of blue sky between crags and clouds was like a river full of fleecy sails and wisps of silver. Above towered a pall of dark cloud, full of the shades of approaching night.

"Oh, beautiful!" breathed the girl, with all her worship of nature. That wild world of sunset grandeur and loneliness and beauty was hers. Over there, under a peak of the black range, was the place where she had been found, a baby, lost in the forest. She belonged to that, and so it belonged to her. Strength came to her from the glory of light on the hills.

Pronto shot up his ears and checked his trot.

"What is it, boy?" called Columbine. The trail was getting dark. Shadows were creeping up the slope as she rode down to meet them. The mustang had keen sight and scent. She reined him to a halt.

All was silent. The valley had begun to shade on the far side and the rose and gold seemed fading from the nearer. Below, on the level floor of the valley, lay the rambling old ranch house, with the cabins nestling around, and the corrals leading out to the soft hay-fields, misty and gray in the twilight. A single light gleamed. It was like a beacon.

The air was cold with a nip of frost. From far on the other side of the ridge she had descended came the bawls of the last straggling cattle of the round-up. But surely Pronto had not shot up his ears for them. As if in answer a wild sound pealed down the slope, making the mustang jump. Columbine had heard it before.

"Pronto, it's only a wolf," she soothed him.

The peal was loud, rather harsh at first, then softened to a mourn, wild, lonely, haunting. A pack of coyotes barked in angry answer, a sharp, staccato, yelping chorus, the more piercing notes biting on the cold night air. These mountain mourns and yelps were music to Columbine. She rode on down the trail in the gathering darkness, less afraid of the night and its wild denizens than what awaited her at White Slides Ranch.

THE LAST OF
THE GREAT SCOUTS

BY HELEN CODY WETMORE

Embroider as they might the life and times of Buffalo Bill Cody, Western pulp fiction writers like Ned Buntline couldn't begin to do justice to the man himself. This 1899 account in The Last of the Great Scouts, *written by his sister, serves as a fitting and illuminating final entry of an era—real and imagined—long gone by.*

Since 1893 the "Wild West" exhibitions have been restricted to the various cities of our own land. Life in "Buffalo Bill's Tented City," as it is called, is like life in a small village. There are some six hundred persons in the various departments. Many of the men have their families with them; the Indians have their squaws and papooses, and the variety of nationalities, dialects, and costumes makes the miniature city an interesting and entertaining one.

The Indians may be seen eating bundles of meat from their fingers and drinking tankards of iced buttermilk. The Mexicans, a shade more civilized, shovel with their knives great quantities of the same food into the capacious receptacles provided by nature. The Americans, despite what is said of their rapid eating, take time to laugh and crack jokes, and finish their repast with a product only known to the highest civilization—ice-cream.

When the "Wild West" visited Boston, one hot June day the parade passed a children's hospital on the way to the show-grounds. Many of the little invalids were unable to leave their couches. All who could do so ran to the open windows and gazed eagerly at the passing procession, and the greatest excitement prevailed. These more fortunate little ones described, as best they could, to the little sufferers who could not leave their beds the wonderful things they saw. The Indians were the special admiration of the children. After the procession passed, one wee lad, bedridden by spinal trouble, cried bitterly because he had not seen it. A kind-hearted nurse endeavored to soothe the child, but words proved unavailing. Then a bright idea struck the patient woman; she told him he might write a letter to the great "Buffalo Bill" himself and ask him for an Indian's picture.

The idea was taken up with delight, and the child spent an eager hour in penning the letter. It was pathetic in its simplicity. The little sufferer told the great exhibitor that he was sick in bed, was unable to see the Indians when they passed the hospital, and that he longed to see a photograph of one.

The important missive was mailed, and even the impatient little invalid knew it was useless to expect an answer that day. The morning had hardly dawned before a child's bright eyes were open. Every noise was listened to, and he wondered when the postman would bring him a letter. The nurse hardly dared to hope that a busy man like Buffalo Bill would take time to respond to the wish of a sick child.

"Colonel Cody is a very busy man," she said. "We must be patient."

At perhaps the twentieth repetition of this remark the door opened noiselessly. In came a six-foot Indian, clad in leather trousers and wrapped in a scarlet blanket. He wore a head-dress of tall, waving feathers, and carried his bow in his hand.

The little invalids gasped in wonder; then they shrieked with delight. One by one, silent and noiseless, but smiling, six splendid warriors followed the first. The visitors had evidently been well trained, and had received explicit directions as to their actions.

So unusual a sight in the orderly hospital so startled the nurse that she could not even speak. The warriors drew up in a line and saluted her. The happy children were shouting in such glee that the poor woman's fright was unnoticed.

The Indians ranged themselves in the narrow space between the cots, laid aside their gay blankets, placed their bows upon the floor, and waving their arms to and fro, executed a quiet war-dance. A sham battle was fought, followed by a song of victory. After this the blankets were again donned, the kindly red men went away, still smiling as benignly as their war paint would allow them to do. A cheer of gratitude and delight followed them down the broad corridors. The happy children talked about Buffalo Bill and the "Wild West" for weeks after this visit.

North Platte had long urged my brother to bring the exhibition there. The citizens wished to see the mammoth tents spread over the ground where the scout once followed the trail on the actual war-path; they desired that their famous fellow-citizen should thus honor his home town. A performance was finally given there on October 12, 1896, the special car bearing Will and his party arriving the preceding day, Sunday. The writer of these chronicles joined the party in Omaha, and we left that city after the Saturday night performance.

The Union Pacific Railroad had offered my brother every inducement to make this trip; among other things, the officials promised to make special time in running from Omaha to North Platte.

When we awoke Sunday morning, we found that in some way the train had been delayed, that instead of making special time we were several hours late. Will telegraphed this fact to the officials. At the next station double-headers were put on, and the gain became at once perceptible. At Grand Island a congratulatory telegram was sent, noting the gain in time. At the next station we passed the Lightning Express, the "flyer," to which usually everything gives way, and the good faith of the company was evidenced by the fact that this train was side-tracked to make way for Buffalo Bill's "Wild West" train. Another message was sent over the wires to the officials; it read as follows: "Have just noticed that Lightning Express is side-tracked to make way for Wild west. I herewith promote you to top seat in heaven."

The trip was a continued ovation. Every station was thronged, and Will was obliged to step out on the platform and make a bow to the assembled crowds, his appearance being invariably greeted with a round of cheers. When we reached the station at North Platte, we found that the entire population had turned out to receive their fellow-townsman. The "Cody Guards," a band to which Will presented beautiful uniforms of white broadcloth trimmed with gold braid, struck up the strains of "See, the Conquering Hero Comes." The mayor attempted to do the welcoming honors of the city, but it was impossible for him to make himself heard. Cheer followed cheer from the enthusiastic crowd.

We had expected to reach the place some hours earlier, but our late arrival encroached upon the hour of church service. The ministers discovered that it was impossible to hold their congregations; so they were dismissed, and the pastors accompanied them to the station, one reverend gentleman humorously remarking: "We shall be obliged to take for our text this morning 'Buffalo Bill and his Wild West,' and will now proceed to the station for the discourse."

Will's tally-ho coach, drawn by six horses, was in waiting for the incoming party. The members of his family seated themselves in that conveyance, and we passed through the town, preceded and followed by a band. As we arrived at the home residence, both bands united in a welcoming strain of martial music.

My oldest sister, Julia, whose husband is manager of "Scout's Rest Ranch," when informed that the "Wild West" was to visit North Platte, conceived the idea of making this visit the occasion of a family reunion. We had never met in an unbroken circle since the days of our first separation, but as a result of her efforts we sat thus that evening in my brother's home. The next day our mother-sister, as she had always been regarded, entertained us at "Scout's Rest Ranch."

The "Wild West" exhibition had visited Duluth for the first time that same year. This city has a population of 65,000. North Platte numbers 3,500. When he wrote to me of his intention to take the exhibition to Duluth, Will offered to make a wager that his own little town would furnish a bigger crowd than would the city of my residence. I could not accept any such inferred slur upon the Zenith City, so accepted the wager, a silk hat against a fur cloak.

October 12th, the date of the North Platte performance, dawned bright and cloudless. "To-day decides our wager," said Will. "I expect there will be two or three dozen people out on this prairie. Duluth turned out a good many thousands, so I suppose you think your wager as good as won."

The manager of the tents evidently thought the outlook a forlorn one. I shared his opinion, and was, in fancy, already the possessor of a fine fur cloak.

"Colonel, shall we stretch the full canvas?" asked the tentman.

"Every inch of it," was the prompt response. "We want to show North Platte the capacity of the 'Wild West,' at any rate."

As we started for the grounds Will was evidently uncertain over the outcome, in spite of his previous boast of the reception North Platte would give him. "We'll have a big tent and plenty of room to spare in it," he observed.

But as we drove to the grounds we soon began to see indications of a coming crowd. The people were pouring in from all directions; the very atmosphere seemed populated; as the dust was nearly a foot deep on the roads, the moving populace made the air almost too thick for breathing. It was during the time of the county fair, and managers of the Union Pacific road announced that excursion trains would be run from every town and hamlet, the officials and their families coming up from Omaha on a special car. Where the crowds came from it was impossible to say. It looked as if a feat of magic had been performed, and that the stones were turned into men, or, perchance, that, as in olden tales, they came up out of the earth.

Accustomed though he is to the success of the show, Will was dumfounded by this attendance. As the crowds poured in I became alarmed about my wager. I visited the ticket-seller and asked how the matter stood. "It's pretty close," he answered. "Duluth seems to be dwindling away before the mightiness of the Great American Desert."

This section of the country, which was a wilderness only a few years ago, assembled over ten thousand people to attend a performance of the "Wild West."

Omaha, where the opening performance of this exhibition was given, honored Will last year by setting apart one day as "Cody Day." August 31st was devoted to his reception, and a large and enthusiastic crowd gathered to do the Nebraska pioneer honor. The parade reached the fair-grounds at eleven o'clock, where it was fittingly received by one hundred and fifty mounted Indians from the encampment. A large square space had been reserved for the reception of the party in front of the Sherman gate. As it filed through, great applause was sent up by the waiting multitude, and the noise became deafening when my brother made his appearance on a magnificent chestnut horse, the gift of General Miles. He was accompanied by a large party of officials and Nebraska pioneers, who dismounted to seat themselves on the grand-stand. Prominent among these were the governor of the state, Senator Thurston, and Will's old friend and first employer, Mr. Alexander Majors.

As Will ascended the platform he was met by General Manager Clarkson, who welcomed him in the name of the president of the exposition, whose official duties precluded his presence. Governor Holcomb was then introduced, and his speech was a brief review of the evolution of Nebraska from a wilderness of a generation ago to the great state which produced this marvelous exposition. Manager Clarkson remarked, as he introduced Mr. Majors: "Here is the father of them all, Alexander Majors, a man connected with the very earliest history of Nebraska, and the business father of Colonel Cody."

This old pioneer was accorded a reception only a shade less enthusiastic than that which greeted the hero of the day. He said:

"Gentlemen, and My Boy, Colonel Cody: [Laughter.] Can I say a few words of welcome? Friend Creighton and I came down here together to-day, and he thought I was not equal to the occasion.

Gentlemen, I do not know whether I am equal to the occasion at this time, but I am going to do the best for you that I can. Give me your hand, Colonel. Gentlemen, forty-three years ago this day, this fine-looking physical specimen of manhood was brought to me by his mother—a little boy nine years old—and little did I think at that time that the boy that was standing before me, asking for employment of some kind by which I could afford to pay his mother a little money for his services, was going to be a boy of such destiny as he has turned out to be.

"In this country we have great men, we have great men in Washington, we have men who are famous as politicians in this country; we have great statesmen, we have had Jackson and Grant, and we had Lincoln; we have men great in agriculture and in stock-growing, and in the manufacturing business men who have made great names for themselves, who have stood high in the nation.

"Next, and even greater, we have a Cody. He, gentlemen, stands before you now, known the wide world over as the last of the great scouts. When the boy Cody came to me, standing straight as an arrow, and looked me in the face, I said to my partner, Mr. Russell, who was standing by my side, 'We will take this little boy, and we will pay him a man's wages, because he can ride a pony just as well as a man can.' He was lighter and could do service of that kind when he was nine years old. I remember when we paid him twenty-five dollars for the first month's work. He was paid in half-dollars, and he got fifty of them. He tied them up in his little handkerchief, and when he got home he untied the handkerchief and spread the money all over the table."

Colonel Cody: "I have been spreading it ever since."

A few remarks followed indicative of Mr. Majors's appreciation of the exhibition, and he closed with the remark, "Bless your precious heart, Colonel Cody!" and sat down, amid great applause.

Senator Thurston's remarks were equally happy. He said:

"Colonel Cody, this is your day. This is your exposition. This is your city. And we all rejoice that Nebraska is your state. You have carried the fame of our country and of our state all over the civilized world; you have been received and honored by princes, by emperors and by kings; the titled women in the courts of the nations of the world have been captivated by your charm of manner and your splendid manhood. You are known wherever you go, abroad or in the United States, as Colonel Cody, the best representative of the great and progressive West. You stand here today in the midst of a wonderful assembly. Here are representatives of the heroic and daring characters of most of the nations of the world. You are entitled to the honor paid you today, and especially entitled to it here.

"This people know you as a man who has carried this demonstration of yours to foreign lands, and exhibited it at home. You have not been a showman in the common sense of the word. You have been a great national and international educator of men. You have furnished a demonstration of the possibilities of our country that has advanced us in the opinion of all the world. But we who have been with you a third, or more than a third, of a century, we remember you more dearly and tenderly than others do. We remember that when this whole Western land was a wilderness, when these representatives of the aborigines were attempting to hold their own against the onward tide of civilization, the settler and the hardy pioneer, the women and the children, felt safe whenever Cody rode along the frontier; he was their protector and defender.

"Cody, this is your home. You live in the hearts of the people of our state. God bless you and keep you and prosper you in your splendid work."

Will was deeply touched by these strong expressions from his friends. As he moved to the front of the platform to respond, his appearance was the signal for a prolonged burst of cheers. He said:

"You cannot expect me to make adequate response for the honor which you have bestowed upon me to-day. You have overwhelmed my speaking faculties. I cannot corral enough ideas to attempt a coherent reply in response to the honor which you have accorded me. How little I dreamed in the long ago that the lonely path of the scout and the pony-express rider would lead me to the place you have assigned me to-day. Here, near the banks of the mighty Missouri, which flows unvexed to the sea, my thoughts revert to the early days of my manhood. I looked eastward across this rushing tide to the Atlantic, and dreamed that in that long-settled region all men were rich and all women happy. My friends, that day has come and gone. I stand among you a witness that nowhere in the broad universe are men richer in manly integrity, and women happier in their domestic kingdom, than here in our own Nebraska.

"I have sought fortune in many lands, but wherever I have wandered, the flag of our beloved state has been unfurled to every breeze: from the Platte to the Danube, from the Tiber to the Clyde, the emblem of our sovereign state has always floated over the 'Wild West.' Time goes on and brings with it new duties and responsibilities, but we 'old men,' we who are called old-timers, cannot forget the trials and tribulations which we had to encounter while paving the path for civilization and national prosperity.

"The whistle of the locomotive has drowned the howl of the coyote; the barb-wire fence has narrowed the range of the cow-puncher; but no material evidence of prosperity can obliterate our contribution to Nebraska's imperial progress.

"Through your kindness to-day I have tasted the sweetest fruit that grows on ambition's tree. If you extend your kindness and permit me to fall back into the ranks as a high private, my cup will be full.

"In closing, let me call upon the 'Wild West, the Congress of Rough Riders of the World,' to voice their appreciation of the kindness you have shown them today."

At a given signal the "Wild West" gave three ringing cheers for Nebraska and the Trans-Mississippi Exposition. The cowboy band followed with the "Red, White, and Blue," and an exposition band responded with the "Star-Spangled Banner." The company fell into line for a parade around the grounds, Colonel Cody following on his chestnut horse, Duke. After him came the officials and invited guests in carriages; then came the Cossacks, the Cubans, the German cavalry, the United States cavalry, the Mexicans, and representatives of twenty-five countries.

As the parade neared its end, my brother turned to his friends and suggested that as they had been detained long past the dinner-hour in doing him honor, he would like to compensate them by giving an informal spread. This invitation was promptly accepted, and the company adjourned to a cafe, where a tempting luncheon was spread before them. Never before had such a party of pioneers met around a banquet-table, and many were the reminiscences of early days brought out. Mr. Majors, the originator of the Pony Express line, was there. The two Creighton brothers, who put through the first telegraph line, and took the occupation of the express riders from them, had seats of honor. A. D.

Jones was introduced as the man who carried the first post office of Omaha around in his hat, and who still wore the hat. Numbers of other pioneers were there, and each contributed his share of racy anecdotes and pleasant reminiscences.